Ius Gentium

Comparative Perspectives on Law and Justice

Volume 42

More information about this series at http://www.springer.com/series/7888

Macarena Sáez
Editor

Same Sex Couples - Comparative Insights on Marriage and Cohabitation

Springer

Editor
Macarena Sáez
Washington College of Law
American University
Washington
District of Columbia
USA

ISSN 1534-6781 ISSN 2214-9902 (electronic)
Ius Gentium
ISBN 978-94-017-9773-3 ISBN 978-94-017-9774-0 (eBook)
DOI 10.1007/978-94-017-9774-0

Library of Congress Control Number: 2015938908

Springer Dordrecht Heidelberg New York London

Cover design: eStudio Calamar, Berlin/Figueres

Printed on acid-free paper

Springer Science+Business Media B.V. Dordrecht is part of Springer Science+Business Media (www.springer.com)

Contents

About the Authors

Estefanía Vela Barba is an Associate Professor and Head of the Sexual and Reproductive Rights Area of the Law Division at the *Centro de Investigación y Docencia Económica*, CIDE, in Mexico. Professor Vela Barba holds a law degree from *Instituto Tecnológico Autónomo de México*, ITAM, in Mexico, and an LL.M. from Yale Law School in the United States.

Dr. Başak Başoğlu is Assistant Professor of Civil Law at Istanbul Kemerburgaz University, Faculty of Law. She received her law degree and JD from Istanbul University and her LL.M. in business law degree from Istanbul Bilgi University. She specializes and publishes in the areas of family law, contract law, international sales law, tort law and environmental law.

Dr. Ayelet Blecher-Prigat is a member of the Law Faculty at the Sha'arey Mishpat Law College in Israel, and co-manages its Center for the Rights of the Child and the Family. She is a co-editor of the *Family in Law* journal, a peer-reviewed interdisciplinary journal (in Hebrew). Dr. Blecher-Prigat holds a JSD and an LL.M. (*Kent scholar* 1999) degree from Columbia Law School in the United States, and an LL.B. (*magna cum laude)* from Tel-Aviv University in Israel. Before joining Israel's Bar, Dr. Blecher-Prigat clerked for Israeli Supreme Court Justice Strasberg-Cohen (1997–1998). Her research interests are family law and inheritance law, and she has published various articles on these issues in leading journals within and outside Israel.

Toni Holness is a Public Policy Associate with the American Civil Liberties Union (ACLU) of Maryland, United States. Before joining the ACLU, Ms. Holness was a Staff Attorney with Maryland Legal Aid and a Georgetown University Law Center Women's Law and Public Policy Fellow. She is a graduate of Temple University in the United States, where she completed a JD and a Master of Arts in Economics. She completed her undergraduate degree at the University of Pennsylvania in the United States.

Natalia Ramírez-Bustamante is an attorney, philosopher and a Masters of Law from the University of the Andes in Colombia. She is an SJD candidate at Harvard Law School. Her fields of interest include critical legal theory, labor law, gender issues and social change and law reform.

Macarena Sáez is a Fellow in International Legal Studies and the Faculty Director of the Impact Litigation Project at American University Washington College of Law, in the United States. She teaches in the areas of family law, comparative law, and international human rights. Professor Sáez holds a law degree from the University of Chile School of Law, and an LL.M. from Yale Law School in the United States.

José María Lorenzo Villaverde is from Galicia, Spain, where he completed his studies in law and journalism at the University of Santiago the Compostela. He is a PhD candidate at the University of Copenhagen, writing on comparative family law and the legal recognition of same-sex couples in Spain and Denmark. He was a Researcher at Leiden Law School with the EU funded project "FamiliesAnd-Societies," focusing on a questionnaire on comparative family law among several European countries. His main areas of interest are family law, sexual orientation law, legal culture and private international law in family matters.

Chapter 1
Introduction

Macarena Sáez

Abstract This chapter summarizes the legal developments of same-sex couples analyzed in the following chapters. It shows that a global discussion on same-sex couples' recognition has sparked discussions on the role of marriage and the legal concept of the family even in countries where same-sex couples are still invisible.

Until the end of the twentieth century marriage was the only union considered legitimate to form a family. Today more than 40 countries have granted rights to same sex couples, including at least 19 that have included same-sex marriage within their family law systems.[1] Every day there is a new bill being discussed or a new claim being brought to court seeking formal recognition of same-sex couples or of families formed by individuals of the same sex.

This worldwide trend is creating new rights for individuals of diverse sexual orientations and gender identities. In countries where marriage has been granted to same-sex couples, a whole new set of rules has emerged. Immigration regulations, tax statutes, inheritance rights, adoption, surrogacy, and presumption of paternity favoring the husband are some of the areas that have been deeply changed by same-sex marriage. These legal changes have benefited thousands of gays and lesbians who now have access to rights and benefits traditionally exclusive to the heterosexual married family.

[1]By September of 2014 same-sex marriage was available in Argentina, Belgium, Brazil, Canada, Denmark, France, Iceland, Luxembourg, Netherlands, New Zealand, Norway, Portugal, South Africa, Spain, Sweden, United Kingdom, Uruguay, parts of the United States, and parts of Mexico. Foreign same-sex marriages were recognized in Israel. Civil unions or some partnership agreement model was available for same-sex couples at least in Australia, Austria, Colombia, Croatia, Czech Republic, Ecuador, Germany, Hungary, Ireland, Lichtenstein, Slovenia, Venezuela.

M. Sáez (✉)
Washington College of Law, American University, Massachusetts Ave. N.W. 4801,
Washington, DC 20016, USA
e-mail: msaez@wcl.american.edu

M. Sáez (ed.), *Same Sex Couples - Comparative Insights on Marriage and Cohabitation*, Ius Gentium: Comparative Perspectives on Law and Justice 42,
DOI 10.1007/978-94-017-9774-0_1

These changes have also benefited more people and in more areas than marriage. If gays and lesbians are treated equally in the strict regulatory framework of family law, it gets harder to argue for a differentiated treatment in other areas such labor or housing. Thus, the discussion on marriage has expanded the debate to other areas where gay and lesbian individuals have also suffered discrimination. Additionally, the discussion on same-sex marriage has made visible other individuals who have been politically identified as part of the same group through the now generally identifiable acronym LGBTI,[2] even though redress for the rest of the group, mainly transgender and intersex people, may not be found in marriage. Same-sex marriage has not automatically granted intersex individuals the right to marry. Nor has it allowed for transgender individuals to get a prompt and accessible procedure to gender reassignment or get a simple change of name in their official ID cards. The same-sex marriage debate, however, has made visible, in some places for the first time, the existence of transgender and intersex individuals and the problems of discrimination and violence they face every day.

Same-sex marriage has sparked discussions on the role of family and marriage in countries where legislatures and judges had (and in some places still have) no intention to open up family structures. In every continent there is today scholarly discussion on same-sex marriage, and in every continent there is at least one country that has broken the rigid marriage paradigm as the only gateway to family formation, and as a strictly heterosexual institution. Same-sex marriage was often preceded by models of same-sex partnership.

For same-sex marriage to be possible as a legal institution, it was necessary to accept first that couples of the same sex existed and, regardless of legal prohibitions, made decisions with economic consequences for the individuals involved and others. For example, the death of a person brings sadness to her surviving partner regardless of her sex, but in countries where there is no recognition of same-sex associations death also brings the fear of losing all economic assets jointly accumulated. It also brings the real possibility of eviction from a rented property. Legal protection of same-sex partners is ultimately a matter of fairness. Equality, however, requires more than protecting the weakest party of an emotional association. It requires the recognition of such association as a family unit. It is in this context that the debate on same-sex marriage at different levels is as transformative of family law as same-sex marriage itself. Same-sex marriage has changed the world of family law by making it possible for the first time to envision families that originate in emotional relations between individuals of the same sex, and by allowing individuals the possibility of having legal families regardless of their sexual orientation and gender identity. The mere fact of same-sex marriage being possible in an increasing number of countries each year has the impact of bringing the debate about family formations to countries where this discussion is still at the level of mere hypotheticals. In many countries where there is no

[2]There are several variations of the acronym from LGBT to include Lesbian, Gay, Bisexual and Trans individuals. There is also LGBTI to include intersex, and LGBTQ to include "queer."

recognition of same-sex couples or LGBTI individuals, these theoretical discussions are the beginning of a legal transformation. They are one more element of bigger movements that involve civil society, policy makers and scholars, all doing their share in imagining, and then implementing, changes that shift the role of marriage and family law in general.

This book explores the tension between same-sex marriage and traditional structures of family law. It moves from countries that have recognized same-sex marriage and are now adjusting to a new family law structure, to countries where same-sex marriage is viewed as a foreign institution, only possible as an academic theoretical conversation. The book covers analyses of countries as diverse as Turkey, Israel, Jamaica, Colombia, Mexico, Spain, and the United States. It is divided in chapters that look at each country's individual experience in recognizing same-sex couples in general, and same-sex marriage in particular. From systems that still deny the existence of same-sex emotional relations, to systems that have reinforced marriage through the recognition of same-sex marriage, we see countries in transition, dealing with a tension between rigid concepts of family and flexible family structures that allow for protection of families outside the realm of the heterosexual married family. There are some common elements among countries that have recognized same-sex marriage or that are in the process of recognition. At the same time, countries that deny the legal existence of same-sex couples and their families also share common elements.

Chapter 2 is a constitutional analysis of Act 13/2005 that in 2005 opened marriage to same-sex couples in Spain. Professor Jose Maria Lorenzo starts with an examination of different constitutional interpretations about the amendment to the Spanish Civil Code that changed all references of a man and a woman to gender neutral references. The amendment not only opened marriage to same-sex couples but it granted all rights and benefits, including parental rights, to the same-sex spouse of a biological mother or father. The analysis shows that even though a constitutional court may decide a statute to be constitutional or unconstitutional, courts have more than just two options, and in fact their legal reasoning may have the effect of closing a discussion almost irreversibly leaving only in the hands of political majorities the possibility of a change. In the case of same-sex marriage, the Constitutional Court could have interpreted the Spanish Constitution as mandating marriage equality and declaring heterosexual marriage unconstitutional. The Court, however, chose another path by which it interpreted the Constitution as giving special protection to heterosexual marriage, and allowing, at the same time, for the legislature to elevate other types of association to the same category. Given that same-sex marriage does not affect, nor hinders marriage between individuals of different sex, there was nothing in the Constitution that would obstruct the legislature in the political process of deciding to expand marriage to individuals of the same sex.

Professor Lorenzo ends his analysis with a word of caution. Although same-sex marriage was declared constitutional by the Spanish Constitutional Court, same-sex marriage was not, through the Court's decision, equalized to heterosexual marriage. There is still a fundamental difference between one and the other. Whereas the heterosexual marriage enjoys a constitutional protection that prevents its modification through the regular political process, same-sex marriage can still be modified by the majorities if they chose to do so. As time goes by, stripping away the right to marriage from same-sex couples will become harder and harder. Its constitutional legitimacy, however, will derive then from a different source than today.

Chapter 3 provides a historical analysis of legal marriage in Mexico in order to explain the most recent developments triggered both by legislative and adjudicative processes. Professor Estefania Vela Barba shows that as marriage's ends change, the concept of marriage has changed too. The heterosexual element in marriage was necessary when marriage was specially linked to procreation. She describes the legal construction of marriage in Mexico as a "means-to-ends" logic. Historically, Vela argues, the legal definition of marriage and its regulatory framework had a specific purpose in mind. Men and women were naturally assigned different roles—with women being the exclusive bearers of procreation—and marriage being the channel to ensure procreation in a particular order. She then explains the legal developments that first enhanced those different roles between men and women but that later moved towards a more egalitarian idea of men and women. This move from a pre-assigned role within the family and a gender specific type of marriage to families with flexible functions, was the consequence of the secularization of marriage. Once marriage was no longer under the control of the Catholic Church it became subject to changes by the legislature and to constitutional control by the Supreme Court. The State may had replicated the religious marriage in the Civil Code, but could not ensure its immutability once it entered the legal realm.

This Chapter highlights the role of international law in reshaping both marriage and the family. The reforms of Mexican civil codes in different states were triggered not only by new Mexican constitutions and constitutional amendments. They were also influenced by new international commitments that Mexico subscribed and that would also apply to marriage and family. These changes created a family law framework that, at least in theory, was based on equality between men and women, the acceptance of family formations outside marriage, and the need of the State to protect existing families, regardless of marriage. Vela shows how family law became more protective of diverse family formations when more leftists governments were in power. These changes did not happen at the same pace in adjudication processes. For example, the chapter analyzes the discussion of the Mexican Supreme Court on marital rape. The denial of rape between spouses, in place in Mexican law through legal interpretations and not through express law until 2005, reflects an understanding of marriage essentially tied to procreation. That year, however, the Supreme Court recognized that rape can exist within marriage and reinforced the idea of marriage as a partnership tied to mutual support more than to procreation.

The chapter also gives a brief account of the LGBT rights movement in Mexico prior to the Supreme Court decisions on same-sex marriage. It shows that the intersection between a shifting understanding of the role and purpose of marriage, and a more visible, stronger LGBT movement, created the right momentum for same-sex marriage in Mexico.

Chapter 4 provides a brief analysis of the status of same-sex marriage in the United States after the U.S. Supreme Court issued its two first decisions related to same-sex marriage in June of 2013. Although these decisions were not about the constitutionality of same-sex marriage, they triggered fast changes at state and federal level throughout the country, with judges in states historically conservative issuing decisions favoring marriage equality. The chapter shows that what was unpredictable 20 years ago—marriage equality nationwide—is today a real possibility. At the same time, the chapter shows that not all decisions on same-sex marriage provide the same framework for the future of family protections. Although same-sex marriage may now be an option in several states, families formed outside the institution of marriage are still unprotected and the marriage debate has not opened any more spaces for them. That is a difference with other countries, included Spain, Colombia, Mexico, and Israel. The legal reasoning behind other countries' decisions on same-sex marriage tend to be based on principles of equality and autonomy that could, in the future, become the basis for the protection of unmarried families, regardless of their gender, sexual orientation, and perhaps sexual connotation. U.S. courts, however, have mostly based their decisions on the value of marriage as an institution that perfects society, leaving little space for a legal development in the future affording legal recognition to families formed outside marriage.

Chapter 5 analyses the development of LGBTI rights in Colombia. With a well-developed case law, the Constitutional Court of Colombia (CCC) has become known in Latin America for its rich analysis and articulated decisions based on equality and autonomy. Ms. Natalia Ramirez-Bustamante gives an excellent summary of the history of Colombia's Constitutional Court decisions on LGBTI rights based on individualistic analysis of constitutional rights and how this approach has hindered, at the end, same-sex marriage recognition. The Chapter analyses how Family Law as an area of protection and regulation of families has changed in Colombia through the increasing recognition of same-sex couples and it warns of the risks of an LGBTI movement focused on same-sex marriage to the detriment of the recognition of other family formations outside marriage.

Colombia, like Canada and Australia, started challenging the married family first, and the heterosexual family after. With a constitutional protection of both the married and the unmarried family, Colombia has been legally recognizing mutual rights and obligations of unmarried couples, as if their associations were only different to married couples in the way they were created. Natalia Ramirez-Bustamante explains that during a first period the CCC was willing to recognize individual LGBTI rights but not their family associations. At the same time, it advanced the recognition of unmarried heterosexual couples. During this period, the CCC justified the dichotomy between individual recognition of LGBTI rights and exclusion of same-sex couples in a supposedly heterosexual character of the natural family recognized by the Colombian Constitution and the connection between family and procreation. Despite this distinction, the Court was slowly recognizing the rights of unmarried heterosexual couples. This constitutional development paved the way for the later recognition of same-sex couples' rights viewed as private associations instead of family associations, and, later, to discuss same-sex couples' rights within the framework of family law as well. The chapter goes beyond an analysis of marriage and provides a reflection on the role of family law and the types of associations that it ought to protect or regulate. It highlights the paradox of LGBTI rights advocates pushing for same-sex marriage while statistics seem to indicate that heterosexual couples are moving away from that institution completely. Natalia Ramirez-Bustamante explains two of the most important reasons for the advocacy of same-sex marriage. The first one has to do with a right to equality that in practical terms includes the right to adoption. The second one has to do with the weight of the word marriage, which makes same-sex couples "morally indistinct" from heterosexual couples. Ramirez-Bustamante challenges the long-term effects of the marriage demand for its risk of reinforcing a system that legitimizes some families—the married families—to the detriment of all others. Same-sex marriage becomes, then, "unacceptably conservative." This chapter is, at the end, a call for a reconceptualization of the same-sex marriage debate to one that includes a discussion of the types of families the Colombian society (and others as well) should protect and embrace.

1.1 The Road Towards the Recognition of Same-Sex Couples

The movement towards the recognition of same-sex couples began in Europe. It was a European country the first one to implement a registered partnership regime, and it was a European country the first one to expand marriage to same-sex couples.[3] Spain was the third country in the world to recognize same-sex marriage after the Netherlands and Belgium. Although same-sex couples were able to marry in Spain since 2005, only in 2012 the Spanish Constitutional Court settled the issue of same-sex marriage by declaring it constitutional.[4] From 2005 and until this decision, same-sex couples married in Spain enjoyed all the benefits and rights of marriage, but were uncertain about the future of their marriage. The decision not only ended this uncertainty, but it did so with a strong analysis on the rights protected by the Spanish Constitution. As mentioned, Chap. 2 of this book gives a detailed account of the arguments presented to the Spanish Constitutional Court and the legal reasoning chosen by the Court favoring the constitutionality of same-sex marriage. Three more chapters provide similar analyses. Chapters 3, 4, and 5 examine courts' decisions in the area of same-sex marriage.

All these chapters share a common thread: they look at legal reasoning as the source of change in the understanding of marriage and the family in different

[3]In June of 1989 Denmark passed the first Registered Partnership Act in the world. The Netherlands enacted *Staatsblad van het Koninkrijk der Nederlanden 2001, nr. 9 (11 January)*, the first statute on same-sex marriage, which became available on April 1, 2001.

[4]*STC 198/2012, of 6th November2012.* Boletin Oficial del Estado (BOE) N. 286, November 28, 2012, pp. 168–219.

countries. We can see from these decisions common arguments provided by groups or government officers opposing to same-sex marriage and similar arguments to advance same-sex marriage as constitutionally possible or even as a constitutional mandate. Three elements stand out as similar in these decisions: First, whether procreation (and therefore heterosexuality) was an essential element of marriage. If procreation was not essential to marriage, an alternative essential element had to be found. This element was found in the right of each individual to make decisions about his/her intimate life, including the decision to share a life with another person; second, the concept of human dignity seems to have tipped the balance in favor of same-sex marriage; and third, all these decisions assume that our understanding of constitutional concepts or institutions may vary in time.

1.1.1 Procreation and Choice

We learn from Chaps. 2, 3, 4, and 5 that the procreative role of marriage was a recurrent argument brought to courts in Spain, Mexico, Colombia and the United States. Heterosexuality was essential to marriage because the objective of marriage was procreation and only heterosexual relationships led to procreation. The counter argument, also common to all these countries, was that procreation could not be essential to marriage. Otherwise, governments could prohibit marriages between elderly people, as well as between people with the inability or no desire to procreate. In none of these countries opponents to same-sex marriage seem to have advanced the argument of procreation to the point of affirming that heterosexual marriages not leading to procreation could be prohibited. An alternative narrative about the essence of marriage brought to courts related to individual choice: marriage was a mutual agreement to share a life plan. These chapters show a tension between a vision of marriage as an institution with a specific role to fulfill in society (procreation), and a vision of marriage as an individual choice within the right of individuals to develop their own life plans. Courts in Mexico, Colombia and Spain speak of a constitutional right to free development of one's individuality.[5] Courts in the United States speak of a liberty interest and a right to privacy embedded in the Due Process Clause of the Constitution. All of them point out to a right to autonomy that prevails over societal conceptions of marriage.

With the exception of a few U.S. state court decisions, these decisions interpreted their constitutions as giving priority to the role marriage played in the life of each person, instead of the role marriage played in the structure of society. Het-

[5]The literal translation of "*Libre desarrollo de la personalidad*" would be "free development of personality." The concept, however, refers to protecting the right of each individual to her own individuality. The Colombian Constitutional Court has stated that "There is a violation of this right when a person is arbitrarily impeded of reaching or pursuing legitimate aspirations or of freely valuing and choosing the circumstances that give meaning to her life." Corte Constitucional de Colombia, Sentencia T 532/92, Sept 23, 1992.

erosexuality was not, therefore, essential to marriage and neither was procreation. What prevailed was the right of individuals to make decisions regarding their life plans. Even the 2012 decision of the Colombian Constitutional Court reached this conclusion, even though this decision did not make same-sex marriage available in Colombia. Chapter 5 explains the development of the Constitutional Court towards a strong protection of sexual orientation and gender identity. Through several decisions about civil unions, access to social security and pensions, among other topics, the Constitutional Court treated sexual orientation as a protected category subject to heightened scrutiny. In the 2012 decision on same-sex marriage the Court applied the same standards of protection and referred to its previous case law. It reinforced its case law on free development of one's individuality as including decisions related to a person's sexual orientation. It recognized the lack of constitutional protection for same-sex couples in the area of marriage, but deferred to the legislature the determination of the model of protection same-sex couples would be afforded. Despite not being a decision favorable to same-sex marriage, the Court's legal reasoning is similar to the Spanish Constitutional Court and the Mexican Supreme Court decisions on same-sex marriage in its rejection of the procreative role of marriage and the reinforcement of individuals to choose their life's plan.

1.1.2 Human Dignity

Another element common to all these decisions was the use of human dignity to justify the right of individuals to make their own life plans. This element gives a final blow to an idea of marriage that would exclude some individuals for their inability or lack of interest in procreating. All these decisions speak of human dignity as linked to a right to autonomy.

They all talk about human dignity as a justification for protecting the free development of one's individuality or the sphere of privacy to make intimate decisions involving marriage and family. None of these decisions seem to develop a concept of human dignity and the chapters that analyzed these decisions do not provide information on how or why human dignity was a prominent element in the decisions. These analyses, however, make clear that at least for these courts there was a connection between the right to autonomy (free development of one's individuality, liberty interest or right to privacy) and the recognition of human dignity. This is less apparent in the 2013 decision of the U.S. Supreme Court *United States v. Windsor*, than in the decisions of Mexico, Spain and Colombia. Chapter 4 provides an account of the different uses of the concept of dignity by the U.S. Supreme Court in the *Windsor* decision, where it seems that the court used two different concepts of dignity. Unquestionably the decision speaks of human dignity as linked to autonomy and privacy. It also speaks, however, of an institutional dignity provided by the marriage institution itself.

1.1.3 *Evolution of Concepts*

Arguments provided against same-sex marriage in the legal proceedings reviewed in these chapters were often justified in a historical understanding of marriage as a union between one man and one woman. Courts could not deny that marriage had been historically a heterosexual institution. The question all these courts had to answer was how much the history of marriage should weigh in a constitutional interpretation of the right to marry. In all these countries historical interpretations were dismissed because other interpretative tools provided a more accurate understanding of the constitutional protection at hand. All of them, including the United States Supreme Court, understood that institutions evolve. In the *Windsor* decision, the U.S. Supreme Court referred to the tension between the historical and current understanding of marriage:

> The limitation of lawful marriage to heterosexual couples, which for centuries had been deemed both necessary and fundamental, came to be seen in New York and certain other States as an unjust exclusion . . . ..
>
> [Same-sex marriage in New York] reflects both the community's considered perspective on the historical roots of the institution of marriage and its evolving understanding of the meaning of equality.[6]

The U.S. Supreme Court provided an evolving concept of equality. The Spanish Court considered that marriage as an institution had evolved. The Colombian and Mexican courts also understood marriage as an evolving concept.

1.2 Legal Systems That Deny Same-Sex Couples

Chapters 6, 7, and 8 of the book transition the analysis from countries that either recognized or are in a direct process to full recognition of same-sex marriage to countries where same-sex marriage is currently a normative impossibility. Chapter 6 shows a country that while denying the possibility of same-sex marriages celebrated locally, it has, in practical terms, come to accept same-sex marriages celebrated abroad. The lack of recognition of same-sex marriage in Israel does not derive of any expressed prohibition, but from the fact that no formal religion in Israel recognizes such unions. Same-sex couples, therefore, are in the same situation as interfaith marriages when the religion of each spouse does not recognize their marriage, or individuals with no religion. Israel is an example of flexibility, with a Supreme Court that has decided issues related to same-sex couples in pragmatic terms. Thus, same-sex couples married abroad have been able to register their marriages just as any opposite-sex couple married abroad has. These and other developments make Israel a fascinating family law model. By now, there are decisions relating to same-sex

[6] *United States v. Windsor*, 133 S. Ct. 2675, 2689, 2692–2693, 186 L. Ed. 2d 808 (2013).

second parent adoption and other issues that go beyond same-sex marriage. The judiciary has played an important role in protecting diverse families in Israel. With a family law system that leaves to religious denominations what is accepted and what is rejected, judges could have taken a hands-off approach concluding that what is not recognized by religious law, must remain invisible to secular law as well. They have, however, used the principle of equality to register marriages celebrated abroad regardless of the sex of its members.

Chapter 7 enters directly to the reality of same-sex couples in a region where animosity towards LGBTI individuals has become international news. Ms. Toni Holness starts her analysis with a clear account of the violence that LGBTI individuals suffer in the Caribbean region. Violence, many times in the form of torture and murder, is often tolerated and sometimes even authored by state officers. The role of family law in such environment cannot be the primary concern of a community that must put all its energy in survival and safety. Despite this bleak scenario, reality also shows that even in adverse conditions, families form. People fall in love, support and care for each other regardless of their sex, sexual orientation and gender identity. This chapter provides a thorough description of the marriage regulations in different countries of the Commonwealth Caribbean. Not all of these regulations have an expressed heteronormative construction. All of them however, have been consistently applied to the exclusion of same-sex couples. These interpretations are complemented with harsh anti sodomy statutes or buggery laws, which are the primary concern of LGBTI groups in the region. As long as anti sodomy statutes remain in place, it will be hard to advance any type of formal recognition of same-sex couples. This Chapter may provide one of the few, if not the only, thorough review of marriage regulations in the region. LGBTI activists and family law scholars will find here a good starting point for thinking of strategies for the formal recognition of same-sex couples. For example, the fact that non-Commonwealth Caribbean countries have been more flexible and open to same-sex couples could impact future normative changes in the Commonwealth Caribbean. Additionally, Ms. Holness shows that at least some post colonialist marriage regulations were structured mirroring British regulations. Marriage heteronormativity, thus, was inherited from the British Empire and marriage could well follow mutations similar to the ones suffered in the United Kingdom.

In some countries of the region, such as Trinidad, the law recognizes and regulates unmarried heterosexual couples. Many of the Western countries that have recognized same-sex marriage started first by recognizing the role of family law in protecting families socially constructed, regardless of the existence of a formal marriage. Once societies make that shift from a family law that mandates what families must be, to one that protects families formed outside the law, the recognition of same-sex couples tend to follow sooner than later. When unmarried heterosexual couples are accepted the door is open to protect associations that *function* as families. When this happens, it becomes very difficult to justify why heterosexuality is essential to that *functioning* of the family.

The review of anti sodomy statutes also shows the influence of Great Britain. These statutes were a colonialist imposition. At the same time, in those places where

Great Britain still has legal influence, such as in the British Overseas Territories, those statutes have been repealed. There are, therefore, some possibilities of change. Once anti sodomy statutes are lifted, debates on recognition of same-sex families become more common, and the opportunity for legal amendments arise.

Chapter 8 provides another example of a country that struggles with social resistance to same-sex couples and LGBTI individuals in general, and a push for some form of recognition of same-sex couples. Turkey is in a unique position between the Eastern and Western world, with a foot in the European Union and its standards of equality and non-discrimination on the basis of sexual orientation, and another in a system of family law deeply embedded in traditional marriage as a patriarchal, heterosexual institution. As mentioned, some countries that do not recognize same-sex marriage have moved towards the recognition of heterosexual unmarried couples. This is the case, for example, of Trinidad, where recognition of heterosexual family associations outside marriage is legally and socially accepted while homophobia has prevented giving any visibility to same-sex families. Turkey's family law, we learn from this chapter, is still strictly centered on the heterosexual marriage as the exclusive gateway to family formation. This position makes the argument of discrimination based on sexual orientation harder in the context of family law. The differentiation is between married and unmarried couples. The discrimination comes from the fact that same-sex couples cannot access marriage, while heterosexual couples—as long as they meet all legal requirements—could marry if they wish to do so. Many heterosexual couples, however, cannot marry given their specific circumstances, or have not married by the time they needed legal protection. In any case, it is clear that the road towards same-sex couples' recognition may be harder in Turkey than in other countries. The commonly used argument that there is no difference between the family functions performed by unmarried heterosexual couples and unmarried same-sex couples cannot be made simply because unmarried heterosexual couples are as invisible as same-sex couples.

1.3 Conclusion

This volume shows the legal development towards the recognition of same-sex marriage in different countries. Spain. Mexico, the United States and Colombia have accepted or are in the path towards full acceptance of same-sex marriage thanks to the role of their courts. Israel's legal system formally does not recognize same-sex marriage not because of a stance against it, but because family law is regulated by personal religious law. Israel's courts, however, have allowed for the registration of same-sex marriages performed abroad, creating a system where in practical terms same-sex marriages enjoy at least certain rights. This book shows a group of countries where same-sex couples are still invisible both to legal and social systems. Turkey and countries in the Commonwealth Caribbean are still at a stage where gay and lesbian individuals suffer discrimination. Courts are not willing to side with individual rights when it comes to family law, but instead, they have chosen to reinforce institutional roles within the family. Thus, marriage is a hierarchical institution where men and women fulfill different functions. In these countries, however, there are efforts from civil society and academia to show the problems produced by this lack of recognition. Even in these countries there is a movement aimed at breaking down barriers in family law. The fact that the world around these countries is changing also has an impact. The analysis of decisions on same-sex marriage in different countries can provide courts in countries with incipient litigation in the area of family law and same-sex couples with new arguments that may support their legal reasoning. Decisions that support same-sex couples are the result of arguments brought by opposing parties that refer not only to local statutes, but also to legal principles that may transcend their national boundaries. At the same time, these decisions apply international law not only when it is binding for them. International law is sometimes used to support decisions as some sort of trend in the international arena. International human rights also play an important role. The European Court of Human Rights decisions with regards to sexual orientation and family law will sooner or later help move some boundaries in Turkey and in other countries of the region. Hopefully the Inter-American Court of Human Rights will do the same in countries of the Caribbean region as well as in the Americas. The role of these courts, however, must be accompanied by academic discussions, such as the ones presented here, on the role of legal systems in protecting or discriminating against individuals and their families.

Chapter 2
And the Story Comes to an End: The Constitutionality of Same-Sex Marriages in Spain

José María Lorenzo Villaverde

Abstract In January 2005 the Spanish Government introduced a bill amending the Civil Code to allow same-sex marriage. The bill was approved in July of 2005 with a small majority and the Conservative Popular Party challenged the new Act's constitutionality before the Spanish Constitutional Court. In 2012 the Constitutional Court decided the challenge upholding the constitutionality of the same-sex marriage statute. This chapter presents an overview of the debate on the constitutionality of Act 13/2005. It discusses the constitutional basis for the enactment of the statute as well as the arguments presented to challenge its constitutionality. It also presents a brief comparative analysis between the Spanish decision on same-sex marriage and the decision by the Constitutional Court of Portugal in the same issue.

In March of 2004, the Spanish Socialist Party (PSOE) won the General Elections and established a new majority. In January 2005, the Government introduced a bill amending the Civil Code (CC) to allow same-sex couples[1] to marry. When the Congress approved the bill in a second reading, it became Act 13/2005 of

This chapter is part of a PhD thesis to be submitted by the author at the Faculty of Law of the University of Copenhagen. With the exception of the provisions of the Spanish and Portuguese Constitutions, translations from the Spanish and Portuguese languages are done by the author.

[1]The expressions "same-sex marriage" or "gender-neutral marriage" are used indistinctly, acknowledging that the notion of "sex" refers to a biological category whilst "gender" is a social construct. See further SCHUSTER, A.: "Gender and Beyond: Disaggregating Legal Categories" in Schuster (Ed.): *Equality and Justice: Sexual Orientation and Gender Identity in the XXI Century*, Editrice Universitaria Udinese srl, Udine, Italy, (2011), p. 31 and ff.

J.M. Lorenzo Villaverde (✉)
Faculty of Law, University of Copenhagen, Studiestræde 6, 1455 Copenhagen, Denmark
e-mail: jovi@jur.ku.dk; jose.m.lorenzo.villaverde@gmail.com

M. Sáez (ed.), *Same Sex Couples - Comparative Insights on Marriage and Cohabitation*, Ius Gentium: Comparative Perspectives on Law and Justice 42,
DOI 10.1007/978-94-017-9774-0_2

July 1st (hereinafter referred as "Act 13/2005" or "the Act").[2] The Bill was passed with 187 votes in favor, 147 against and 4 abstentions. The Conservative Popular Party (PP) presented an appeal against its constitutionality before the Spanish Constitutional Court (TC).[3] The Council of the State,[4] the General Council of the Judiciary (CGPJ)[5] and the Royal Academy of Jurisprudence and Legislation (RAJL)[6] respectively issued reports on the matter. There have been political, legal and social debates with arguments both in favor and against the Act.

The Spanish Constitution (CE) and the principles and values contained in it are the starting point and the basis of Family Law in Spain and, therefore, most of the legal debate has revolved around the constitutionality of the Act.[7] After 7 years, the TC decided the appeal against the constitutionality of Act 13/2005 through STC 198/2012[8] in which the Court rejected the appeal and affirmed the constitutionality of gender-neutral marriages in Spain.

---

[2]*Act 13/2005, of 1st July, amending the Civil Code with regards to the right to marry. Boletin Oficial del Estado* (BOE) N. 157, of 2nd July 2005, pp. 23632–23634.

[3]*Appeal against constitutionality nr. 6864-2005, relative to Act 13/2005, of 1st July, amending the Civil Code with regards to the right to marry.* Accepted for consideration by decision of the TC of 25th October 2005. *Boletín Oficial del Estado* (BOE) N. 273 of 25th November 2005, pp. 37313–37313.

[4]*Report of the Council of State n. 2628/2004, of 16th December 2004*, available at http://www.boe.es/buscar/doc.php?id=CE-D-2004-2628. The Council of the State is an advisory body which main duty is issuing reports and opinions on legislative drafts. See further, on the Council of the State, SÁNCHEZ NAVARRO, Á.J.: *Consejo de Estado, función consultiva y reforma constitucional*, Reus, Madrid, (2007).

[5]*Study on the amendment of the Civil Code regarding marriage between persons of same sex, of 26th January 2005*, available at http://www.poderjudicial.es/cgpj/es/Poder-Judicial/Consejo-General-del-Poder-Judicial/Actividad-del-CGPJ/Informes/Estudio-sobre-la-reforma-del-Codigo-Civil-en-materia-de-matrimonio-entre-personas-del-mismo-sexo. The General Council of Judiciary is the ruling body of the Judiciary and one of its functions is issuing reports on legislative drafts. This report was particularly against the enactment of the Act 13/2005, based on its possible unconstitutionality and on its "inconvenience," although there was an important number of dissenting votes against the decision of the majority of the CGPJ. See further on the General Council of the Judiciary, its composition and functioning, BALLESTER CARDELL, M.: *El Consejo General del Poder Judicial: su función constitcional y legal*, Consejo General del Poder Judicial, Madrid, (2007).

[6]*Report issued by the Royal Academy of Jurisprudence and Legislation relative to the bill amending the Civil Code with regards to the right to marry, of 14th March 2005,* available in *Anales de la Real Academia de Jurisprudencia y Legislación Núm 35 (2005)* pp. 939–941

[7]See, LÓPEZ AGUILAR, J.F.: "Los criterios constitucionales y políticos inspiradores de la reforma del Derecho Civil en materia matrimonial", *Actualidad Jurídica Aranzadi núm. 655 (digital edition)*, (2005).

[8]*STC 198/2012, of 6th November 2012.* STC is the usual abbreviation to refer to a judgment by the TC, while ATC is the usual abbreviation for a writ. Both abbreviations are hereinafter used in this chapter. The judgments and writs of the Spanish Constitutional Court are available at http://hj.tribunalconstitucional.es/HJ/en.

This chapter presents an overview of the debate on the constitutionality of Act 13/2005 through six different sections: Sect. 2.1 discusses the constitutional basis for the enactment of Act 13/2005; Sect. 2.2 analyzes the challenges to the constitutionality of the Act based on Article 32 CE; Sect. 2.3 examines relevant case law of the TC with regards to the notion of "institutional guarantee" vis a vis subjective rights; Sect. 2.4 focuses on the only occasion prior to STC 198/2012 where the TC discussed the "principle of heterosexuality"[9] in marriage; Sect. 2.5 discusses the debate and solution to the constitutionality of same-sex marriages in Portugal, which was decided 2 years before the Spanish case; Sect. 2.6 analyzes different aspects of STC 198/2012.

2.1 Constitutional Basis of the Debate on Same-Sex Marriage

2.1.1 Equality

Article 14 of the CE contains an Equality Clause that states: "Spaniards are equal before the law and may not in any way be discriminated against on account of birth, race, sex, religion, opinion or any other personal or social condition or circumstance." The principle of equality must be understood in light of Article 9.2 CE, which sets an obligation on the State to promote equality while removing all obstacles that may impede its enjoyment. Article 14 CE also contains an open clause, as other "personal or social conditions or circumstances" may eventually be included within its scope. Sexual orientation is not expressly mentioned. The grounds expressly mentioned are subject to a more strict scrutiny by the TC when they are claimed.[10] Otherwise, the standard of review used by the Court is general scrutiny.[11]

---

[9]The expressions "principle of heterosexuality" (also "heterosexual principle" or "heterosexual element") and "heterosexuality" to refer to gender diversity in marriage are used by the TC in its case law and, often, by the Spanish legal scholarship. These expressions will also be used in this Chapter, even though they are not totally accurate. The so-called "principle of heterosexuality" refers to marriage conceived as a bilateral relationship where gender diversity is one of its elements, but it does not directly refer to the sexual orientation of the spouses.

[10]See *STC 81/1982, of 21st December 1982* and *STC 128/1987 of 16th of July 1987*.

[11]Some authors like GAVIDIA SÁNCHEZ, have considered sexual orientation within the ground of sex and, hence, included in the expressly mentioned grounds of Article 14 CE. However, discrimination based on sex is clearly different from that based on sexual orientation, and therefore an opposite-sex marriage where both husband and wife have the same rights and obligations seems in accordance with the ground of sex as mentioned in the Article 14 CE. Those, either men or women, who experience an attraction to people of their same sex are the ones affected by a regulation allowing only opposite-sex marriages, because of their sexual orientation. See further GAVIDIA SÁNCHEZ, J.V.: "La libertad de elegir como cónyuge a otra persona del mismo sexo y de optar entre el matrimonio y una unión libre (análisis crítico de la constitucionalidad del matrimonio homosexual y del llamado divorcio express)" in Gavidia Sánchez (Ed.): *La reforma del matrimonio (Leyes 13 y 15/2005)*, Marcial Pons, Madrid, (2007), pp. 25–77.

The TC has never established a set of criteria that should be followed in order to add a new ground to the expressly mentioned by Article 14 and that could trigger a stricter scrutiny by the TC. *Martín Sánchez* has argued that it may be possible to integrate sexual orientation as an expressly mentioned protected ground against discrimination. The argument requires an analysis of Article 14 CE in light of Article 10.2 CE,[12] which establishes that any interpretation of fundamental rights and liberties included in the CE must be done in line with the international treaties and agreements ratified by Spain. Since Spain is a Member State of the EU it is bound by its Treaties. The Treaty of the Functioning of the European Union expressly mentions the ground of sexual orientation as a suspicious ground for discrimination in its Articles 10 and 19.1. Thus, *Martín Sánchez* has argued that sexual orientation could and should be assimilated to the grounds already included in Article 14 CE.

The Charter of Fundamental Rights of the European Union, which currently has the same status as the Treaties, mentions sexual orientation in Article 21. Moreover, even if the European Convention of Human Rights (ECHR) does not include sexual orientation in the wording of its Article 14, the European Court of Human Rights (ECtHR) has reiterated in several occasions that sexual orientation must be considered as if it expressly appeared in the article itself.[13] Nevertheless, even though this interpretation may lead to the inclusion of sexual orientation as an assimilated ground to those expressly mentioned, that does not necessarily lead to the conclusion that there is a constitutional obligation to open marriage to same-sex couples.[14]

If we assume that sexual orientation is subject to strict scrutiny, some criteria must be fulfilled in order to assess whether legislation establishing some kind of differentiation is constitutional or not.[15] These criteria are:

- Comparability of factual situations.
- Existence of a *tertium comparationis*.
- The legislation must pursue a legitimate, objective, proportional and reasonable aim. When strict scrutiny applies, this aim has to be based on a constitutional purpose. Mere compatibility of the aim with the CE is insufficient to consider such differentiation constitutional.[16]

Still, application of these criteria does not automatically impose the legislature a constitutional obligation to open marriage to same-sex couples. It could be argued

[12]MARTÍN SÁNCHEZ, M.: *Matrimonio homosexual y constitución*, Tirant lo Blanc, Valencia, (2008), pp. 90–100.

[13]See, *inter alia*, the cases of the ECtHR: *Salgueiro da Silva Mouta v. Portugal*, of 21 December 1999, para. 28; S.L. v Austria, of 9 January 2003, para. 37; E.B. v. France, of 22 January 2008, paras. 91, 93.

[14]See, *inter alia*, *Schalk and Kopf v. Austria*, of 24 June 2010.

[15]See MARTÍN SÁNCHEZ, M.: *Matrimonio homosexual y constitución*, *op.cit.* pp. 35–100 and FERNÁNDEZ SEGADO, F.: *El Sistema Constitucional Español*, Dykinson, Madrid, (1992), pp. 190–209.

[16]MARTÍN SÁNCHEZ, M.: *Matrimonio homosexual y constitución*, *op.cit.* p. 99.

that there would be no different treatment if factual situations are different and the legislator is simply providing different legal consequences to situations that were originally in a different legal framework.[17]

Following Article 14 CE, it could eventually be argued that legal institutions other than marriage may ensure equality as in the case of introducing legislation on registered partnerships with protections similar to marriage. Opening marriage to same-sex couples, however, is possibly the best way to fulfil the mandate of Article 9.2 CE, which seeks to promote "conditions which ensure that the freedom and equality of individuals and of the groups to which they belong may be real and effective" and remove "the obstacles which prevent or hinder their full enjoyment." Among the different options open to the legislator, the one which eliminates the most differences is the one that best fulfils Articles 14 and 9.2 CE.

2.1.2 Dignity

Human dignity appears in Article 10.1 CE. Also, Article 11 CE considers dignity as one of the highest values of the legal system.[18] Moreover, dignity is linked to principles of equality and liberty, and all fundamental rights and freedoms included in Title I of the CE. Does the exclusion of same-sex couples from marriage, exclusion based on sexual orientation, contradict the principle of dignity? Some jurisdictions, like South Africa, consider the prohibition of same-sex marriage a contradiction with the value dignity.[19] The CE, however, does not allow a similar inference. Nonetheless, even if an exclusively opposite-sex marriage policy is unlikely unconstitutional on the basis of the principle of dignity,[20] such principle supports the enactment of Act 13/2005, in the same way as explained above with regards to equality.

[17]See *STC 148/1985* of 25th November and FERNÁNDEZ SEGADO, F.: *El Sistema Constitucional Español*, *op.cit.* pp. 190–209. FERNÁNDEZ SEGADO points out the possibility of "discriminating by no establishing differences", which would occur if the legislature did not establish different legal consequences to different factual situations. This approach has never been followed by the TC.

[18]Following this interpretation, MARTÍN SÁNCHEZ, M.: *Matrimonio homosexual y constitución*, *op.cit.* See also *STC 337/1994,* of 23rd December 1994.

[19]See further, decision of the Constitutional Court of South Africa *Minister of Home Affairs and Another v. Fourie and Another (CCT 60/04) [2005] ZACC 19; 2006 (3) BCLR 355 (CC); 2006 (1) SA 524 (CC) (1 December 2005)*.

[20]For an opposite point of view, see MARTÍN SÁNCHEZ, M.: *Matrimonio homosexual y constitución*, *op.cit.*, pp. 100–111.

2.1.3 Liberty

Article 1.1 CE recognizes the principle of liberty as a high value within the Spanish legal system. Moreover, Article 10.1 CE establishes that the "free development of the personality" is a "foundation of political order and social peace." Some political parties highlighted the importance of the free development of personality during the parliamentary debate of Act 13/2005.[21] Same-sex marriage may be seen as a step towards the fulfilment of the constitutional value of liberty.[22] Even though other options like registered partnerships are possible, the introduction of a gender neutral marriage seems the best way to fulfil both constitutional provisions of Articles 1.1 and 10.1 CE.

2.2 Challenges to the Constitutionality of Act 13/2005: Article 32 CE and Heterosexuality as a Defining Element in Marriage

The first four challenges to the constitutionality of Act 13/2005 came from Spanish judges in charge of civil registries where same-sex couples attempted to get married. According to Article 163 CE, "when a judicial body consider, within a proceeding, that a regulation with legal status, applicable to the proceeding, and upon the validity of which the judgment depends, may be contrary to the Constitution, will bring the matter before the Constitutional Court in the circumstances, manner and subject to the consequences established by law, which shall in no case create a stay."[23] In each case the TC dismissed the constitutionality issue on procedural grounds and did not review the request on the merits.[24]

Later, the PP appealed the constitutionality of Act 13/2005 (hereinafter referred as "Appeal 6864-2005" or " the Appeal"). The Appeal argued that the Act violated several articles of the CE. The key one was Article 32 CE. After 7 years, STC 198/2012 affirmed the constitutionality of the Act.

---

[21] See, e.g. *DS Congreso de los Diputados N. 78 of 17th March 2005* available at http://www.congreso.es/public_oficiales/L8/CONG/DS/PL/PL_078.PDF.

[22] In a similar way, GAVIDIA SÁNCHEZ, J.V.: *La libertad de elegir como cónyuge a otra persona del mismo sexo y de optar entre el matrimonio y una unión libre (análisis crítico de la constitucionalidad del matrimonio homosexual y del llamado divorcio express)*, *op.cit.*, pp. 32–37.

[23] This way of challenging the constitutionality of an Act is named *cuestión de inconstitucionalidad*, literally "question of unconstitutionality". See further FERNÁNDEZ SEGADO, F.: *El Sistema Constitucional Español*, *op.cit.* p. 1082 and ff and PÉREZ ROYO, J.: *Curso de Derecho Constitucional*, Marcial Pons, Madrid, (1998), p. 691 and ff.

[24] *ATC 505/2005*, of 13th December 2005, *ATC 508/2005*, of 13th December 2005, *ATC 59/2006*, of 15th February 2006 and *ATC 12/2008*, of 16th January 2008.

Prior to STC 198/2012, the TC had never defined the content of the concept of marriage as contained in the CE. It had, however, referred to the marriage institute, the *de facto* unions and the "guarantee of institute"[25] in previous judgments. As mentioned, the Council of the State, the CGPJ, and the RAJL issued three reports, respectively.

The TC faced three possible positions with regards to the constitutionality of gender-neutral marriages: it is unconstitutional,[26] it is constitutionally possible, or it is constitutionally mandated. The three positions contain different perspectives and nuances.

Appeal 6864-2005 stated that Act 13/2005 did not respect the guarantee of the marriage institute recognized in the Constitution. Article 32 CE establishes the right to marry as follows:

> Men and women have the right to marry with full legal equality.
>
> The law shall regulate the forms of marriage, the age at which it may be entered into and the required capacity therefore, the rights and duties of the spouses, the grounds for separation and dissolution, and the consequences thereof.

There is no definition of marriage in the CE and it does not mention its elements.[27] Rather, it establishes the right to marry and involves an institutional guarantee following Article 53.1 CE: "the rights and liberties recognized in Chapter Two of the present Title are binding for all public authorities. The exercise of such rights and liberties, which shall be protected in accordance with the provisions of Article 161, 1a), may be regulated only by law [understood as acts or statutes passed by parliament] which shall, in any case, respect their *essential content*" (emphasis added). As the CE recognizes marriage as an institutional guarantee, it becomes a constitutional guarantee.

What is the concept of marriage recognized in the CE and how should the essential content that the legislator must respect be understood? The key question is whether the so-called "heterosexual element" or "principle of heterosexuality", that is, gender diversity, is part of the essential content of marriage, by determining the meaning of the terms "man" and "woman" in Article 32 CE.

Article 149.1.8ª CE reserves to the central State (as opposed to the Autonomous Communities) the enactment of rules related to the implementation of legal norms, including those needed for their interpretation. Article 3 of the Spanish Civil Code

---

[25]The term "institute" is, broadly, used within the field of private law and "institution", most often, within the field of public law. However, for the purposes of this Chapter, the terms "institute" and "institution" will be used to refer to marriage indistinctly, as well as the expressions "institutional guarantee", "guarantee of institution" or "guarantee of institute."

[26]This was supported by *Appeal 6864-2005* and the *Reports* of the CGPJ and the RAJL.

[27]In the same way: GARCÍA RUBIO, M.P.: "Viejos y nuevos apuntes sobre la constitucionalidad del matrimonio homosexual" in Álvarez González (Ed.): *Estudios de Derecho de Familia y Sucesiones (dimensiones interna e internacional)*, Fundación Asesores Locales, Santiago de Compostela, (2009), pp. 171–197 and ASÚA GONZÁLEZ, C.I.: "El matrimonio hoy: sus perfiles jurídicos ad intra y ad extra", *Teoría y Derecho. Revista de Pensamiento Jurídico*, vol. 2, (2007), pp. 7–27.

(CC) lays down the general rules of interpretation as follows: "Legal norms shall be interpreted according to the proper sense of their words, in relation to the context, historical and legislative background, and social reality of the time when they shall be applied, taking into account their spirit and purpose."[28] These are the grammatical, historical and dynamic criteria.

2.2.1 Grammatical Criterion

Appeal 6864-2005 stressed the relevance of the grammatical interpretation of Article 32 CE according to the "proper sense of its words" of both the expression "man and woman" and the term "marriage."

Article 32 CE is the only article in the Constitutional text where "man" and "woman" are expressly mentioned. Other articles of the CE use terms and expressions such as "everyone has the right to . . . ", "every person", "the citizens", and so on. What is, therefore, the constitutional significance of this express reference to "man" and "woman"?

The appellants agreed with the arguments set forth in the report written by the Council of the State. This report stated that the reference to "man" and "woman" in Article 32 CE had a double purpose: on the one hand, it referred to the full legal equality between a man and a woman. Thus, the provision ensured that the legislature could not pass marriage regulations setting inequalities based on the sex of the spouses that could violate the principle of equality of Article 14 CE. On the other hand, the report of the Council of the State stated, this explicit mention to gender diversity meant that compliance with the equality clause of Article 14 CE in relation to Article 32 CE must start from what is laid down in Article 32.1 CE.[29] The Council of the State in its report, however, reached a different conclusion than the appellants. Whereas the appellants argued that the Act was unconstitutional, the Council of the State supported the interpretation that opposite-sex marriage was the only marriage constitutionally protected. It considered, however, that the legislator

[28] Traditionally, the rules for interpretation of norms have been introduced in the Civil Code, but these rules must comply with the CE, as this is hierarchically superior. However, and even though, the TC is only subject to the CE and the Organic Act of the Constitutional Court (LOTC), these criteria may be used, and are actually used, by the TC. See further BALAGUER CALLEJÓN, M.L.: *Interpretación de la Constitución y ordenamiento jurídico*, Editorial Tecnos, Madrid, (1997), pp. 78–80. See also ALONSO GARCÍA, E.: *La interpretación de la Constitución*, Centro de Estudios Constitucionales, Madrid, (1984), pp. 77–84, where the author is of the opinion that the TC could use and create new criteria for interpretation. Cfr, the *Report of the CGPJ,* p. 23.

[29] In a same way, although with different conclusions, GAVIDIA SÁNCHEZ has supported that the reference to the gender diversity in Article 32 CE is a special rule from the Article 14 CE. Therefore, without this reference to "man" and "woman" an opposite-sex only marriage would be unconstitutional by virtue of the equality clause of the Article 14 CE, see GAVIDIA SÁNCHEZ, J.V.: *La libertad de elegir como cónyuge a otra persona del mismo sexo y de optar entre el matrimonio y una unión libre (análisis crítico de la constitucionalidad del matrimonio homosexual y del llamado divorcio express), op.cit.,* p. 29.

could introduce a gender-neutral marriage. In other words, it concluded that same-sex marriage was a constitutional option for the legislature.

An accurate interpretation of the Act requires reading the paragraph as a whole: "men and women have the right to marry with full legal equality." Before the approval of the CE, and during the Franco dictatorship, married women were clearly discriminated against. Article 32 CE eliminated any possibility of legislation that differentiated on the basis of sex with regards to marriage.

A grammatical interpretation does not conclude that the heterosexual principle is an essential element in marriage as described in Article 32 CE. Furthermore, Article 32 CE does not state at the end "man and woman have the right to marry *with each other*." Alternatively, it is possible to argue that such reference may have been unnecessary because the Constituent Assembly in 1978 did not contemplate same-sex marriage. That claim, however, involves a historical criterion and not simply a grammatical one.

The Appeal also claimed that a grammatical interpretation of the term "marriage" would lead to the unconstitutionality of same-sex marriage. Appellants pointed out that the reform came to modify the "traditional, constitutional and legal conception of marriage as a union between a man and a woman," giving marriage "a different meaning from the one that it has always had."[30] Additionally, the appellants also stated that "marriage is, in its basic and central core, an institution of a precise outline which responds to the logic of the nature and social needs of our species."[31] They relied on, among others, old legal texts, like the Provisional Act of Civil Marriage of 1870, the Civil Code of 1889 or the Act of Civil Marriage of 1932, and even medieval texts like *Las Siete Partidas* or Las *Decretales,*[32] in order to conclude that *matrimonio* (marriage) came from *matris munium* ("care of the mother") and, therefore, it involved the idea of procreation and the union of a man and a woman.

However, the argument that marriage means a monogamous union between a man and a woman to further procreation may be challenged. First, marriage does not have a universal outline and definition, neither in time, nor in space. This is clear from the introduction of divorce, which challenged the traditional concept of marriage as an indissoluble bond or the existence of polygamous marriages in different countries. Second, marriage was once the only source of family relations and its main function was procreation. Now, Article 39 CE protects the family regardless of the existence of a marriage bond and infertility is no longer a ground for annulment. Moreover, gender neutral marriages already exist in other jurisdictions. *Asúa González* holds that the lack of a precise definition of "marriage" in the Spanish Civil Law is the result, in part, of the deliberate removal of marriage regulations from Civil Law to Canon Law in the pre-constitutional past, when the civil marriage was subsidiary to the canonical marriage.[33] In fact, Article 32 CE,

---

[30] *Appeal 6864-2005, FJ 1.*

[31] *Ibid.*

[32] *Ibid., FJ 2. Las Decretales* is actually Canon Law.

[33] ASÚA GONZÁLEZ, C.I.: "El matrimonio hoy: sus perfiles jurídicos ad intra y ad extra", *op.cit.* pp. 17–18.

especially in its second paragraph, may be considered a confirmation of the State's jurisdiction in marriage law, against that of Canon Law.[34] In any case, it does not seem accurate to claim a universal concept of marriage.

CGPJ's report also supported sex/gender diversity as essential to the concept of marriage. It enumerated definitions of marriage provided by different scholars, all of them including heterosexuality as a defining element of marriage. The report, however, erred by providing definitions written in the Spanish pre-constitutional period and others that still include indissolubility as an essential element of marriage, even though divorce has been legal in Spain since 1981.[35] The same could apply to the element of heterosexuality, which must be analyzed taking into account the current constitutional context.

The definition of marriage in the Dictionary of the Royal Academy of the Spanish Language (RAE) has also been used to support a grammatical interpretation of marriage as essentially requiring a male and a female. *Martínez de Aguirre* used this argument, in the context of a grammatical interpretation, in order to conclude that heterosexuality was a necessary element of the meaning of the term "marriage" in Spain.[36] The RAE, however, covers the Spanish language in many countries which do not have regulation on same-sex marriages. The RAE does not automatically modify the dictionary's definitions based on changing legislation in a particular country. Nevertheless, in 2012 the RAE added same-sex marriage to its definition of marriage: "In some jurisdictions, the union between two people of the same-sex, established by some rituals or legal formalities, with the aim of establishing a community of life and interests." Furthermore, Spanish is only one of the four languages spoken in Spain, together with Catalan, Galician and Basque. The *Institut d'Estudis Catalans*, the *Real Academia Galega* and the *Euskaltzaindia* have modified the definition of marriage for the Catalan, Galician and Basque languages, respectively, including, in the concept of marriage, that of two persons of the same sex.

Another argument against the value of a concept established by the RAE, following *Gavidia Sánchez*, is that definitions given by the RAE and other language scholars must be deemed irrelevant because they "lack democratic legitimacy."[37] Following this argument, definitions given by an institution like the RAE, which is not part of the structure of the Spanish "social and democratic State, subject to the rule of law" (Article 1.1. CE), should not bound the TC when following the

---

[34] In a similar way, although to support different arguments, DE PABLO CONTRERAS, P.: "La Constitución y la Ley 13/2005, de 1 de julio, de reforma del Código Civil en materia de derecho a contraer matrimonio" in Martínez de Aguirre Aldaz (Ed.): *Novedades legislativas en materia matrimonial*, Consejo General del Poder Judicial, Madrid, (2008), p. 72.

[35] *Act 30/1981, of 7th July 1981.*

[36] MARTÍNEZ DE AGUIRRE ALDAZ, C. and DE PABLO CONTRERAS, P.: "National Report: Spain", *Journal of Gender, Social Policy and the Law*, vol. 19, 1 (2011), p. 294.

[37] GAVIDIA SÁNCHEZ, J.V.: *La libertad de elegir como cónyuge a otra persona del mismo sexo y de optar entre el matrimonio y una unión libre (análisis crítico de la constitucionalidad del matrimonio homosexual y del llamado divorcio express), op.cit.*, pp. 24–25.

grammatical criterion of interpretation. Accordingly, the expression "proper sense of the words" contained in Article 3 CC must not be understood as referring to the meaning described in a given dictionary drafted by a royal academy of the Spanish language. Such assumption would be an unacceptable limitation to the work of legal interpretation by the TC.

A grammatical analysis clearly concludes that opposite-sex marriages are constitutionally protected. It does not, however, lead to the conclusion that same-sex marriages are constitutionally forbidden. This conclusion does not close the debate on the constitutionality of same-sex marriage. A grammatical "proper sense of the words" analysis is likely the first criterion used to interpret the constitutionality of a statute, but it needs to be contrasted with other criteria, and it is not necessarily the element that will prevail.[38] A grammatical criterion, alone, is not a sufficient element of interpretation.

2.2.2 *Historical Criterion*

The historical criterion attempts to ascertain the intent of the Constituent Assembly. Appeal 6864-2005 stated that "the Constitution does not allow the public powers to change the sense of the words used by the Constituent [Power]."[39] The appellants argued that the Constituent Assembly of 1978 took the concept of marriage prevalent in 1978 and in the Spanish legal tradition and placed it at a constitutional level, the maximum level on the normative hierarchy. This approach followed an interpretation which reproduced the intention of the Constituent Assembly. Constitutional concepts and institutions would be "frozen in time" unless a constitutional amendment took place. Accordingly, the Appeal rendered Act 13/2005 unconstitutional because it does not respect the essential element and the intention of the Constituent Power.

The history of the Constituent Assembly's discussion, however, shows that in 1978 most of the debate about the meaning of Article 32 CE focused on paragraph two with regards to the possibility of legal divorce, as well as the recognition of canonical marriages.[40] With regards to the first paragraph of Article 32 CE, the discussion was mainly about ensuring equality between husband and wife before and during marriage, and upon its dissolution, and this may explain its wording. Issues related to homosexuality were left to discussions on Criminal Law, with

---

[38] ALBALADEJO, M., *Derecho Civil I, introducción y parte general*, pp. 150–153.

[39] *Appeal 6864-2005, FJ 1.*

[40] See *DS Congreso de los Diputados N. 72 of 23rd May 1978, pp. 2610 and ff; N. 107 of 11th July 1978, pp. 4073 and ff.* See also *DS Senado N. 45, of 29th August 1978, pp. 2000 and ff; N. 61, of 28th September 1978, pp. 3042 and ff.* Reports of the debates of both the Congress and the Senate can be found at http://www.congreso.es/portal/page/portal/Congreso/Congreso/Publicaciones?_piref73_2342619_73_1340041_1340041.next_page=/wc/refrescarLegislatura.

the aim of decriminalizing homosexual sexual practices. It is, thus, clear that the dominant concept of marriage in 1978 Spain included the "heterosexual principle".

The dissolubility/indissolubility of the marital bond, however, was a matter of significant importance during the debates of the Constituent Assembly. Some of the arguments used to avoid including the term "dissolution" in the Constitution were similarly used a quarter of century later as arguments against same-sex marriages. Two amendments were introduced (and finally rejected) during the constitutional debates to leave the term "dissolution" out of the CE.[41] They were introduced by two members of parliament representing the political party *Alianza Popular* (AP).[42]

Opponents to divorce argued that indissolubility was a universal element of marriage. Likewise, appellants argued that the universal character of marriage included heterosexuality. Additionally, opponents of divorce used the "unique" regulation of divorce in the Constitution. For example, *López Bravo y De Castro* claimed the CE would be one of the very few constitutions to include dissolution of marriage in its text. Similarly, Appeal 6864-2005 argued that Spain would be the exception among countries by recognizing same-sex marriages. Opponents of divorce denied the need for dissolution of marriage. In this sense, *Mendizábal Uriarte*, in 1978, pointed out that including the term "dissolution" in the CE was not necessary because marriage was already dissoluble by death. Similarly, appellants argued that a prohibition of same-sex marriage did not discriminate against homosexuals on the basis of sexual orientation. In 2005, the appellants stated that nobody was discriminated against on the grounds of sexual orientation with regards to marriage because homosexuals were allowed to marry, as long as they married someone of their opposite sex.[43] Both opponents of divorce and of same-sex marriage argued that regulating dissolution/same-sex marriage went against a desirable consensus. Furthermore, appellants, like opponents to divorce, used previous legislation to support their definition of marriage. Finally, both opponents of divorce and appellants showed disdain for surveys that favored divorce/same-sex marriage. Therefore, it appears that appellants attempted to breathe new life into failed arguments used by opponents to divorce to challenge dissolubility of marriage almost three decades earlier.

It is self-evident, as the appellants correctly argued, that the historical criterion used to interpret constitutional norms shows that the Constituent Assembly solely contemplated opposite-sex marriage. The historical criterion, however, is only one of many possible criteria to consider. One significant problem with using the historical criterion is that the Constitution becomes a static document unable to adapt not only to social changes but also to terms whose contents may evolve with time.[44]

---

[41] *DS Congreso de los Diputados N. 107, of 11th July 1978, pp. 4074 and ff.*

[42] The two members were *López-Bravo y De Castro* and *Mendizábal Uriarte Alianza Popular* changed the name to *Partido Popular* (PP) some years later. It is, therefore, the same party that appealed against the constitutionality of the Act 13/2005.

[43] Also in the *Report of the CGPJ*, p. 19.

[44] BALAGUER CALLEJÓN, M.L.: *Interpretación de la Constitución y ordenamiento jurídico*, *op.cit.* pp. 80–83.

The TC has only used the debates of the Constituent Assembly as an interpretative source in a few cases, and its use has not led to freeze constitutional concepts.[45] Moreover, in some decisions, the TC has considered the Constituent Assembly's debates as a criterion that works better when combined with others.[46] In other cases it has rejected an interpretation according to the intention of the Constituent Assembly because it did not reconcile with the "reality of the time" in which the law currently applied.[47]

Using the historical approach as the main source of constitutional interpretation could lead to absurd results. For example, a new Constituent Assembly could approve a new Constitution with the intention of including same-sex couples within the concept of marriage and, still, keep the same wording as the current Article 32 CE. The intention of the Constitution can be ambiguous because it reflects a compromise between political parties. Furthermore, in the specific case of Spain, the legislature may have left some issues unanswered as a result of the period known as "political transition" from dictatorship to democracy in which the Constituent Assembly drafted the Constitution.[48]

2.2.3 *Dynamic (Sociological) Criterion*

The Appeal did not discuss the sociological criterion, but article 3.1 CC expressly mentions it.[49] A statutory interpretation can account for the social reality of the time in which laws are applied. It could be argued, however, that the understanding of marriage in 2005, when Act 13/2005 was passed, still included the principle of heterosexuality. In June 2004, however, the Centre of Sociological Research (CIS) conducted a poll in which 66.2 % of Spaniards were in favor of opening marriage to same-sex couples, while 26.5 % were against. The poll also revealed that 69.4 % were in favor of legislation on partnerships, while only 11.6 % were against.[50] The difference between the percentage of people favouring same-sex marriage and favoring a different regulation (i.e. registered partnership) was not significant. Additionally, the decision to Appeal 6864-2005 was issued 7 years after it was

[45] *STC* of 1st November 1981, regarding Commercial Law.

[46] *STC* of 13th February 1981, regarding "freedom of chair" in universities.

[47] *STC* of 20th July 1981, regarding Tax Law. On the use of the historical criterion by the TC, see further ALONSO GARCÍA, E.: *La interpretación de la Constitución, op.cit.* pp. 148–153.

[48] As GARCÍA RUBIO pointed out, taking the idea from the Canadian Constitutional Court, the Constitution would be a "living tree", GARCÍA RUBIO, M.P.: *Viejos y nuevos apuntes sobre la constitucionalidad del matrimonio homosexual, op.cit.*, p. 180.

[49] It is also central in the Preamble of Act 13/2005.

[50] *Barómetro de Junio. Estudio n° 2568 de junio de 2004, Centro de Investigaciones Sociológicas.*

lodged. In those years, more than 20.000 same-sex marriages were celebrated.[51] The dynamic interpretation requires taking into account the reality of the time in which laws are applied. It requires, therefore, considering the social reality of during the years Act 13/2005 was in force.

In conclusion, only the historical criterion suggests the configuration of marriage in the CE 1978 as including the principle of heterosexuality. By using a dynamic interpretation, the concept of marriage would adapt to the reality of the time in which the Constitution applies, including the reality of the number of same-sex couples who got married, and the acceptance of same-sex marriage by Spaniards. Finally, the grammatical criterion of interpretation is not conclusive of marriage as an essentially heterosexual institution.

2.3 The Constitutional Court and the Development of the Concepts of Constitutional Guarantee and Subjective Right

After the enactment of Act 13/2005, some legal scholars held that the constitutionality of the Act depended on whether Article 32 CE contained a pure subjective right to marry, which meant that the legislator was not allowed to abolish opposite-sex marriage but could be allowed to extend it to same-sex couples, or if it contained guarantee of the institution of marriage, which limited the choices of the legislator.[52] Considering Article 32 CE as a mere subjective right[53] involves that the essential content of marriage is not referred to a constitutionally guaranteed institution, but to the essential content of a fundamental right like the right to marry. A constitutional guarantee over marriage, however, limits the role of the legislator, becoming, in principle, a more conservative solution and bringing the possibility of freezing the Constitution.[54]

In the relationship between fundamental rights and the concept of institutional guarantee it is important to distinguish between the subjective and the objective

[51] From 2005 to 2011, 22.124 same-sex marriages were contracted in Spain, source: National Institute of Statistics, www.ine.es

[52] DÍEZ PICAZO, L.: "En torno al matrimonio entre personas del mismo sexo", (2007) www.indret.com, (last seen: September 2014), pp. 11–12.

[53] ROCA TRÍAS held that there would not be a guarantee of institute, and only a subjective right, as the institutional protection is already secured and such interpretation would be confirmed by the Charter of Fundamental Rights of the EU: ROCA TRÍAS, E.: "La familia y sus formas", *Teoría y Derecho. Revista de Pensamiento Jurídico*, vol. 2, (2007), p. 58. See also RODRÍGUEZ, Á.: "Treinta y dos", *Diario La Ley n° 6643 (digital edition)*, (2007).

[54] See *STC 26/1987*, of 27th February 1987, regarding the "autonomy of the universities". In this judgement, the Court stated that the fundamental right, understood as absolute fundamental right or subjective right, offers more resistance to the legislator, whilst the guarantee of institution is more vulnerable. In the case of marriage it appears to be the opposite, taking into account the second paragraph of Article 32 CE and Article 53.1 CE.

(or institutional) dimensions of fundamental rights, and between the latter and the concept of institutional guarantee. In STC 53/1985,[55] the TC explained the objective dimension of fundamental rights:

> It is not only the negative obligation of the State not to damage the individual nor the institutional sphere protected by fundamental rights, deduced from the obligation of submission of all powers to the Constitution, but also the positive obligation of contributing to the effectiveness of the mentioned rights and values linked to those rights, even when there is no subjective claim from the citizen.

The objective dimension of a fundamental right contrasts with the traditional liberal conception of fundamental rights where the State has a passive duty to protect. The objective dimension obliges the State to act in order to guarantee the exercise of those fundamental rights.

The institutional guarantee differs from this objective (institutional) dimension because the institutional guarantee's main purpose is *keeping* the "master image" of an institution. The objective dimension of a fundamental right demands a *positive action* from the State. The existence of an objective dimension of a fundamental right, however, does not exclude that some rights contain, together with the subjective right, an institutional guarantee.[56] Previously to STC 198/2012, the TC used the concept of institutional guarantee in a confusing way by referring to concepts that do not respond to characteristics of an institution, but rather, respond to the objective dimension of a right, as in STC 12/1982[57] or STC 9/2007.[58] Although at times the differences between objective dimension and institutional guarantee are unclear or mistaken, both fundamental right and institutional guarantee can coexist.[59]

---

[55] *STC 53/1985*, of 11th April 1985, *FJ 4th*.

[56] See CIDONCHA MARTÍN, A.: "Garantía institucional, dimensión institucional y derecho fundamental: balance jurisprudencial",(2009), http://espacio.uned.es/fez/eserv.php?pid=bibliuned:TeoriayRealidadConstitucional-2009-23-50050&dsID=PDF, (last seen: September 2014), pp. 149–188.

[57] *STC 12/1982*, of 31st March 1982 dealt with the right to manage and use images and sounds via television, connected to Article 20.1 CE which recognizes "the right to freely express and disseminate thoughts, ideas and opinions trough words, in writing or by any other means of communication." The TC mentioned that the notion of "free public opinion" was a guaranteed institution. However, "free public opinion" responds to the characteristics of the objective dimension of the right in the sense that the State must carry out a positive action in order to ensure such free public opinion.

[58] *STC 9/2007*, of 15th January 2007 dealt also with the notion of "free public opinion." Another example is *STC 254/1993*, of 20th July 1993, with regards to the use of data processing and the protection of honor and personal and family privacy.

[59] In the same way, BAÑO LEÓN pointed out that the notion of subjective right and institutional guarantee intertwine and, both together, become part of the notion of fundamental right, BAÑO LEÓN, J.M.: "La distinción entre derecho fundamental y garantía institucional en la Constitución Española", *Revista Española de Derecho Constitucional*, vol. 24 (septiembre-diciembre), (1988), pp. 169–170.

The TC has held in various occasions that fundamental rights have this double character as subjective rights and institutional guarantees. Two cases illustrate this double character. First, this double character was early confirmed by STC 37/1987,[60] regarding the right to property, stating that:

> It is a recognized right, as it has been established by this Court in STC 111/1983, FJ 8th, from its institutional and individual dimensions, and it constitutes, from the latter point of view, a subjective right which *gives in, in order to become an economic equivalent, when the interest of the community legitimates its expropriation* (emphasis added).

The decision further stated that:

> The social dimension of the private property, as *institution* called to satisfy collective needs, is consistent with the image contemporary society has of the right [to private property] (emphasis added).

This "social function" is part of the objective dimension of a right[61] but it does not exclude that such "social function" can frame the institutional guarantee as well. Moreover, the TC recognized the guarantee of the institution of family[62] and referred to marriage as an institution in the relevant ATC 222/1994[63] which will be analyzed later.

Following *Ramos Chaparro*,[64] the first paragraph of Article 32 CE expresses the aspect of marriage in which liberty and individual autonomy prevail (the subjective right), and the second paragraph describes marriage as an institution. Regardless of whether an institutional guarantee exists in Article 32 CE, the issue of defining what this guarantee involves remains. What is the essential content included in this Article, connected with the guaranteed institution? Is the so-called "principle of heterosexuality"[65] part of the institutional guarantee and, hence, it eliminates the possibility of opening marriage to new realities?

Prior to STC 198/2012, the TC dealt with the terms "essential content" and "constitutional guarantee of institution." Two decisions that discussed these terms are STC 11/1981[66] and STC 32/1981.[67] Neither decision dealt with family law issues. One referred to the right of workers to strike and the other to the guarantee of provincial autonomy within the structure of the territorial State. Both, however, help to an understanding of these terms.

In STC 11/1981,[68] the TC pointed out two ways of defining the "essential content" of a right. The first approach looked at the legal nature of every right:

---

[60] *STC 37/1987*, of 26th March 1987, *FJ 2nd*.

[61] See CIDONCHA MARTÍN, A.: "Garantía institucional, dimensión institucional y derecho fundamental: balance jurisprudencial", *op.cit.* (last date seen: September 2014), p. 182 and ff.

[62] See, for all, *STC 203/2000*, of 27th July 2000, *FJ 4th*.

[63] *ATC 222/1994*, of 11th July 1994.

[64] RAMOS CHAPARRO, E.: "Objecciones jurídico-civiles a las reformas del matrimonio", *Actualidad Civil, vol. 10, 1 (digital edition)*, (2005), p. after note 3.

[65] See *supra* note 9.

[66] *STC 11/1981*, of 8th April 1981.

[67] *STC 32/1981*, of 28th July 1981.

[68] *Id.*, supra note 66, *FJ 8th*.

> Those faculties or possibilities of exercising a right necessary for the right to be recognized as belonging to the described type [of rights]. Without them, the right shall not belong to that type any longer and shall become part of another type of rights, losing its nature. Moreover, it must be taken into account the historical moment in every case and the conditions inherent to democratic societies, when dealing with constitutional rights.

The second approach looked at the legally protected interests as a core of subjective rights. Thus, the TC pointed out that the essential content of the right refers to:

> The part of the right which is totally necessary for those legally protected interests (....) to be actually, concretely and effectively protected. Therefore, this essential content is exceeded or not fulfilled when the right is subject to limitations which make it impracticable or more difficult to be exercised than it is reasonable or subject to limitations that divest the right of the necessary protection.

Both approaches complement each other. Framing and defining an essential content requires both approaches. The first approach takes into account the dynamic criterion of interpretation which analyzes the "historical moment" in which a right is exercised and the laws apply. In the above mentioned STC 37/1987[69] regarding the right to property, the TC pointed out that:

> In its double dimension, as institution and subjective right, [property] has experienced such a deep transformation in our century that it can no longer be conceived as a legal concept framed exclusively by the abstract type described in article 348 of the Civil Code... [therefore] the intention of the appellants of identifying its essential content [of the right to private property] by exclusively focusing on what the Civil Code, back in the nineteenth century, established in its article 348, must be rejected as groundless. Such intention is not taking into account the modulations and changes the institution of private property, in general, and the agrarian property, in particular, have undergone.

Is it applicable to marriage what the TC said about property? Marriage and the concept of family have evolved and it is no longer possible to identify them with those contained in the civil codes of the nineteenth century.[70] This argument undermines the appellants' use of the historical criterion. It will be discussed below if, and how, the TC uses this argument in its STC 198/2012.

Regarding the second approach, it is difficult to understand how Act 13/2005, which involves an extension of the right to marry, may be seen as a limitation of the right itself, since opposite-sex married couples are protected in the same way as before Act 13/2005 was passed.[71] In TC's decision STC 32/1981,[72] which dealt with local autonomy, the Court explained the concept of institutional guarantee by saying that:

---

[69] *STC 37/1987*, of 26th March 1987, *FJ 2nd*.

[70] In the same way, VALPUESTA FERNÁNDEZ, R.: "Reflexiones sobre el Derecho de Familia", *Teoría del Derecho. Revista de Pensamiento Jurídico*, vol. 2, (2007), p. 76.

[71] In a similar way, PRATS ALBENTOSA, L.: "La nueva regulación del derecho matrimonial español: bases y principios" in Morales Moreno and Míquel González (Ed.): *Anuario de la Facultad de Derecho de la Universidad Autónoma de Madrid, n° 10: Derecho, sociedad y familia: cambio y continuidad*, Boletín Oficial del Estado y Universidad Autónoma de Madrid, Madrid, (2006), p. 22.

[72] *STC 32/1981*, of 28th July 1981, *FJ 3rd*.

> The institutional guarantee does not ensure a specific content or a determined sphere of competence, but rather the preservation of an institution in recognizable terms according to the image that the social conscience has [of that institution] in each time and place. Such guarantee is unknown when the institution is limited in a way that is basically deprived of its possibilities of real existence as institution, becoming a simple name.

Thus, three elements must be met in an institutional guarantee: (a) the institution has a core the legislator must respect, (b) that core is not determined, but rather it connects to the image the social conscience has of it in a particular point in space and time, and (c) it must not be reduced to a simple name. The first element accounts for the historical interpretation, and therefore the "core" responds to a fixed content established in 1978, and it relates to a certain idea of "freezing" such "core". The second element, however, contrasts with the first element suggesting that the content is not expressly fixed and it needs to be recognized in a given time and place by the social conscience. Like in STC 11/1981 and STC 37/1987, the TC referred to the reality of the time (and place) and, therefore, such reality must be taken into account.

The definition of guarantee clarifies that the essential content of the institution is not respected when the legislature changes it to the point of making it unrecognizable. At the same time, however, the essential content is not respected if the legislature does not allow the institution to adapt to changes, becoming unrecognizable by the current social conscience.

The third element mandates that the legislature may not reduce the institution to a simple name. It could be argued that the creation of a new legal institute such as a registered partnership reduces marriage to a simple name, as there would be two institutions with same or similar content and functions. The name "marriage," however, has a symbolic power that "registered partnership" does not have.[73]

2.4 Same-Sex Couples and Marriage According to the Constitutional Court Prior to STC 198/2012

Before STC 198/2012 on the constitutionality of Act 13/2005, the TC only briefly referred to the "heterosexual principle" in marriage in a brief writ in 1994, ATC 222/1994.[74] In that case writ, the survivor partner of a same-sex cohabiting couple, requested a widower's pension. The claimant argued that his situation was different from opposite-sex cohabitants because same-sex couples were not allowed to marry and this would involve indirect discrimination. The TC, however, dismissed the claim by pointing out that:

---

[73] ASÚA GONZÁLEZ refered to it as the "fight for the name." Indeed, it was one of the key factors (together with the adoption) at the centre of discussion from those positions opposed to same-sex marriage, see ASÚA GONZÁLEZ, C.I.: "El matrimonio hoy: sus perfiles jurídicos ad intra y ad extra", *op.cit.*, p. 14.

[74] *ATC 222/1994*, of 11th July 1994.

> The union between two persons of the same sex is not a legally regulated institution, and there is no constitutional right to its establishment, unlike marriage between a man and a woman, which is a constitutional right (article 32.1 CE) that generates, *ope legis*, a multiplicity of rights and duties (STC 184/90).[75]

From that perspective, the TC concluded that:

> The full constitutionality of the heterosexual principle must be admitted as qualifier of the matrimonial bond, as it is stated in our Civil Code. The Public Powers might allow a privileged treatment to the family union of a man and a woman compared to a same-sex union. However, the legislator can create a system in order to provide homosexual partners with full rights and benefits of marriage, as the European Parliament advocates.[76]

The TC did not recognize a constitutional obligation to open marriage to same-sex couples. Nonetheless, it pointed out that the legislature may create a system that provides full rights and benefits of marriage, following the European Parliament's (EP) Resolution. As the EP referred to both registered partnerships and marriage, it could be interpreted that the TC, in this writ, was allowing legislators the freedom to introduce same-sex marriage or registered partnerships.

Following ATC 222/1994, the role of the heterosexual principle appeared fully constitutional to define marriage in a given place and time (that is, Spain and 1994). The TC, however, did not refer to it as an essential element of marriage. ATC 222/1994 disregarded the argument that same-sex couples were suffering indirect discrimination and it stated that the legislator had broad freedom to frame the Social Security System in favor of the "familial bond."[77] By referring to the family based on traditional opposite-sex marriage as "familial bond," the TC differed from previous decisions. For example, in STC 222/1992[78] the Court stated that the CE did not identify and limit family to the family based on marriage. Indeed, marriage and family are regulated in the CE in different chapters (marriage in Chapter II on "Rights and Liberties" and family in Chapter III on "Principles governing Economic and Social Policy"). Article 39 CE and the TC case law, which has extended some protection given to marriage to those couples under cohabitation demonstrate that every marriage involves a family but not every family is based on marriage.

Finally, ATC 222/1994 referred to the Civil Code to conclude that requiring heterosexuality as a qualifier for marriage was constitutional. But this statement

---

[75]Id. *FJ 2nd.*

[76]The TC referred to the *Resolution on equal rights for homosexuals and lesbians in the EC, A3-0028/94.*

[77]The TC has been reluctant to extend rights with regards to Social Security to cohabitants in previous case law, *inter alia*, *STC 184/1990* and *STC 66/1994*. The solution given by the TC in *ATC 222/1994* seems consistent with these previous judgments which dealt with opposite-sex cohabitation. However, the TC recognized cohabitants for the purposes of subrogation in rental contracts (*inter alia*, *STC 222/1992* and *STC 47/1993*). This has been criticized as it seems that the TC has a different perspective depending on if the case has a negative impact on the public budget, see PÉREZ VILLALOBOS, M.C.: *Las leyes autonómicas reguladoras de las parejas de hecho*, Editorial Civitas, Madrid, (2008), p. 145. It is unclear whether the solution would have been the same if the case of ATC 222/1994 dealt with rental contracts instead of a pension from the Social Security system.

[78]*STC 222/1992*, of 12th December 1992.

may be seen as an inversion of the normative hierarchy, by using the CC to define constitutional concepts. In sum, ATC 222/1994 held that the principle of heterosexuality was constitutional but it did not conclude that passing gender neutral marriage legislation would be unconstitutional. In fact, ATC 222/1994 underlined that legislators had broader options. One could reasonably say that this decision left open the possibility of later declaring a same-sex marriage statute constitutionally forbidden, constitutionally mandated or constitutionally possible. Nonetheless, ATC 222/1994 seemed to follow the last option by stating that although opposite-sex marriage was constitutionally guaranteed, the legislature had a broad margin of action.

2.5 Lessons from Portugal: Acórdãos 359/2009 and 121/2010

Portugal introduced same-sex marriages in 2010. Some months later, its Constitutional Court (TCRP) decided on the constitutionality of the statute. Although Portugal approved gender-neutral marriage legislation 5 years later than Spain, its Constitutional Court acted faster. An overview of the Portuguese case may help to gain a better understanding of the Spanish situation and to outline similarities and differences between the Portuguese decision and STC 198/2012.

Portugal legalized same-sex cohabitation through Act 7/2001,[79] amending Act 135/1999.[80] Those acts provided few rights.[81] In 2010, however, the Portuguese Congress passed Act 9/2010,[82] legalizing same-sex marriage, but excluding same-sex married couples from adoption.[83]

The Portuguese Constitution (CRP) refers to marriage and family in its Article 36:

> Everyone has the right to form a family and to marry under conditions of full equality.
>
> The law shall regulate the requisites for and the effects of marriage and its dissolution by death or divorce, regardless of the form in which it was entered into.

---

[79] *Act 7/2001, of 11th May, protecting de facto unions.*

[80] *Act 135/1999, of 28th August, protecting de facto unions.*

[81] On *de facto* unions in Portugal, see DE OLIVEIRA, G. and PEREIRA COELHO, F.: *Curso de Direito de Familia, vol. 1*, Coimbra Editora, Coimbra, (2008), pp. 52–93, MARTINS, R.: "Same-Sex Partnerships in Portugal. From De Facto to De Jure?", *Utrecht Law Review*, vol. 4, 2 (2008); LORENZO VILLAVERDE, J.M.: "Las uniones de hecho (del mismo y de distinto sexo) y su consideración como familia en Portugal: una visión a la luz del art 36 de la Constitución de la República Portuguesa", *Derecho de Familia. Abeledo Perrot*, vol. 48, (2011).

[82] *Act 9/2010, of 31st May, allowing civil marriage between persons of the same sex.*

[83] RAPOSO named this restriction a "castrated marriage", see RAPOSO, V.L.: "Crónica de um casamento anunciado (o casamento entre pessoas do mesmo sexo)", *Revista do Ministério Público*, vol. Oct-Dec 2009, 120 (2009), pp. 188–189.

Additionally, Constitutional Act 1/2004[84] expressly established sexual orientation as a prohibited ground for discrimination, based on the Equality Clause of Article 13 CRP.

The relevant articles of the Portuguese Civil Code (CCRP), prior to the enactment of Act 9/2010, stated the following:

> Article 1577: Marriage is a contract celebrated between two persons of the opposite sex who seek to form a family by a full community of life, according to the provisions of this Code.
>
> Article 1628: It is legally inexistent .... e) the marriage entered into by two persons of same sex.

Act 9/2010 repealed the requirement of opposite sex in Article 1577 CCRP and eliminated the legal inexistence of marriage as laid down in Article 1628 e) CCRP.

Before the enactment of Act 9/2010, the TCRP had already discussed same-sex marriages. *Acordão*[85] 359/2009[86] referred to a female same-sex couple whose marriage application was rejected. After unsuccessfully appealing, the case reached the TCRP. The issue was whether Articles 1577 and 1628 e) CCRP were unconstitutional. The couple argued that the concept of marriage in the Portuguese Civil Code could not be understood as a historically received concept of marriage because it would result in an inversion of the normative hierarchy with the Civil Code defining constitutional concepts. Moreover, that definition of marriage denied same-sex couples access to a legal institution that was perceived as a "symbolic good." The couple argued that since marriage represented a "symbolic good," any legislation allowing same-sex couples to enter into a registration scheme different from marriage would not be enough to guarantee equality.

The TCRP in *Acordão* 359/2009 rejected the appeal but pointed out some relevant arguments. The decision stated that the concept of marriage at the time of the approval of the CRP (1976) included the heterosexual principle.[87] It recognized, however, that requirements and legal effects of marriage were subject to change by legislation. The TCRP also stated that the inclusion of sexual orientation in the Equality Clause of Article 13 CRP did not impose an obligation to regulate same-sex marriages.[88] At the same time, the Court declared that constitutional guarantees

---

[84] *Constitutional Act 1/2004, of 24th July, sixth constitutional review.*

[85] I will keep the term *Acordão* in Portuguese to refer to the judgements of the TCRP. The judgments of the Portuguese Constitutional Court are available at http://www.tribunalconstitucional.pt/tc/acordaos/.

[86] *Acordão 359/2009*, of 9th July 2009.

[87] *Ibid., Fundamento 10.*

[88] *Ibid.* The TCRP referred to the opinion of the constitutionalists GOMES CANOTILHO, J.J. and MOREIRA, V.: *Constituição da República Portuguesa, anotada: artigos 1° a 107°, vol. 1*, Coimbra Editora, Coimbra (2007), p. 568 and MIRANDA, J. and MEDEIROS, R.: *Constituição Portuguesa Anotada, Tomo I: Introdução Geral, Preâmbulo, artigos 1° a 79°*, Wolters Kluwer Portugal, Coimbra Editora, Coimbra, (2010), p. 820.

did not "freeze" in time constitutional concepts.[89] It further asserted that unmarried same-sex couples could also become a family even if not married.[90] In the end, the Court concluded that it was the role of the legislature, and not of the TCRP, to adapt marriage regulation to every historical moment.[91]

Similarly to Spain, it is possible to identify three positions supported by similar arguments: those who supported same-sex marriage as a constitutional obligation,[92] those who supported the position that same-sex marriage was constitutionally forbidden,[93] and those who supported the position that it was constitutionally possible.[94]

---

[89] *Ibid.*

[90] *Ibid., Fundamento 15.*

[91] *Ibid., Fundamentos 11 and 12.*

[92] See, *inter alia*, PAMPLONA CÔRTE-REAL, C.: "Da inconstitucionalidade do Código Civil – artigos 1577°, 1628°, alínea e), e disposições conexas – ao vedar o acceso ao instutito do casamento a casais do mesmo sexo" in Pamplona Côrte-Real, Moreira and Duarte D'almeida (Ed.): *O casamento entre pessoas do mesmo sexo: Três pareceres sobre a inconstitucionalidade dos artigos 1577° e 1628° alínea e) do Código Civil*, Edições Almedina SA, Coimbra, (2008); MOREIRA, I.: "Da inconstitucionalidade das normas resultantes da leitura conjugada do artigo 1577° do Código Civil e da alínea e) do artigo 1628° do mesmo Código, nos termos das quais duas pessoas do mesmo sexo não podem contrair casamento e, se o fizerem, é o mesmo tido por inexistente" in ibid. (Ed.),; DUARTE D'ALMEIDA, L.: "Casamento Civil e <sexo diferente>: Sobre a inconstitucionalidade das normas expressas pelos artigos 1577°, e 1628°, alínea e), do Código Civil" in ibid. (Ed.),; MÚRIAS, P.: "Un símbolo como bem juridicamente protegido – parecer", (2008) http://muriasjuridico.no.sapo.pt/PMuriasParecerCPMS.pdf, (last date seen: November 2013).

[93] See, *inter alia*, BARROSO, I.M.: "Casamento civil entre pessoas do mesmo sexo: um <<direito fundamental>> á medida da lei ordinária?", *Lex Familiae – Revista Portuguesa de Direito da Familia*, vol. 7, 13 (2010), pp. 57–82, DE OLIVEIRA, G. and PEREIRA COELHO, F.: *Curso de Direito de Familia, vol. 1, op.cit.* p. 203 and ff; SANTOS, D.: *Mudam-se os tempos, mudam-se os casamentos? O casamento entre pessoas do mesmo sexo e o Direito português*, Coimbra Editora, Coimbra, (2009), pp. 342 and ff, specially. However, DE OLIVEIRA, in DE OLIVEIRA, G.: "Portugal! Um país de contrastes" in Costa (Ed.): *Metamorfosi del matrimonio e altre forme di convivenza affetiva*, Libreria Bonomo Editrice, Bologna, (2007), p. 181, stated that there is no obstacle for opening marriage to same-sex couples.

[94] See RAPOSO, V.L.: "Crónica de um casamento anunciado (o casamento entre pessoas do mesmo sexo)", *op.cit.* p. 179 and ff. This author rejected that the CRP established a prohibition on same-sex marriages. She mentioned that it could eventually be possible to name it differently (that is, creating a registration scheme for same-sex partnerships, see p. 179), but she was of the opinion that, taking into account a dynamic interpretation of the CRP, if not now, same-sex marriage could become constitutionally obliged in the future (p. 182) and supported same-sex marriage versus registered partnership (pp. 186 and ff.). See also GOMES CANOTILHO, J.J. and MOREIRA, V.: *Constituição da República Portuguesa, anotada: artigos 1° a 107°, vol. 1, op.cit.* pp. 567–568, MIRANDA, J. and MEDEIROS, R.: *Constituição Portuguesa Anotada, Tomo I: Introdução Geral, Preâmbulo, artigos 1° a 79°, op.cit.*, pp. 811 and 819–821.

The historical interpretation was discussed among the legal scholarship.[95] This interpretation connected with the guarantee of the institution of marriage contained in the CRP and its essential content, which must be respected.[96] Some scholars considered sex/gender diversity as part of the essential content of the marriage institution.[97] Under that interpretation same-sex marriage had to be unconstitutional because it violated a constitutional guarantee. Other scholars claimed that the "heterosexual element" in marriage was not essential.[98] From this perspective, legislators had the option (or even the obligation) to open up marriage to same-sex couples. This argument followed a dynamic interpretation.[99] Some legal scholars

---

[95]GOMES CANOTILHO, J.J. and MOREIRA, V.: *Constituição da República Portuguesa, anotada: artigos 1° a 107°, vol. 1, op.cit.*, pp. 567–568, MIRANDA, J. and MEDEIROS, R.: *Constituição Portuguesa Anotada, Tomo I: Introdução Geral, Preâmbulo, artigos 1° a 79°*, *op.cit.*, p. 811 and 819.

[96]See GOMES CANOTILHO, J.J. and MOREIRA, V.: *Constituição da República Portuguesa, anotada: artigos 1° a 107°, vol. 1, op.cit.*, p. 561; MIRANDA, J. and MEDEIROS, R.: *Constituição Portuguesa Anotada, Tomo I: Introdução Geral, Preâmbulo, artigos 1° a 79°*, *op.cit.*, p. 819; DE OLIVEIRA, G. and PEREIRA COELHO, F.: *Curso de Direito de Familia, vol. 1, op.cit.*, pp. 112–114 In a different way, MURIAS considered the theory of the guarantee of institute (or institution) groundless, see MÚRIAS, P.: "Un símbolo como bem juridicamente protegido – parecer", *op.cit.* (last date seen: November 2013), p. 16 and ff.

[97]*Inter alia*, BARROSO, I.M.: "Casamento civil entre pessoas do mesmo sexo: um <<direito fundamental>> á medida da lei ordinária?", *op.cit.* p. 65; SANTOS, D.: *Mudam-se os tempos, mudam-se os casamentos? O casamento entre pessoas do mesmo sexo e o Direito português, op.cit.*, pp. 303–306 and 342 and ff; MACHADO, J.E.M.: "A (in)definição do casamento no Estado constitucional: Fundamentos meta-constitucionais e deliberação democrática" in De Oliveira, Machado and Martins (Ed.): *Família, consciência, secularismo e religião*, Wolters Kluwer Portugal, Coimbra Editora, Coimbra, (2010), p. 65.

[98]See GOMES CANOTILHO, J.J. and MOREIRA, V.: *Constituição da República Portuguesa, anotada: artigos 1° a 107°, vol. 1, op.cit.*, pp. 567–568; MIRANDA, J. and MEDEIROS, R.: *Constituição Portuguesa Anotada, Tomo I: Introdução Geral, Preâmbulo, artigos 1° a 79°*, *op.cit.*, pp. 819–821; PAMPLONA CÔRTE-REAL, C.: *Da inconstitucionalidade do Código Civil – artigos 1577°, 1628°, alínea e), e disposições conexas – ao vedar o acceso ao instutito do casamento a casais do mesmo sexo*, *op.cit.* pp. 21–22; RAPOSO, V.L.: "Crónica de um casamento anunciado (o casamento entre pessoas do mesmo sexo)", *op.cit.*, pp. 182–183.

[99]The possibility or convenience of a dynamic interpretation, in order to give the legislator the option (or in order to impose the obligation) of opening up marriage to same-sex couples, has been present in the debate among the legal scholarship, *inter alia*: MIRANDA, J. and MEDEIROS, R.: *Constituição Portuguesa Anotada, Tomo I: Introdução Geral, Preâmbulo, artigos 1° a 79°*, *op.cit.*, p. 815; DE OLIVEIRA, G.: *Portugal! Um país de contrastes*, *op.cit.* p. 181; PAMPLONA CÔRTE-REAL, C.: *Da inconstitucionalidade do Código Civil – artigos 1577°, 1628°, alínea e), e disposições conexas – ao vedar o acceso ao instutito do casamento a casais do mesmo sexo*, *op.cit.* p. 24; MOREIRA, I.: "Da inconstitucionalidade das normas resultantes da leitura conjugada do artigo 1577° do Código Civil e da alínea e) do artigo 1628° do mesmo Código, nos termos das quais duas pessoas do mesmo sexo não podem contrair casamento e, se o fizerem, é o mesmo tido por inexistente" in ibid. (Ed.), p. 37; RAPOSO, V.L.: "Crónica de um casamento anunciado (o casamento entre pessoas do mesmo sexo)", *op.cit.*, p. 181. On the other hand, BARROSO denied a dynamic interpretation not only with regards to the CRP but also with regards to the Universal Declaration of Human Rights which could eventually be used to interpret article 36 CRP, taking

argued that an interpretation that sticks to the historical concept of marriage prior to the approval of the CRP involved an inversion of the normative hierarchy by giving priority to civil legislation (particularly former Articles 1577 and 1628 e) CCRP) over the CRP.[100] It was also pointed out that procreation was not an essential element of marriage,[101] becoming the heterosexual element irrelevant.[102] Some opponents to same-sex marriage also mentioned the Judeo-Christian tradition.[103] Additionally, the symbolism of marriage (as opposed to any other alternatives to regulate same-sex couples, such as registered partnerships or civil unions)[104] was relevant not only in scholarly discussions but in political debates as well.[105]

---

into account article 16.2 CRP, see BARROSO, I.M.: "Casamento civil entre pessoas do mesmo sexo: um <<direito fundamental>> á medida da lei ordinária?", *op.cit.*, p. 63.

[100]PAMPLONA CÔRTE-REAL, C.: *Da inconstitucionalidade do Código Civil – artigos 1577°, 1628°, alínea e), e disposições conexas – ao vedar o acceso ao instutito do casamento a casais do mesmo sexo*, *op.cit.* p. 23; MOREIRA, I.: "Da inconstitucionalidade das normas resultantes da leitura conjugada do artigo 1577° do Código Civil e da alínea e) do artigo 1628° do mesmo Código, nos termos das quais duas pessoas do mesmo sexo não podem contrair casamento e, se o fizerem, é o mesmo tido por inexistente" in ibid. (Ed.), p. 35. However, BARROSO used the argument of the normative hierarchy in a different way: he pointed out that opening up marriage to same-sex couples in the CCRP and then interpreting Article 36 CRP in the light of such amendment would be an inversion of the normative hierarchy, see BARROSO, I.M.: "Casamento civil entre pessoas do mesmo sexo: um <<direito fundamental>> á medida da lei ordinária?", *op.cit.*, p. 68 and 80.

[101]DE OLIVEIRA, G.: *Portugal! Um país de contrastes*, *op.cit.*, p. 181; GOMES CANOTILHO, J.J. and MOREIRA, V.: *Constituição da República Portuguesa, anotada: artigos 1° a 107°, vol. 1*, *op.cit.* p. 567; MIRANDA, J. and MEDEIROS, R.: *Constituição Portuguesa Anotada, Tomo I: Introdução Geral, Preâmbulo, artigos 1° a 79°*, *op.cit.* p. 809; RAPOSO, V.L.: "Crónica de um casamento anunciado (o casamento entre pessoas do mesmo sexo)", *op.cit.* p. 176; MOREIRA, I.: *Da inconstitucionalidade das normas resultantes da leitura conjugada do artigo 1577° do Código Civil e da alínea e) do artigo 1628° do mesmo Código, nos termos das quais duas pessoas do mesmo sexo não podem contrair casamento e, se o fizerem, é o mesmo tido por inexistente*, *op.cit.* pp. 50–52; DUARTE D'ALMEIDA, L.: "Casamento Civil e <sexo diferente>: Sobre a inconstitucionalidade das normas expressas pelos artigos 1577°, e 1628°, alínea e), do Código Civil" in ibid. (Ed.), pp. 68–69.

[102]However, DUARTE SANTOS, denying the constitutionality of same-sex marriages, considers that, even though procreation is not necessarily essential, marriage is "potentially procreative", see SANTOS, D.: *Mudam-se os tempos, mudam-se os casamentos? O casamento entre pessoas do mesmo sexo e o Direito português*, *op.cit.*, p. 327 and ff.

[103]MACHADO, J.E.M.: *A (in)definição do casamento no Estado constitucional: Fundamentos meta-constitucionais e deliberação democrática*, *op.cit.*, p. 9 and ff.

[104]MÚRIAS, P.: "Un símbolo como bem juridicamente protegido – parecer", *op.cit.* (last date seen: September 2014), p. 28; DUARTE D'ALMEIDA, L.: *Casamento Civil e <sexo diferente>: Sobre a inconstitucionalidade das normas expressas pelos artigos 1577°, e 1628°, alínea e), do Código Civil*, *op.cit.* p. 59. However, DUARTE SANTOS, even admitting the power of such symbolism, gave more weight to the idea of marriage as potentially procreative, see SANTOS, D.: *Mudam-se os tempos, mudam-se os casamentos? O casamento entre pessoas do mesmo sexo e o Direito português*, *op.cit.* p. 326 and 328 and ff.

[105]For a summary of the political debate and initiatives in Portugal, see SANTOS, D.: *Mudam-se os tempos, mudam-se os casamentos? O casamento entre pessoas do mesmo sexo e o Direito português*, *op.cit.*, p. 72 and ff.

Once Act 9/2010 was approved, the Portuguese President lodged an appeal against the constitutionality of the new legislation. The TCRP, in its *Acordão* 121/2010[106] followed a similar line of argument as in *Acordão* 359/2009. The Court provided some relevant arguments that complement its previous decisions:

- In 1976 the legislature did not discuss same-sex marriages. It was an unknown political and legal issue.[107]
- The CRP contains an institutional guarantee of marriage but such institutional guarantee could not become more important than the fundamental right.[108]
- The Universal Declaration of Human Rights could not be used to provide a restrictive interpretation of the Constitution, as a broader protection should be favored.[109]
- The legislature must take into account the social reality (dynamic interpretation).[110]
- Sex/gender diversity was not within the essential content of marriage.[111]

2.6 The Spanish Constitutional Court and Its Long Awaited Decision STC 198/2012

Seven years after the enactment of Act 13/2005, the TC decided appeal 6854-2005.[112] The decision was long awaited and the demand from LGBT groups and social and political forces supporting the Act urging for a final decision increased. The situation of thousands of same-sex married couples was uncertain and some feared the TC would find the Act unconstitutional. After the general elections of 2011, a change in the government from the centre-left PSOE to the conservative PP took place. The new government, supported by the party which challenged the constitutionality of the Act, decided to wait for the decision of the TC before considering actions on the matter. Finally, the TC issued STC 198/2012 of 6th November, declaring the Act constitutional. The decision was not unanimous, with eight votes in favor and three dissenting votes.[113]

---

[106] *Acordão 121/2010,* of 8th April.

[107] *Ibid., Fundamento 18.*

[108] *Ibid., Fundamento 19.*

[109] *Ibid., Fundamento 20.*

[110] *Ibid., Fundamento 22.*

[111] *Ibid.*

[112] Unfortunately, 7 years is within the average time the TC takes to deliver a decision, http://politica.elpais.com/politica/2012/04/01/actualidad/1333311471_924226.html (last accessed: September 2014).

[113] In favor: magistrates Pascual Sala Sánchez (President), Pablo Pérez Tremps, Adela Asúa Batarrita, Luis Ignacio Ortega Alvarez, Francisco Pérez de los Cobos Orihuel, Encarnación Roca

The decision focused on the possible violation of Article 32 CE. The other provisions of the CE claimed by the appellants to support the unconstitutionality of the Act were disregarded by the Court, since a violation of Article 32 CE would lead to the violation of the remaining provisions. With regards to these provisions, however, it is noteworthy mentioning two considerations by the TC. First, the Court, based on previous case law, rejected the idea of "discrimination by no differentiation" derived from the Equality Clause of Article 14 CE.[114] There is "no subjective right to unequal legal treatment,"[115] even if affirmative action is constitutionally possible. Second, regarding Article 39 CE, the TC noted that marriage and family were "two different constitutional goods."[116] Thus, the TC, did not identify family with the one which has its origin in marriage nor with the one which main purpose is procreation. By separating family from marriage and procreation the constitutional notion of family covered a plurality of family models, from marriages with no offspring to single parents and also *de facto* unions,[117] with or without children. Additionally, the ECHR applies to Spain and the European Court of Human Rights has stated that same-sex couples are covered by the right to family life of Article 8 ECHR.[118] In STC 198/2012 the TC referred to Article 10.2 CE which mandates that "principles relating to the fundamental rights and liberties recognized by the Constitution shall be interpreted in conformity with the Universal Declaration of Human Rights and the international treaties and agreements thereon ratified by Spain."

When discussing if Act 13/2005 violated the constitutional provision on marriage of Article 32 CE, the TC stated that this provision contained both a fundamental right to marry and an institutional guarantee.[119] How did the Court discuss the institutional guarantee of marriage in STC 198/2012? The Court acknowledged that

---

Trías and Fernando Valdés Dal-Ré; dissenting votes: magistrates Ramón Rodríguez Arribas, Andrés Ollero Tassara and Juan José González Rivas; concurrent vote: magistrate Manuel Aragón Reyes. Magistrate Francisco José Hernando Santiago was challenged because he participated in the preparation of the report issued by the CGPJ and did not take part in this decision. There is a publicly known distinction between so-called "progressive" and "conservative" magistrates, depending on whether their appointment was suggested by the conservative PP or the centre-left PSOE. The three dissenting votes correspond to magistrates known as "conservative". The magistrate Francisco José Hernando Santiago, who did not participate, is also known as "conservative". Such unofficial distinction between the members of the TC highlights the significance of political influence in the Court.

[114] *STC 198/2012, FJ 3rd.* See *supra* note 17.

[115] *Ibid.*

[116] *Ibid. FJ 5th.* See *supra* Sect. 2.4 "Same-Sex Couples and Marriage According to the Constitutional Court prior to STC 198/2012".

[117] See, *inter alia, STC 222/1992 of 11th December 1992, FJ 4th and 5th; STC 116/1999, of 17th June 1999, FJ 13th; STC 19/2012 of 15th February 2012, FJ 5th.*

[118] See, *inter alia, Schalk and Kopf v. Austria, 24th June 2010.*

[119] *STC 198/2012, FJ 7th.* See *supra* Sect. 2.3 "The Constitutional Court and the Development of the Concepts of Constitutional Guarantee and Subjective Right".

the notion of marriage in 1978, when the Constitution was approved, entailed the union between a man and a woman. It also pointed out, however, that a literal interpretation of Article 32 CE did "not entail that [the Constituent Assembly] excluded [the possibility of allowing same-sex couples to marry]."[120] Nonetheless, according to the TC, a purely grammatical or historical interpretation of the constitutional text was not accurate. It stated that it was necessary to use a dynamic interpretation of the institutional guarantee of marriage because Law is "a social phenomenon linked to the reality where it develops," and it is connected to the notion of "legal culture".[121] According to the TC, legal culture could not be understood from a purely literal, systematic or original interpretation. It required the use of other factors as well, such as the social reality, the opinion of legal scholars and advisory bodies, the law of socio-culturally similar jurisdictions, and the case law of international courts as well as opinions and reports issued by international bodies.[122]

The rule of interpretation set forth in Article 10.2 CE was understood in STC 198/2012 as an evolutionary or dynamic rule of interpretation.[123] When discussing whether the guarantee of marriage had been respected, that is, if the "master image" of the marriage institution had been kept when Act 13/2005 was introduced,[124] the Court relied on case law by the ECtHR and on EU Law. Thus, the Court acknowledged that the implementation of same-sex marriages is neither obliged nor forbidden by the ECHR and EU Law but that a broad margin of appreciation is given to their Member States. The Court also relied on comparative law, legal scholarship and social reality to conclude that the legal image of marriage is not unrecognized in the current Spanish social reality and Article 32 CE provides a margin broad enough to include same-sex couples.[125] The Court, in sum, declared the total accordance of Act 13/2005 with the constitutionally guaranteed marriage institution. The constitutionality of a registration scheme for same-sex couples, however, was not excluded. Therefore, STC 198/2012 considered same-sex marriages constitutionally possible but not a constitutional obligation.

This decision is also important because the TC for the first time provided a definition of marriage as a "community of affection which generates a bond of mutual aid between two persons who are equal within this institution and who freely decide to join a common project of family life by giving their consent and

[120]*Ibid., FJ 8th.*

[121]*Ibid., FJ 9th.*

[122]*Ibid.*

[123]*Ibid.*

[124]See Sect. 2.3, "The Constitutional Court and the Development of the Concepts of Guarantee and Subjective Right".

[125]Following the definition of guarantee of institution given in *STC 32/1981*, of 28th July, *FJ 3rd*. See *supra* Sect. 2.3, "The Constitutional Court and the Development of the Concepts of Guarantee and Subjective Right".

expressing it expressly according to the established formalities."[126] The TC did not define marriage as containing gender/sex diversity but it stressed the importance of affection, equality between members of the couple (monogamy is, thus, a defining element) and free will of the spouses. It is, therefore, a definition in accordance with the Equality Clause of Article 14 CE and the free development of personality of Article 10.1 CE.

The decision gave an opportunity to the TC to analyze the notion of "essential content" of a subjective right with regards to the right to marry of Article 32 CE, using the approach taken in its 1981 decision STC 11/1981 as the starting point.[127] The Court ascertained some elements of this essential content: (a) full legal equality between spouses; (b) need of mutual consent to marry; and (c) freedom not to marry.[128] As the Court stated, this notion gave and gives a broad margin to the legislature to both regulate the formalities of marriage, age, legal capacity, rights and duties, etc. as established by Paragraph 2 of Article 32 CE, and to regulate other types of unions, which means that the option of a registration scheme is constitutionally possible.[129]

The decision made reference to ATC 222/1994,[130] which stated that the so-called "principle of heterosexuality" was fully constitutional. This time the Court clarified that ATC 222/1994 could not be understood as a constitutional prohibition to introduce gender-neutral marriage legislation but it only meant that an exclusively opposite-sex marriage regime was constitutional.

In STC 198/2012, the Court also identified the objective dimension of the right to marry with the institutional guarantee of marriage.[131] It focused, therefore, on the subjective right to ascertain whether the essential content of marriage had been respected by Act 13/2005. The TC concluded that the subjective right to marry for opposite-sex couples had not been subject to any type of limitation as a consequence of the enactment of Act 13/2005 and had not been denaturalized because of it.[132]

Despite the TC's statement that it was not its role to judge the opportunity or convenience of enacting Act 13/2005, but only to determine the constitutionality of such Act, the Court seemed to welcome the new legislation as positive. It stated that the legislation was based on dignity and free development of personality. This assessment was criticized by the concurrent vote of Magistrate Manuel Aragón Reyes. He pointed out that it was not the role of the TC to assess if the choice

[126] *STC 198/2012, FJ 9th.*

[127] See *supra* Sect. 2.3, "The Constitutional Court and the Development of the Concepts of Guarantee and Subjective Right".

[128] *STC 198/2012, FJ 10th.*

[129] *Ibid.*

[130] See *supra* Sect. 2.4. "Same-Sex Couples and Marriage According to the Constitutional Court prior to STC 198/2012".

[131] *STC 198/2012, FJ 10th.*

[132] *Ibid.*

made by the legislature was convenient or timely.[133] Magistrate Aragón Reyes also disagreed with the dynamic interpretation used by the majority vote, stating that the TC could not become a "permanent constituent power."[134] He pointed out that, following a historical interpretation, the Constituent of 1978 excluded same-sex marriages. Magistrate Aragón Reyes, however, agreed that the principle of heterosexuality was no longer an essential element of the guarantee of marriage based on the current social conscience and legal culture of Spain.[135]

The main arguments of the three dissenting votes can be summarized as follows: (a) marriage is an institution that pre-dated the Spanish Constitution;[136] (b) following a historical interpretation, same-sex marriage had been excluded by the Constituent Assembly; (c) they rejected that the rule of interpretation set forth in Article 10.2 CE, with regards to international human rights treaties led to the constitutionality of Act 13/2005;[137] (d) marriage has an essential purpose which same-sex marriage does not respect;[138] (e) they rejected a dynamic interpretation of Article 32 CE and stated that the introduction of same-sex marriages would have required a constitutional reform;[139] f) the legislature could protect same-sex couples through other legal regimes different from marriage.

---

[133]*STC 198/2012, concurrent vote Magistrate Manuel Aragón Reyes, FJ 1st.*

[134]*Ibid. FJ 2nd.*

[135]Although Aragón Reyes rejected the dynamic interpretation of the guarantee, he considered the essential content of the guarantee as "historically changeable" and, hence, a certain idea of evolution to keep the image of the guarantee of institution recognizable for the social conscience is present. *STC 198/2012, concurrent vote of Magistrate Aragón Reyes, FJ 2nd.*

[136]Magistrates Ollero Tassara mentioned that marriage is an "anthropological" reality. *STC 198/2012, dissenting vote of Magistrate Ollero Tassara, FJ 5th.*

[137]Magistrates González Rivas and Ollero Tassara referred to this point. González Rivas pointed out that the broad margin left by international courts meant that the Court was not obliged to introduce same-sex marriage and, in connection with the wording of the Constitution, same-sex marriage was excluded. *STC 198/2012, dissenting vote of Magistrate González Rivas, FJ 3rd.* Ollero Tassara stressed that Constitutional case law cannot be dependent on "foreign decisions." *STC 198/2012, dissenting vote of Magistrate Ollero Tassara, FJ 6th.*

[138]Rodríguez Arribas talked about marriage as a "sexual union which natural purpose is the perpetuation of human species." *STC 198/2012, dissenting vote of Magistrate Rodríguez Arribas, FJ 1st.* Ollero Tassara embraced the idea of a "social function" of marriage which, although he did not explicitly mention it, seems to refer to procreation as well. *STC 198/2012, dissenting vote of Magistrate Ollero Tassara, FJ 2nd and 3rd.* Similarly, González Rivas, without expressly mentioning procreation, referred to the "essential purpose" of marriage. *STC 198/2012, dissenting vote of Magistrate González Rivas, FJ 4th.* "after" well."

[139]Ollero Tassara pointed out that the TC should be prevented from becoming a "third chamber" (together with the Congress and the Senate). *STC 198/2012, dissenting vote of Magistrate Ollero Tassara, FJ 1st.*

2.7 Conclusion

The Spanish Constitutional Court took 7 years to decide on the constitutionality of Act 13/2005. STC 198/2012 shows that the TC used similar arguments to those used by the Portuguese Constitutional Court 2 years before, when deciding on the same issue. The TC had previously discussed marriage in relation to same-sex unions in 1994 (ATC 222/1994). STC 198/2012 did not contradict its previous decision and, at the same time, it declared same-sex marriage constitutional.

As mentioned above,[140] prior to the TC's decision many scholars discussed that the decision on the constitutionality of same-sex marriages in Spain would depend on whether the TC would decide that Article 32 CE contained a mere subjective right to marry or if it was an institutional guarantee of marriage, which would limit the role of the legislature. STC 198/2012 stated that Article 32 included both a constitutional right and an institutional guarantee. This approach is exactly the same as the one adopted by the Portuguese Constitutional Tribunal in its *Acordão* 359/2009 and, more importantly, in its *Acordão* 121/2010. According to the Portuguese Court, Article 36 CRP had such double character, as a guarantee and as a fundamental right. Therefore, both courts put the focus on the interpretation of the guarantee of the institution and on what its essential content entails.

Both courts rejected the identification between family and marriage and declared that family was a broader concept than marriage. This perspective meant that, in accordance with the European Court of Human Rights, same-sex unmarried couples could constitute a family regardless of whether they were allowed to marry or not. It also involved a reaffirmation that marriage is not linked to procreation. The procreation argument, however, was present in the dissenting votes to STC 198/2012, either implicitly, as in the case of Magistrates González Rivas and Ollero Tassara, or explicitly, in the dissenting vote of Magistrate Rodríguez Arribas.[141] Contrary to these statements, marriage is a socially constructed institution and there is no legal basis, neither in the CE nor in the CC, to conclude that procreation is a purpose of marriage.[142]

Both the TC and the TCRP rejected a constitutional interpretation based solely on the historical criterion. The TC also stated that, although the Constituent Assembly of 1978 understood marriage as a union between a man and a woman, it did expressly exclude a gender-neutral legislation. Likewise, the TCRP, in its *Acordão* 121/2010, considered same-sex marriages in 1976 (when the CRP was approved) a legally and politically unknown issue. However, the concurrent vote of Magistrate Aragón Reyes in the Spanish decision underlined that the Constituent Assembly and the legal culture in 1978 understood marriage as made up of opposite-sex

[140] See *supra* Sect. 2.3. "The Constitutional Court and the Development of the Concepts of Constitutional Guarantee and Subjective Right".

[141] See *supra* note 138.

[142] See *supra* Sect. 2.2. "Challenges to the Constitutionality of Act 13/2005: Article 32 CE and heterosexuality as a defining element in marriage".

couples. Both approaches can be combined nonetheless. A purely historical criterion suggests that the Constituent Assembly, in the context of 1978, understood marriage as a heterosexual union but, as an unknown issue at the time, it did not expressly exclude same-sex couples in the wording of the CE. However, this lack of express reference to same-sex couples involves a grammatical criterion of interpretation and not a purely historical one. The three dissenting votes considered marriage as an institution pre-existent to the approval of the CE which was simply received by the constitutional text.[143] Although not expressly mentioned in STC 198/2012, the TC implicitly rejected this argument which would involve an acceptance of pre-constitutional definitions of constitutional concepts instead of an understanding of the CE as a starting point in itself.

The Spanish decision did not seem to clearly distinguish between the historical and the grammatical criteria of interpretation and they appear to be mixed or blurred at times. Regarding the grammatical interpretation, the judgment simply mentioned that "Article 32 CE only identifies the holders of the right to marry and not who they may marry with although, we must emphasize, a systematic approach makes it clear that it is not possible to conclude that there was a will to extend the right to same-sex unions in 1978."[144] However, as two different criteria of interpretation, the grammatical criterion should have been treated more thoroughly. Even if an analysis of the Constituent Assembly's discussions suggests that the concept of marriage for the Constituent Assembly was that of opposite-sex couples, a grammatical interpretation of Article 32.1 CE on marriage may bring a different conclusion. The mere reference to "man" and "woman" does not conclude that Article 32 CE prohibited same-sex marriages but rather that it was forbidden to discriminate against on the basis of sex when entering into marriage, during marriage and upon its dissolution. Consequently, though related, both criteria deserve a separate analysis.

The TC gave strong consideration to a dynamic interpretation of the guarantee of the institution of marriage. The Court relied on previous decisions and it was consistent with its previous approach to the understanding of the concept of constitutional guarantee.[145] The guarantee must, thus, be recognized in accordance to the image the social conscience has of it in each time and place.[146] A dynamic interpretation of the institutional guarantee allows it to be recognizable in each time

[143]This approach has as a consequence a coincidence between the concept of marriage in the CE and in the CC. Supporters of this coincidence of concepts have been, *inter alia*, CAÑAMARES ARRIBAS, S.: *El matrimonio homosexual en derecho español y comparado*, Iustel, Madrid, (2007), p. 132 and MARTÍNEZ DE AGUIRRE ALDAZ, C. and DE PABLO CONTRERAS, P.: *Constitución, derecho al matrimonio y uniones entre personas del mismo sexo*, Rialp, Madrid, (2007), pp. 76–80. This is also the position of the CGPJ in its Report of 26th January 2005, pp. 42–43.

[144]*STC 198/2012, FJ 8th.*

[145]See *supra* Sect. 2.3. "The Constitutional Court and the Development of the Concepts of Constitutional Guarantee and Subjective Right".

[146]As defined in *STC 32/1981*. See *supra* Sect. 2.3. "The Constitutional Court and the Development of the Concepts of Constitutional Guarantee and Subjective Right".

and place. This understanding of institutional guarantees is the same as the one adopted by the TCRP in both *Acordão* 359/2009 and *Acordão* 121/2010 where it also supported a dynamic approach to the concept of institutional guarantees in order to avoid "freezing" them in time. This approach was criticized by the dissenting votes to STC 198/2012 that demanded the need of a constitutional amendment to include same-sex couples within the institutional guarantee of marriage. Otherwise, the argument went, there would be a "constitutional mutation" without following the regulated procedure for its amendment.[147] This argument, however, must be disregarded in the context of previous definitions of the constitutional guarantee in the TC case law. If we understand that the guarantee must keep the image of the institution in a given *time* and *place*, it is not difficult to conclude that freezing the institutional guarantee in time, with the consequence of losing its "image" in current society, would involve a violation of such guarantee and a mutation in itself. Additionally, STC 198/2012 connected the dynamic interpretation of Article 32 CE with the rule of Article 10.2 CE in order to interpret rights according to international treaties ratified by Spain. By connecting a dynamic interpretation of the institutional guarantee with Article 10.2 CE, the TC understands that any future interpretation of Article 12 of the European Convention of Human Rights by the European Court of Human Rights that would include same-sex couples would influence the interpretation of Article 32 CE in the future.

The TC assessed the introduction of same-sex marriage as a step forward in the guarantee of dignity and free development of personality in order to achieve the full effectiveness of fundamental rights.[148] A model that eliminates more differences between opposite and same-sex couples, in this case, the introduction of a gender-neutral marriage law, seems to be the one that better fulfills Articles 14, 9.2, 10.1, 11, 1.1 and 10.1 CE. Thus, the principle of heterosexuality contained in the marriage regulation in the CC before Act 13/2005 was constitutional but it did not prevent the legislature from opening it up to homosexual relationships.[149] Both the Spanish and Portuguese Courts agreed that the decision on how to legally recognize same-sex couples was in the hands of the legislature. There are, however, some differences between the Spanish and the Portuguese decisions:

---

[147] *STC 198/2012, dissenting votes of: Magistrate Rodríguez Arribas, FJ 2nd; Magistrate Ollero Tassara, FJ 5th; Magistrate González Rivas, FJ 6th.*

[148] *STC 198/2012, FJ 11th.*

[149] Among the legal scholars supporting same-sex marriage as constitutionally possible prior to Act 13/2005. See DE AMUNÁTEGUI RODRÍGUEZ, C.: "Argumentos a favor de la posible constitucionalidad del matrimonio entre personas del mismo sexo", *Revista General de Legislación y Jurisprudencia*, 3 (2005), p. 32 and GAVIDIA SÁNCHEZ, J.V.: "Uniones homosexuales y concepto constitucional de matrimonio", *Revista Española de Derecho Constitucional*, vol. 61, (2001), p. 50. For an opposite opinion, MARTÍNEZ DE AGUIRRE ALDAZ, C. and DE PABLO CONTRERAS, P.: *Constitución, derecho al matrimonio y uniones entre personas del mismo sexo*, *op.cit.*, pp. 76–80.

First, The Portuguese Equality Clause of Article 13.2 CRP contains, since Constitutional Act 1/2004, a reference to sexual orientation which does not expressly exist in the case of the CE. The mention to sexual orientation, however, did not entail the automatic constitutionality of regulations on same-sex couples in Portugal.[150] At the same time, the fact that sexual orientation is not expressly mentioned as a ground in Article 14 CE does not mean that it is allowed to discriminate on the basis of sexual orientation in Spain either.

Second, Article 36.1 of the Portuguese Constitution mentions that "everyone has the right to form a family and to marry under conditions of full equality," whilst the Spanish Constitution expressly refers to "man" and "woman." In spite of this different wording, in Portugal some scholars had suggested that the reference to "everyone" had to be understood as limited to "man" and "woman," in light of Article 16.2 CRP and the Universal Declaration of Human Rights.[151] Similarly, the interpretation of the Spanish provision on marriage also triggered heated debate. In Spain and Portugal some legal scholars argued that the constitutional marriage provisions had the purpose of avoiding the discriminations on the grounds of sex that existed in the pre-democratic periods in both countries (in the case of Portugal, the *Estado Novo*).[152] As mentioned by the Portuguese Court the issue of same-sex marriages was, simply, unknown at the time of the approval of the Constitution.[153]

Third, the question of normative hierarchy was not as deeply debated in Spain as it was in Portugal, not even among legal scholars. In both jurisdictions, however, it was stated that the starting point to an understanding of the concept of marriage is the constitutional text and not the civil legislation. In Spain, before the approval of Act 13/2005, there was no provision in the CC similar to Articles 1577 and 1628 e) of the Portuguese Civil Code. Thus, some authors had even argued that same-sex marriages were not forbidden in Spain, even before 2005, especially since Act 30/1981 of 7th July, which had abolished impotence as an impediment to marriage.[154]

[150]In this sense, the TCRP in *Acordão 359/2009*, p. 10. See also MIRANDA, J. and MEDEIROS, R.: *Constituição Portuguesa Anotada, Tomo I: Introdução Geral, Preâmbulo, artigos 1° a 79°, op.cit.,* p. 819 and GOMES CANOTILHO, J.J. and MOREIRA, V.: *Constituição da República Portuguesa, anotada: artigos 1° a 107°, vol. 1, op.cit.,* p. 568. In a similar way, the inclusion of sexual orientation in the Swedish Constitution (the other constitution of a European country which expressly mentions it) was not conclusive of an obligation of opening marriage to same-sex couples (I wish to thank CAROLINE SÖRGJERD for enlightening me in the Swedish case).

[151]See BARROSO, I.M.: "Casamento civil entre pessoas do mesmo sexo: um <<direito fundamental>> á medida da lei ordinária?", *op.cit.,* pp. 61–62. He also denied a dynamic interpretation of Article 16.1 of the Universal Declaration of Human Rights.

[152]MIRANDA, J. and MEDEIROS, R.: *Constituição Portuguesa Anotada, Tomo I: Introdução Geral, Preâmbulo, artigos 1° a 79°, op.cit.,* pp. 824–825.

[153]*Acordão 121/2010. Fundamentação 18.*

[154]PRATS ALBENTOSA, L.: *La nueva regulación del derecho matrimonial español: bases y principios, op.cit.,* p. 19. It is relevant, because of the time and the context in which those comments

In sum, both the Spanish and the Portuguese decisions shared a similar reasoning. The Belgian *Cour d'arbitrage* was another court of a European country that had to decide on the constitutionality of same-sex marriages after legislation was introduced in its country.[155] The Belgian Court also concluded in the way of considering same-sex marriage not only constitutional according to the Belgian Constitution but also perfectly compatible with the ECHR and the United Nations International Covenant on Civil and Political Rights, which expressly mentions "man" and "woman" in its Articles 12 and 23.2.

Some final ideas are worth mentioning in relation to the decision of the TC on Act 13/2005. When the constitutionality of an act is challenged, the act usually remains in force until the TC decides on the matter. During the 7 years the appeal was pending, many same-sex couples married, and rights and obligations arose from those marriages. A judgment declaring Act 13/2005 unconstitutional would have created a "legal chaos" in relation to the couples already married.

The solution provided by STC 198/2012 may lead to a problem of legal uncertainty. If same-sex marriage is constitutionally possible but it is not constitutionally mandated, and not included within the constitutional guarantee of marriage, it could mean that the legislature, under a new parliamentary majority, could eventually proceed to repeal Act 13/2005. Although the conservative majority of the PP stated that gender-neutral marriage legislation would remain in force, nothing prevents the possibility of repeal. If we take, however, a dynamic interpretation of the constitutional concepts and the institutional guarantee of marriage, along with a constitutional interpretation that includes the international human rights treaties ratified by Spain (Article 10.2 CE), what was permitted before could eventually become constitutionally mandated.[156] This is a possibility that should not be disregarded, if not now, in a near future.

Bibliography

1. Alonso García, E. 1984. *La interpretación de la Constitución*. Madrid: Centro de Estudios Constitucionales.
2. Asúa González, C.I. 2007. El matrimonio hoy: sus perfiles jurídicos ad intra y ad extra. *Teoría y Derecho. Revista de Pensamiento Jurídico* 2: 7–27.

were made, the opinion of PERE RALUY, judge in charge of the Civil Registry of Barcelona in 1977, just 2 years after the death of General Franco, with the Francoist Civil Code still in force. In an interview, PERE RALUY pointed out that the Civil Code in force did not expressly prevent same-sex couples from marrying as the gender diversity was not expressly demanded anywhere in the Code. Interview with PERE RALUY in DOMINGO LORÉN, V.: *Los homosexuales frente a la ley. Los juristas opinan*, Plaza y Janés S.A., Barcelona, (1977), pp. 138–144.

[155] *Arrêt n° 159/2004*, of 20th October 2004.

[156] In this sense, referring to the Portuguese case, RAPOSO, V.L.: "Crónica de um casamento anunciado (o casamento entre pessoas do mesmo sexo)", *op.cit.*, p. 182.

3. Balaguer Callejón, M.L. 1997. *Interpretación de la Constitución y ordenamiento jurídico*. Madrid: Editorial Tecnos.
4. Ballester Cardell, M. 2007. *El Consejo General del Poder Judicial: su función constitcional y legal*. Madrid: Consejo General del Poder Judicial.
5. Baño León, J.M. 1988. La distinción entre derecho fundamental y garantía institucional en la Constitución Española. *Revista Española de Derecho Constitucional* 24 (septiembre-diciembre), pp. 155–179.
6. Barroso, I.M. 2010. Casamento civil entre pessoas do mesmo sexo: um direito fundamental á medida da lei ordinária? *Lex Familiae – Revista Portuguesa de Direito da Familia* 7(13), pp. 57–82.
7. Cañamares Arribas, S. 2007. *El matrimonio homosexual en derecho español y comparado*. Madrid: Iustel.
8. Cidoncha Martín, A. 2009. *Garantía institucional, dimensión institucional y derecho fundamental: Balance jurisprudencial,* pp. 149–188. http://e-spacio.uned.es/fez/eserv.php?pid=bibliuned:TeoriayRealidadConstitucional-2009-23-50050&dsID=PDF. Last date seen November 2013.
9. De Amunátegui Rodríguez, C. 2005. Argumentos a favor de la posible constitucionalidad del matrimonio entre personas del mismo sexo. *Revista General de Legislación y Jurisprudencia* 3: 351–368.
10. De Oliveira, G. 2007. Portugal! Um país de contrastes. In *Metamorfosi del matrimonio e altre forme di convivenza affetiva*, ed. Costa. Bologna: Libreria Bonomo Editrice.
11. De Oliveira, G., and F. Pereira Coelho. 2008. *Curso de Direito de Familia*, vol. 1. Coimbra: Coimbra Editora.
12. De Pablo Contreras, P. 2008. La Constitución y la Ley 13/2005, de 1 de julio, de reforma del Código Civil en materia de derecho a contraer matrimonio. In *Novedades legislativas en materia matrimonial*, ed. C. Martínez De Aguirre Aldaz. Madrid: Consejo General del Poder Judicial.
13. Díez Picazo, L. 2007. *En torno al matrimonio entre personas del mismo sexo*. www.indret.com. Last date seen November 2013.
14. Domingo Lorén, V. 1977. *Los homosexuales frente a la ley. Los juristas opinan*. Barcelona: Plaza y Janés S.A.
15. Duarte D'almeida, L. 2008. Casamento Civil e <sexo diferente>: Sobre a inconstitucionalidade das normas expressas pelos artigos 1577°, e 1628°, alínea e), do Código Civil. In *O casamento entre pessoas do mesmo sexo: Três pareceres sobre a inconstitucionalidade dos artigos 1577° e 1628° alínea e) do Código Civil*, ed. C. Pamplona Côrte-Real, I. Moreira, and L. Duarte D'almeida. Coimbra: Edições Almedina SA.
16. Fernández Segado, F. 1992. *El Sistema Constitucional Español*. Madrid: Dykinson.
17. García Rubio, M.P. 2009. Viejos y nuevos apuntes sobre la constitucionalidad del matrimonio homosexual. In *Estudios de Derecho de Familia y Sucesiones (dimensiones interna e internacional)*, ed. Álvarez González. Santiago de Compostela: Fundación Asesores Locales.
18. Gavidia Sánchez, J.V. 2007. La libertad de elegir como cónyuge a otra persona del mismo sexo y de optar entre el matrimonio y una unión libre (análisis crítico de la constitucionalidad del matrimonio homosexual y del llamado divorcio express). In *La reforma del matrimonio (Leyes 13 y 15/2005)*, ed. J.V. Gavidia Sánchez. Madrid: Marcial Pons.
19. Gavidia Sánchez, J.V. 2001. Uniones homosexuales y concepto constitucional de matrimonio. *Revista Española de Derecho Constitucional* 61: 11–58.
20. Gomes Canotilho, J.J., and V. Moreira. 2007. *Constituição da República Portuguesa, anotada: artigos 1° a 107°, vol. 1*. Coimbra: Coimbra Editora.
21. López Aguilar, J.F. 2005. Los criterios constitucionales y políticos inspiradores de la reforma del Derecho Civil en materia matrimonial. *Actualidad Jurídica Aranzadi núm.* 655 *(digital edition)*.
22. Lorenzo Villaverde, J.M. 2011. Las uniones de hecho (del mismo y de distinto sexo) y su consideración como familia en Portugal: una visión a la luz del art 36 de la Constitución de la República Portuguesa. *Derecho de Familia. Abeledo Perrot* 48: 199–211.

23. Machado, J.E.M. 2010. A (in)definição do casamento no Estado constitucional: Fundamentos meta-constitucionais e deliberação democrática. In *Família, consciência, secularismo e religião*, ed. G. De Oliveira, J. Machado, and R. Martins. Coimbra: Wolters Kluwer Portugal, Coimbra Editora.
24. Martín Sánchez, M. 2008. *Matrimonio homosexual y constitución*. Valencia: Tirant lo Blanc.
25. Martínez De Aguirre Aldaz, C., and P. De Pablo Contreras. 2011. National report: Spain. *Journal of Gender, Social Policy and the Law* 9-1: 289–307.
26. Martínez De Aguirre Aldaz, C., and P. De Pablo Contreras. 2007. *Constitución, derecho al matrimonio y uniones entre personas del mismo sexo*. Madrid: Rialp.
27. Martins, R. 2008. Same-sex partnerships in Portugal: from De Facto to De Jure? *Utrecht Law Review* 4-1: 194–211.
28. Miranda, J., and R. Medeiros. 2010. *Constituição Portuguesa Anotada, Tomo I: Introdução Geral, Preâmbulo, artigos 1° a 79°*. Coimbra: Wolters Kluwer Portugal, Coimbra Editora.
29. Moreira, I. 2008. Da inconstitucionalidade das normas resultantes da leitura conjugada do artigo 1577° do Código Civil e da alínea e) do artigo 1628° do mesmo Código, nos termos das quais duas pessoas do mesmo sexo não podem contrair casamento e, se o fizerem, é o mesmo tido por inexistente. In *O casamento entre pessoas do mesmo sexo: Três pareceres sobre a inconstitucionalidade dos artigos 1577° e 1628° alínea e) do Código Civil*, ed. C. Pamplona Côrte-Real, I. Moreira, and L. Duarte D'almeida. Coimbra: Edições Almedina SA.
30. Múrias, P. 2008. Un símbolo como bem juridicamente protegido – parecer. http://muriasjuridico.no.sapo.pt/PMuriasParecerCPMS.pdf. Last date seen November 2013.
31. Pamplona Côrte-Real, C. 2008. Da inconstitucionalidade do Código Civil – artigos 1577° 1628° alínea e), e disposições conexas – ao vedar o acceso ao instutito do casamento a casais do mesmo sexo. In *O casamento entre pessoas do mesmo sexo: Três pareceres sobre a inconstitucionalidade dos artigos 1577° e 1628° alínea e) do Código Civil*, ed. C. Pamplona Côrte-Real, I. Moreira, and L. Duarte D'almeida. Coimbra: Edições Almedina SA.
32. Pérez Royo, J. 1998. *Curso de Derecho Constitucional*. Madrid: Marcial Pons.
33. Pérez Villalobos, M.C. 2008. *Las leyes autonómicas reguladoras de las parejas de hecho*. Madrid: Editorial Civitas.
34. Prats Albentosa, L. 2006. La nueva regulación del derecho matrimonial español: bases y principios. In *Anuario de la Facultad de Derecho de la Universidad Autónoma de Madrid, no 10: Derecho, sociedad y familia: cambio y continuidad*, ed. Morales Moreno and Míquel González. Madrid: Boletín Oficial del Estado y Universidad Autónoma de Madrid.
35. Ramos Chaparro, E. 2005. Objecciones jurídico-civiles a las reformas del matrimonio. *Actualidad Civil* 10: 1 (*digital edition*).
36. Raposo, V.L. 2009. Crónica de um casamento anunciado (o casamento entre pessoas do mesmo sexo). *Revista do Ministério Público* Oct–Dec 2009, 120: 157–190.
37. Roca Trías, E. 2007. La familia y sus formas. *Teoría y Derecho. Revista de Pensamiento Jurídico* 2: 49–72.
38. Rodríguez, Á. 2007. Treinta y dos. *Diario La Ley n° 6643 (digital edition).*
39. Sánchez Navarro, Á.J. 2007. *Consejo de Estado, función consultiva y reforma constitucional*. Madrid: Reus.
40. Santos, D. 2009. *Mudam-se os tempos, mudam-se os casamentos? O casamento entre pessoas do mesmo sexo e o Direito português*. Coimbra: Coimbra Editora.
41. Schuster, A. 2011. Gender and beyond: disaggregating legal categories. In *Equality and justice: sexual orientation and gender identity in the XXI century*, ed. A. Schuster. Udine: Editrice Universitaria Udinese srl.
42. Valpuesta Fernández, R. 2007. Reflexiones sobre el Derecho de Familia. *Teoría del Derecho. Revista de Pensamiento Jurídico* 2: 75–79.

Chapter 3
Same-Sex Unions in Mexico: Between Text and Doctrine

Estefanía Vela Barba

Abstract Currently Mexico recognizes same-sex marriage in several states. The Mexican Supreme Court has been instrumental in this recognition, advancing an interpretation of marriage outside its historical and textual interpretation. The current state of same-sex marriage and LGBTI rights in general in Mexico is the consequence of a new interpretation of the role of marriage and the family in the Mexican society, as well as the evolution of the LGBTI movement.

By 2013, Mexico City recognized same-sex marriage. The states of Coahuila, Colima, and Jalisco, recognized different forms of unions, each granting different rights that were exclusive for same-sex couples (solidarity pacts, conjugal unions, and civil unions, respectively). Through litigation, same-sex couples have been able to get married in Oaxaca, Colima, Yucatán, Sinaloa, Chihuahua, Estado de México, Jalisco, Guanajuato, and Nuevo León. Litigation was pending in other states, as well. Same-sex couples could adopt in Mexico City, Colima, and Coahuila. All of these models of recognition, with the exception of Coahuila's solidarity pacts approved in 2007, happened in a lapse of less than 5 years, after Mexico City approved same-sex marriages in 2009 and the Supreme Court affirmed its constitutionality in 2010.

This chapter contends that the recognition of same-sex unions in Mexico is the result of legal changes pushed by the LGBT movement. At the same time, this work shows how these transformations were articulated in a narrative of individual rights. For the last decade this narrative has been gaining force and it has become a source of legitimacy for the courts' decisions in the area. It was through individual rights that the Supreme Court was able to break the logic that previously informed legal reasoning around marriage: an essentialist way of reasoning that guaranteed the perpetuation of its original Catholic doctrine, sometimes in spite of its legal reforms.

E. Vela Barba (✉)
Carretera México- Toluca 3655, Centro de Investigación y Docencia Económicas – DEJ, Col. Lomas de Santa Fe, DF, 01210 Mexico
e-mail: estefania.vela.barba@gmail.com

M. Sáez (ed.), *Same Sex Couples - Comparative Insights on Marriage and Cohabitation*, Ius Gentium: Comparative Perspectives on Law and Justice 42,
DOI 10.1007/978-94-017-9774-0_3

This chapter is structured in three main sections: First, this chapter will review the main transformations of marriage and family law in Mexico, focusing particularly on recent Supreme Court decisions. This section attempts to identify the logic that informed the original doctrine of marriage, and how the framework of fundamental rights, as opposed to the original logic of marriage, has been altering this institution. Second, the chapter reviews changes towards the recognition of civil unions that culminated with same-sex marriage and adoption. The third section analyzes the 2010 Supreme Court decision (*Acción de Inconstitucionalidad* 2/2010) on Mexico City's same-sex marriage legislation, and the 2012 Supreme Court decision (*Amparo en Revisión* 581/2012) that sanctioned same-sex marriage in the State of Oaxaca. This section sketches how the Court responded to the claim about marriage being linked to procreation, and the role that individual rights played as a counter argument.

3.1 Marriage and Family Law in Mexico

3.1.1 The Original Conception of Marriage and the Transformations of Marriage and Family Through History

Civil marriage in Mexico has two notable influences that affect how it functions even today.[1] The first is Catholicism's influence in the inception and understanding of marriage in Mexican society. The second, closely related to the first, is the influence of the Second Scholastic, and through them, of Thomism and Aristotelian reasoning, in the legal construction of marriage.

The first *civil* marriage in Mexico was actually a catholic institution. When the nascent Mexican Nation-State issued in 1857 its first law regulating the Civil Registry, it established that couples should get married before the Catholic Church. If they wanted their unions to have "civil effects," they had to register them before the Civil Registry. When Mexico finally issued a law 2 years later that regulated marriage, including who could get married, how, and why, it replicated the institution of catholic marriage. The statute was passed in the context of the "wars" between the Mexican State and the Catholic Church. During this time, Mexico published a series of statutes, called the *Leyes de Reforma* (Laws of Reform),

[1] I know that scholarship has identified other influences in marriage that perpetuate –or undermine– the functioning of this particular model. Capitalism –and other economic factors–, is one of them. (See, for example, Jane Collier, *Cambio y continuidad en los procedimientos legales zinacantecos,* Haciendo justicia. Interlegalidad, derecho y género en regiones indígenas, 92 (María Teresa Sierra ed.) (CIESAS 2004); and Maxine Molyneux, "Mothers at the Service of the New Poverty Agenda: Progresa/Oportunidades, México's Conditional Transfer Programme", *Social Policy & Administration*, vol. 40, no. 4, (August 2006)).

through which it tried to dismantle the power of the Catholic Church. Among other actions, the government seized control of the Church's properties and enacted the Civil Registry Law and the Law of Marriage, areas previously controlled by the Church. Replicating catholic institutions through legal secular reforms allowed people to comply with Mexico's regulations while remaining truthful to their faith. There was an acceptance of the catholic concept of marriage.[2]

The convergence between the catholic and civil concepts of marriage did not reside solely on the actual definitions, and rights and obligations, that each established. The *basic* structure of marriage, how it was defined and understood, was the same in the catholic and civil marriage institutions. Liberals followed the French Napoleonic Code in their regulation of marriage, while the Catholic Church followed Canon Law. Historian James Gordley claims that both the Napoleonic Code and Canon Law came from the same place: a conceptualist and teleological method of reasoning that Aquinas, following Aristotle, used on marriage, and, that the Second Scholastic, following Aquinas and Aristotle, used to build a doctrine of contract law.[3] This doctrine of contract law survived up until the French Civil Code and even today in most of Mexican civil and family law. It is not that individualism and other modern values did not alter the way contract law or marriage, specifically, operated. The *logic* of these legal institutions, however, and not just only moral or religious beliefs about marriage, made its reform harder.

The first big change to marriage came in 1914 when divorce was understood as the dissolution of the marriage bond and individuals could remarry. The amendment, however, allowed for no-fault divorce only in cases of mutual consent. Otherwise, divorce was granted if there was fault by one of the parties. Fault basis for divorce meant that the "realization of marriage's ends [were] impossible or unjust" or the "discord of the spouses [was] irreparable."[4] The idea of marriage as a union that could only dissolve if the realization of marriage became impossible changed in 2008 when no-fault divorce was allowed.[5] In the early years of the twentieth

---

[2]Pablo Mijangos argues that "that Mexico's 1859 Law on Civil Marriage was the last moment of a long debate about the clergy's incapacity to bring into being the Christian moral order envisioned by the Council of Trent in the sixteenth century. [In] other words, that civil marriage intended first and foremost to *reform* Mexican society within an essentially religious framework, and only as an unintended and long-term consequence did it contribute to the secularization of social life." Pablo Mijangos, "Secularization or Reformation? The Religious Origins of Civil Marriage in Mexico", paper presented at the 2014 annual meeting of the American Historical Association, cited with the author's permission, p. 2.

[3]James Gordley, *The Philosophical Foundations of Modern Contract Doctrine*, Clarendon Press, 1991, pp. 3–4.

[4]Ley de 14 de Diciembre de 1874, reglamentaria de las adiciones y reformas de la Constitución Federal, article 23, section IX (reformed el December 29, 1914).

[5]Código Civil para el Distrito y Territorios Federales en Materia Común y para toda la República en Materia Federal (1928), articles 266–267 (reformed October 3, 2000). For the evolution of divorce, and a list of all the states that now have no fault divorce as an option, *see* Estefanía Vela Barba, "La evolución del divorcio en clave de derechos y libertades" *Nexos: El Juego de la Corte*, August 20, 2013, http://eljuegodelacorte.nexos.com.mx/?p=3004

century, however, marriage suffered two other important changes. The first was the elimination of all distinctions between legitimate and illegitimate children. The second was the recognition of cohabitation between a man and a woman as another form of family formation. *Concubinato,* however, granted little rights to the couple.[6] With time, female concubines started gaining more rights. In the 1973 Social Security Law, for instance, female concubines were included as beneficiaries of social security. Prominently, the female concubines had a right to receive a pension derived from her partners' work disability, age retirement or death, in similar conditions as legal spouses.[7] In 1983, the law established that concubines – men and women– had the obligation to provide each other economic support.[8] In 2000, *concubinato* became a full-fledged alternative to marriage, when it was officially conceived as another source of kinship[9] and was granted "all the rights and obligations *inherent* to the family, as applicable to them."[10] In 2006, thanks to the LGBT movement, Mexico City recognized civil unions as an additional option for couples, both of same and opposite-sex ("*sociedades de convivencia*"). The law stated that these societies would enjoy the same rights and obligations established for concubines.[11] The most prominent difference between *concubinato* and a civil union was its source of formation. While *concubinato* recognized an already established relationship between a man and a woman who had been living together for 2 years, or less if they had a child, a *sociedad de convivencia* was a contract that two people had to sign and register at a government office (not the Civil Registry).[12] These changes are important because marriage stopped being the "only moral way to found a family."[13]

Adoption suffered changes as well. Legally established in 1917, it was originally conceived as an exclusive relationship between the adoptee and the person seeking to adopt.[14] It did not extend to other family members (grandparents, brothers and sisters, etc.). It was not until 1998 that the law included for the first time "full adoption" (*adopción plena*). In this case, the relationship between the adopted child and the birth parents was extinguished. And the adoption created a filial relationship

---

[6]*Ibid.*, articles 383, 1,368, f. V. Diario Oficial de la Federación, México, 1928.

[7]Ley del Seguro Social (1973), articles 92, 152, 155, 164.

[8]Código Civil . . . (1928), article 302 (reformed December 27, 1983).

[9]*Ibid.*, articles 292, 294. (reformed May 25, 2000).

[10]*Ibid.*, article 291-Ter. (reformed May 25, 2000).

[11]Ley de Sociedad de Convivencia para el Distrito Federal, article 5.

[12]Código Civil . . . (1928), article 291-Bis. (reformed May 25, 2000); Ley de Sociedad de Convivencia para el Distrito Federal, Gaceta Oficial del Distrito Federal, November 16, 2006, no. 136, p. 4.

[13]Ley del Matrimonio Civil, no. 5057, July 23, 1859, p. 693 (in Manuel Dublan & Jose Maria Lozano, De las disposiciones legislativas expedidas desde la Independencia de la Republica, tomo VII, Mexico, 1877).

[14]Ley Sobre Relaciones Familiares, Diario Oficial de la Federación, April 14, 1917, tomo V, 4a época, no. 87, pp. 429–430

between the child, the adoptive parents, and their extended family.[15] The recognition of adoption undermines marriage as the exclusive gateway to family formation by accepting that biological reproduction is not the only way to establish parenthood.

With regards to obligations between spouses, changes were triggered by a concern for women's equality. Even in the Law of Marriage of 1859, lawmakers denounced how "in spite of the philosophy of the century and of the great progress of humanity, the woman, that precious half of the human being, still appear[ed] degraded in the old legislation."[16] One of the innovations of the 1870 Civil Code, for example, was to give the mother, along with the father, parental authority (*patria potestad*).[17] Many other changes slowly happened throughout the years.[18] In 1974 the Constitution was amended to include a provision that men and women were "equal before the law."[19] This constitutional amendment gave an important push for the amendment of most states civil codes in Mexico, specifically with regards to marriage. Equality was enshrined in the Constitution and in the civil codes before the amendment. Sex, however, had, until then, been treated as a justified reason to allow a differential treatment between men and women, particularly within marriage. The 1974 constitutional reform was introduced precisely to change this conception. This reform was later complimented in 1981, when Mexico also incorporated the Convention on the Elimination of All Forms of Discrimination Against Women (CEDAW) into its law.[20] Article 16 of CEDAW explicitly established that States must take measures to "eliminate discrimination against women in all matters relating to marriage and family relations," which includes granting them the same rights and responsibilities "during marriage and its dissolution" and "as parents." This move is important because it shattered the "sexed" nature of marriage. Before, marriage had to be between a man and a woman because only a man and a

[15]Código Civil ... (1928), articles 410-A-410-D.

[16]*See* "Circular del Ministerio de Justicia. Remite la ley del matrimonio civil", núm. 5056, July 23, 1859. Mexico. p. 3.

[17]Civil Code of 1870, articles 392, 396. Although only a father could "correct and punish his children temperately and moderately" and, as I affirmed previously, the woman had to ultimately obey him in regards to the education of the children.

Código Civil del Distrito Federal y Territorio de la Baja California, Ministerio de Justicia e Instrucción Pública (Publisher), Mexico (Publisher Location), December 22, 1870 (date of publication).

[18]Venustiano Carranza explicitly referred to the "slavery" women experienced when they were "stuck" with a bad husband and conceived of divorce as a remedy for these women. *See* Exposición de motivos del Decreto que reforma el artículo 23 de la Ley del 14 de diciembre de 1874, reglamentaria de las adiciones y reformas de la Constitución Federal, decretadas el 25 de diciembre de 1873, December 29, 1914. The Law of Family Relationships of 1917 also had a concern with women's equality.

[19]Constitución Política de los Estados Unidos Mexicanos, article 4 (reformed December 31, 1974).

[20]Both the International Covenant on Civil and Political Rights (23.4) and the American Convention on Human Rights (17.4) establish that "The States Parties shall take appropriate steps to ensure the equality of rights and the adequate balancing of responsibilities of the spouses as to marriage, during marriage, and in the event of its dissolution."

woman *together* could fulfill marriage's ends. They were "halves" that, when joined, embodied perfect "conjugal duality." The man was in charge of providing for the family; the woman was in charge of taking care of the family. With equality, these roles could remain the same, or be reversed, or be distributed in other ways. This distribution had nothing to do with the sex of the person, but with their personality and interests.

One of the ends of marriage, since 1859, had been reproduction. The 1974 constitutional reform introduced, together with sex equality, the right of each individual to freely determine the number and spacing of his or her children. In response to the constitutional reform, the law established that, when it came to marriage, the right to decide the number and spacing of children had to be exercised *jointly* by the spouses.[21] This norm survives until today. It has only been altered once, in the year 2000, when the law established that couples had a right to access "any method of assisted reproduction to achieve [having] their own offspring."[22] This was also the year in which the definition of marriage changed and it became the "free union of one man and one woman to form a community of life, in which both offer each other respect, equality and mutual aid, with the *possibility* of procreating children in a free, responsible, and informed manner."[23] That same year, being incapable of copulating was no longer an impediment for marriage if the other spouse knew and accepted it. Historically, this can be viewed as the moment in which procreation stopped being one of the ends of marriage.

Originally infidelity was also grounds for divorce and adultery was a crime. In 1928, fidelity stopped being an explicit obligation of the spouses. Adultery was decriminalized in 2002 and infidelity stopped being a cause for divorce in 2008. With these changes there was no longer a link between the act of having sex and marriage. Additionally, in 2008 the Civil Code allowed people to change their birth certificate to reflect their sex change. This reform is notable for two reasons. The first is that it included *no* prohibition for trans people to get married. If a man became a woman and married a man, this became a valid marriage.[24] The second highlight of this reform is that if trans people were married at the time of their sex change, the procedure did not modify their civil status and the couple remained married in the eyes of the law. If a man, married to a woman, became a woman, the law accepted their marriage –or at least the "obligations" that spawned from it.[25] In the first case, if one considers that many trans people undergo surgery that affects their reproductive capacity, the law is implicitly sanctioning the disconnection between

[21] Código Civil ... (1928), article 162 (reformed December 31, 1974).

[22] *Ibid.*, article 162 (reformed May 25, 2000). p. 8

[23] *Ibid.*, article 146 (reformed May 25, 2000).

[24] I highlight the importance of trans people being able to marry, assuming that there are many that, like the judge in *Corbett v. Corbett* (UK, 1970), argue that they are incapable of fulfilling the ends of marriage, because they are unable to reproduce. The same goes for intersexuals.

[25] Código Civil ... (1928), article 135-Bis (reformed October 10, 2008). Mexico.

marriage and procreation. In the second case, the law is implicitly sanctioning the marriage that exist between two people that are *now* of the same sex.[26]

In December 2009, the law was reformed once more, this time redefining marriage as "the free union of two people for the realization of a community of life, in which both offer each other respect, equality and mutual aid."[27] It no longer included a mention of procreation, or sex diversity in the couple. *Concubinato* was also reformed to expand its effects to same-sex cohabitant couples. And, importantly, adoption was not reformed with the aim of excluding same-sex couples from being able to initiate an adoption process. With this reform, same-sex couples acquired the exact same rights as opposite-sex couples with regards to marriage and cohabitation.

Originally, marriage was an institution regulated almost exclusively by civil law and, marginally, by criminal law. In civil law, the State established the necessary procedures for people to get married; for marriages to get annulled (thus protecting "the essence" of marriage); and procedures for couples to separate (because they were incapable of complying with the "ends" of marriage). Out of all the obligations that marriage spawned, only one could be demanded directly before the State: the obligation of spousal and parental economic support. The rest of the obligations (living together, fidelity, etc.), could not be *demanded*; only their breach could be punished. Infidelity and abandonment of the home were grounds for divorce (which was conceived, originally, as a punishment); infidelity was also a crime (adultery).

In addition to several amendments triggered by social welfare reform, in 1974, the Constitution was amended to include the following norm: "[The law] must protect the organization and development of the family." In that reform, article 123, section XXIX was altered and *social security* became a right of the worker "and [his or her] extended family." The International Covenant on Civil and Political Rights, the International Covenant on Economic, Social, and Cultural Rights, and the American Convention on Human Rights became Mexican law in 1981.[28] Additionally, the General Health Law was passed in 1983.[29] It established that one of the objectives of the National Health System was to "promote the development of the family and the community."[30] The law advanced maternal

[26]The importance of this is not minor. Rafael Rojina Villegas, to this day one of the most read treatise writers on family law, used examples of transexuality and intersexuality to explain why "same *sex*" marriage could not exist, according to doctrine. Rafael Rojina Villegas, *Derecho civil mexicano*, tomo II, ed. 2006 (1962), pp. 250–253.

[27]Código Civil ... (1928), article 146 (reformed December 29, 2009). p. 525.

[28]They were published in the *Diario Oficial de la Federación* on May 20, 1981; March 23, 1981; and May 7, 1981, respectively.

[29]For a brief history of health services in Mexico, *see* Daniel Lopez-Acuña, "Health services in Mexico", *Journal of Public Health Policy*, vol. 1, no. 1, 1980; José Arturo Granados Cosme & Luis Ortiz Hernández, "Descentralización sanitaria en México: transformaciones en una estructura de poder", *Revista Mexicana de Sociología*, vol. 65, no. 3, 2003.

[30]Ley General de Salud (February 7, 1984), Article 6, section IV.

care,[31] determined that "health, educational and labor authorities" had to support and promote . . . cultural activities destined to strengthen the family unit . . . .,[32] and dealt with families with drug addiction and disability issues.[33] In 2003, the General Health Law was reformed to create the System of Social Protection in Health, commonly known as the "popular insurance" (*seguro popular*). It was designed to reach the population that wasn't being covered by the health insurance provided by social security. The "unit of protection," however, became the *family unit*. It was not aimed at protecting the individual or the worker but the family unit, which could consist of: couples married or in *concubinato*, and "the father and/or mother" not joined in matrimony or in cohabitation.[34]

With regard to housing, as early as 1972, the Institute of the National Fund for Workers' Housing was created by law. The loans given to each worker were to be determined considering the number of family members each worker had.[35] In 1983, the Constitution was amended to establish that "every family ha[d] a right to enjoy dignified and decorous housing." In 2006, the Federal Congress passed a law aimed at "establishing and regulating the national policy, programs, instruments and support so that every family might enjoy" this right.[36]

Besides housing, health, and property protections, the other great source of support for families came through support for children. Since 1929, several associations were created for this purpose, such as the National Association for the Protection of Childhood, the National Institute for the Protection of Childhood, the Mexican Institute for the Assistance to Childhood and the Mexican Institution of Childhood Protection. The actions these institutes took ranged from giving mothers' milk and school lunches, and trying to solve the problem of child abandonment and exploitation. The highlight of reforms in this area came in 1977 with the creation of the National System for the Integral Development of the Family –*DIF*, for its initials in Spanish– which, until today, is the organism in charge of taking care of the "most vulnerable" sectors of society, including children, the elderly,[37] and people with disabilities, and promoting policies for the "integration of the family." They offered legal counseling for families; psychological attention and homes for children and teenagers; homes for the elderly, centers for rehabilitation of people

---

[31] *Ibid.*, article 61, section III.

[32] *Ibid.*, article 65, section II.

[33] *Ibid.*, article 174, section IV; 188, section II; 189, section II; 191, section III.

[34] *Ibid.*, articles 77-Bis-1, 77-Bis-4.

[35] Ley del Instituto del Fondo Nacional de la Vivienda para los Trabajadores, article 47, (April 24, 1972).

[36] Ley de Vivienda, article 1 (June 27, 2006).

[37] For a brief overview of the situation of the elderly in Mexico, *see* Mercedes Blanco & Edith Pacheco, "Aging and the Family-Work link: A Comparative Analysis of Two Generations of Mexican Women (1936–1938 and 1951–1953)", *Journal of Comparative Family Studies*, vol. 40, no. 2, 2009.

with disabilities.[38] Since the 1980s, the government has had several programs that supply day-care facilities for mothers. All of these programs are administered through DIF.[39]

To complete the protection of the family, there were also changes to the criminal law system. In addition to civil enforcement, not complying with the obligation of economic support became a punishable crime.[40] Homicides, assaults, rape and sexual abuse received higher sentences if committed against a family member.[41] The crime of femicide was also punished with higher crimes if the perpetrator was emotionally involved with the victim.[42] Family violence was defined as "the physical, psycho-emotional, sexual, economical, patrimonial violence [. . .] that happens [. . .] in or out of the home" against the spouse, concubine, an ascendant, a descendant, the adopted child, the adoptive parent, the ward, or the person with whom a civil union was contracted.[43] In all of these cases, the Criminal Code protects "the family" and not just the marriage bond.

3.1.2 Changes in Legal Reasoning Around Marriage

In spite of all these changes to marriage and the family, marriage was still interpreted according to the functions it fulfilled in society. Decisions on marital rape, loss of parental rights and no-fault divorce show this contradiction between textual reforms to the law and legal reasoning based on traditional concepts of marriage and family.

3.1.2.1 Marital Rape

Marital rape has been addressed by Mexican courts in several decisions. There are two separate rulings by the First Chamber of the Supreme Court of Mexico that framed the issue: one decided in 1994 (*Contradicción de Tesis 5/92*) and the other, reversing the first one, in 2005 (*Solicitud de Modificación de Jurisprudencia 9/2005*).

In the 1994 case, the Supreme Court had to decide a contradiction that existed between two circuit courts over the issue of marital rape. The disputed question was the following: Could there be an act of rape between spouses? One circuit court

---

[38]For a list of the services the DIF provides today, *see* their webpage: http://sn.dif.gob.mx/servicios/

[39]For an overview of the day-care programs, *see* Felicia Knaul & Susan Parker, "Cuidado infantil y empleo femenino en México: evidencia descriptiva y consideraciones sobre las políticas", *Estudios demográficos y urbanos*, vol. 11, no. 3, 1996.

[40]Código Penal para el Distrito Federal (2002), articles 193–199 (reformed July 22, 2005).

[41]*Ibid.*, article 125 (July 16, 2002), article 131 and article 178 (reformed March 18, 2011).

[42]Código Penal para el Distrito Federal (2002), article 148 Bis (reformed July 26, 2011).

[43]Código Penal para el Distrito Federal (2002), article 200 (reformed March 18, 2011).

argued that it was rape in the terms established by the Criminal Code because the statute did not include an exception for spouses when regulating rape. If the law did not include this distinction, judges should not include it. The circuit court cited First Chamber precedents in which it had ruled that the fact that the victim was a prostitute did not excuse the perpetrator from being guilty of rape. If prostitutes were protected, so should spouses. Additionally, if the act was not considered rape, it would amount to allowing spouses to take justice into their own hands, which is expressly prohibited by the Constitution. The circuit court conceded, however, that spouses were subject to rights and obligations and one of those was "contributing to the ends of marriage, which implies perpetuating the species, which can only be achieved through intercourse." This reasoning, however, did not authorize spouses to demand the fulfillment of this duty with violence, "since this would be taking justice into their own hands," violating the Constitution and the rules of treating each other with respect.[44]

Another circuit court considered that forced intercourse among spouses was not rape in the terms established in the Criminal Code. The husband would be "legitimately exercising a right." At most, the court argued, the husband could be "responsible for [. . .] the injuries caused as a result of the violent coitus, but not of the crime of rape."[45] The court argued that at most forced intercourse could serve as a cause for divorce.

The First Chamber of the Supreme Court had to decide which of these two interpretations was correct. For this, it looked at procreation as an end of marriage. To fulfill this end "spouses must submit themselves to the carnal relationship as long as it is carried out normally, that is, as long as coitus is limited to the total or partial introduction of the penis in the feminine sexual organ; since they only have a right to a sexual relationship of this nature."[46]

The Chamber argued that there was a "right to the carnal benefit,"[47] but it accepted that this right had its limits. Prominently, it could not affect "morality, health or some other expressed legal norm." For example, spouses had no right to impose "unnatural sex acts" on each other, since they had not agreed to this type of "carnal joining." The Chamber added that in several situations the rape of the spouse could be possible, such as when the attacking spouse is drunk, is a drug addict, has a venereal disease or AIDS, if the rape occurred in the presence of other people, if the "woman" had an ailment, like paralysis, that prevented her from "producing herself in her sexual relationships," or if the spouses were legally separated. In all of these cases, rape was rape. In all other cases, there could be no marital rape. It could be an "undue exercise of a right," a crime of lesser significance in Mexico City's Criminal Code. But it was not rape.

---

[44] Amparo en Revisión 93/92, Primer Tribunal Colegiado del Sexto Circuito, *cited in* Contradicción de Tesis 5/92, Primera Sala de la Suprema Corte de Justicia de la Nación.

[45] Eugenio Cuello Calón, only referred to by name *in* Amparo en Revisión 447/89, Tercer Tribunal Colegiado del Sexto Circuito, *cited in* Contradicción de Tesis 5/92, Primera Sala de la Suprema Corte de Justicia de la Nación.

[46] Contradicción de Tesis 5/92, Primera Sala de la Suprema Corte de Justicia de la Nación.

[47] *Ibid.*

This case is paradigmatic of how the original doctrine of marriage was used against the text of the law. This case was decided in 1994, more than 100 years after Mexico first adopted a Constitution that guaranteed basic rights to freedom.[48] And 20 years after sex equality was included in the constitutional text, along with the right to choose the number and spacing of children. It was decided almost 15 years after the CEDAW was ratified. In spite of all this constitutional guarantees and international obligations, the Chamber did not even mention a single constitutional or international norm.

Eleven years later, a Circuit Court petitioned the First Chamber to reverse its criteria. It gave several reasons for the reversal. It argued that, although the "conjugal obligation" affected both parties, it had unequal effects. Because of the physical nature of the procreative sexual act, women would generally be the victims of unconsented sex. It presented, therefore, a problem of discrimination on the basis of gender. The Circuit Court also argued that:

> It may well be true that under the current contractualist conception of marriage, our legislation and doctrine consider procreation as one of its ends, and conjugal obligation and mutual fidelity as some of its consequences, [which come to] restrict [the spouses'] sexual freedom [... However], this does not imply that the freedom to refuse [...] to have sex with the spouse disappears, regardless of whether the fact that if this refusal is deemed unjustified the [rejected] spouse might invoke it as a cause for divorce. Sustaining the opposite view would take us back to the conception of marriage in which the woman is considered an object that the man acquires as property, over which he has an absolute and unlimited power, and would [lead us to] disavow the sublime and consensual nature that every sexual union between husband and wife must have.[49]

The First Chamber's response was very brief. First, it admitted that rape in the criminal code did not include an exemption for spouses. It then analyzed the civil code, which did not include an explicit exemption for spouses with regards to rape or a right "to access the sexual act in a violent way" against the other spouse's wishes.[50] After reviewing the civil code and not finding an exemption, the Chamber concluded that although an essential component of marriage was procreation, there was a constitutional right to sexual liberty and a right to decide when to procreate.[51]

The logic of looking at the ends of marriage was not shattered entirely. The Chamber court did not go as far as to establish that the obligation to procreate did not exist. The new interpretation, however, prioritized the individual *constitutional* right to choose the number and spacing of children over the marriage-based right to "carnal access."

---

[48]Although the Constitution of 1824 is celebrated as the first Mexican Constitution, it did not include a chapter on rights and it established catholicism as the State religion. This changed with the 1857 Constitution, which began by proclaiming the rights of man and ultimately – in 1973 – proclaimed the absolute separation between State and Church.

[49]Solicitud de Modificación de Jurisprudencia 9/2005, Primera Sala de la Suprema Corte de Justicia de la Nación, p. 12.

[50]*Ibid.*, p. 33.

[51]*Ibid.*, p. 32.

3.1.2.2 Marriage, Divorce and the Loss of Parental Control

The dispute spawns from two separate cases in which parents had lost their parental rights over their children because they "abandoned" the marital home for over 2 years. In the first case, the father left the marital home with his son because his wife was mentally ill and doctors had recommended the separation. The father and the paternal grandmother took care of the son. In the second case, a mother lost her parental rights over her children because she had abandoned the home for more than 6 months.

The first lower court argued that the loss of parental control was a disproportionate penalty that violated the Mexican Constitution. Following old Supreme Court precedents, the second lower court argued that the loss of parental control was not a sanction because the Civil Code did not establish it as a sanction. The Civil Code merely determined that in a divorce ruling, the judge had to decide over the situation of children.[52] The spouse lost her rights, "but this was not because she was punished."[53] A few lines further, this lower court affirmed that the law did not distinguish at all between the different types of causes for divorce, in order to establish if one was worse than the other, since they all revealed a lack of moral quality of the spouse that would affect the wellbeing of the child because any fault based cause for divorce implied recklessness with regards to the duties that parental control demands.[54] This rationale, the lower court argued, protected the family, complying with constitutional mandates.

In the lower court's decision a bad spouse was automatically a bad parent. Whether it was infidelity or abandonment of the home, fault based divorce revealed "the moral quality" of the spouse involved. What was done against one member of the family was really done against them all. Not complying with *one* end of marriage meant not complying with all the relationships that naturally spawn from marriage, such as parenthood.

In this case, the Court separated the constitutional protection of the family from the constitutional protection of "parental control" (*patria potestad*) and both, from the rights of children.[55] Although they connect, these protections were considered by the Court as independent "guarantees." The Court affirmed that parental control was an institution designed to protect minors, regardless of whether they were born to a marriage, or not; and whether the children were adopted, or not.[56] With this new reasoning the Court sees parenthood not as a natural consequence of marriage but as an independent right of parents.

---

[52] Contradicción de Tesis 21/2006, pp. 15–16.

[53] *Ibid.*, p. 16.

[54] *Ibid.*, pp. 16–17.

[55] *Ibid.*, p. 36.

[56] *Ibid.*, p. 32.

The Court affirmed that the abandonment of the home did not necessarily imply the abandonment of the child.[57] The Court also reasoned that interfering with the parent-child relationship could have the effect of depriving the child of the benefits of the parent's "cultural, ethical, moral, religious formation, as well as [this parent's] patrimonial administration of the [child's] assets."[58]

3.1.2.3 The No-Fault Divorce Case

In 2008, Mexico City introduced no fault divorce in its Civil Code. Spouses could now unilaterally dissolve their marriage upon request, without having to give specific reasons for it. The new law established that all matters related to children and property, had to be decided separately. The First Chamber of the Supreme Court was called to rule on an *amparo*, an individual suit brought by a woman who had been divorced under this new procedure and was challenging it.[59] In this *amparo* procedure the plaintiff claimed that no fault divorce was a violation of article 4, paragraph 1 of the Federal Constitution, a norm that enshrined "the right the family has so that through the laws [. . .] its organization and development are protected."[60] If the family was the basic unit of society the State had to protect it and the legislature could not pass statutes against its survival by considering the will of one of the spouses to be enough to dissolve the marriage bond, without allowing the other spouse to oppose."[61] The plaintiff claim that the reform left the abandoned spouse defenseless.[62]

The plaintiff argued that this reform "violated the *theory of obligations*, [and was] contrary to all legal logic, since marriage is a bilateral act that can only end through the death of one of the parties, through a mutual agreement between the parties that started it, or because of the presence of a grave cause that leads to its termination."[63]

[57] *Ibid.*, pp. 58, 62.

[58] *Ibid.*, p. 62.

[59] In 2011, the state of Hidalgo reformed its civil code as well, to include no fault divorce. A woman challenged this reform, after she too was divorced under this new procedure. The First Chamber of the Supreme Court was called to solve this case as well. I cannot contrast the two cases here, because technically, the Hidalgo case was decided *after* the same-sex marriage case. However, it is interesting because, like the Mexico City no fault divorce case, it is an example of how the original doctrine of marriage is used to argue against changes to the text of marriage. But the difference between both cases is that there is a slight sophistication in the way the doctrine is presented: in the first case (Mexico City no fault divorce case), the plaintiff simply refers to the "doctrine" of marriage; in the second (Hidalgo no fault divorce case), the doctrine is re-inscribed both in the constitutional text and in international treaties. The doctrine gets rearticulated as a matter of rights as well.

[60] Amparo Directo en Revisión 917/2009, p. 22.

[61] *Ibid.*, p. 22.

[62] *Ibid.*, p. 23.

[63] *Ibid.*, p. 2.

The First Chamber conceded that the State had an obligation to protect the family.[64] This protection meant that the State "must establish the best conditions for the full development of [the family] members, since [the family] is and must continue being the unit or best place for the growth and formation of individuals."[65] This implies that it must pay "attention to [. . .] the institutions that keep [families] together."[66] The First Chamber agreed that stability was important, but achieving it "[did] not imply that the spouses, per se, must remain together even if their coexistence [was] impossible."[67] "Since time immemorial," the Chamber wrote, "the State recognized the existence of a legal institution that would allow the dissolution [of the marriage] when coexistence became impossible between the spouses and with the children." Divorce, in this scenario, appeared as a "less harmful solution" than forcing the spouses to remain together in "dysfunctional relationships of abuse or family violence."[68] Divorce was just the State's recognition of a "*de facto* situation."[69]

Protecting the family implied "preventing violence, be it physical or moral, as a consequence of the controversy sparked by fault divorce."[70] This is why no fault divorce, at the same time that it protected the family, also respected "the free development of the personality."[71] If a lack of love[72] was never a valid reason to split up, now it was.

3.2 Towards the Recognition of Same-Sex Couples and Same-Sex Marriage

In 2001, the right to non-discrimination was included in the Mexican Constitution. The text read: "Every form of discrimination motivated by [. . .] gender, [. . .] health conditions, [. . .] *preferences*, or any other that violates human dignity or

[64] *Ibid.*, p. 26. By the way: the Chamber understands "the family" in a broad sense. It can originate with a marriage, but not exclusively. "Common-law marriage, societies of coexistence, and 'free unions'" also constitute family ties. This is a point that in the same-sex marriage case will be fundamental, key to winning the case. What's incredible is that nobody cited this no fault divorce decision as a precedent.

[65] *Ibid.*, p. 25.

[66] *Ibid.*, p. 26.

[67] *Ibid.*, p. 27.

[68] *Ibid.*, p. 27.

[69] *Ibid.*, p. 29.

[70] *Ibid.*, p. 29.

[71] *Ibid.*, p. 39.

[72] *Ibid.*, p. 40. The Chamber uses the word "*desamor*" which could be translated as "unlove."

seeks to annul or diminish the rights and liberties of a person is prohibited."[73] In 2003, the *Federal* Law to Prevent and Eliminate Discrimination was passed. The law established that discrimination, specifically on the grounds of "sexual preferences," "sex," and "health," was prohibited. It also created the National Council to Prevent Discrimination (CONAPRED).[74] This organism is mainly in charge of promoting the right to non-discrimination within the Federal Government.[75] Out of all the institutions that directly or indirectly have promoted LGBT rights, this one has been the most vocal, being involved, especially since 2010, in condemning violence and hate speech against the LGBT community.

Two important things happened in 2006 in Mexico City. First, hate crimes were included in the Criminal Code and, second, the law recognizing civil unions was passed.[76] By "hate crimes" (technically, the crime is called "discrimination"), article 206 of the Criminal Code understands the provocation of hatred or violence; the denial of a right or service; the exclusion of a "person or group of persons" (although the law does not say *exclusion* from what); and the denial or restriction of labor rights "on account of age, sex, civil status, pregnancy, race, ethnic origin, language, religion, ideology, sexual orientation, skin color, nationality, social position or origin, work or profession, economical position, physical characteristics, disabilities or health status or any other that violates human dignity."[77]

Starting in 2001 the law of civil unions was pushed by Enoé Uranga, a lesbian congresswoman in the Mexico City Assembly. She worked closely with a group of lesbian activists in drafting this legislation.[78] In spite of the fact that civil unions were both for same- and opposite-sex couples, it was praised as a gain by the LGBT community. A few months after this law was passed in Mexico City, the "Solidarity Pacts" were approved in the state of Coahuila. These pacts were exclusively for same-sex couples and they altered the couple's civil status. Civil unions could be dissolved, for instance, by marrying another person; a solidarity pact could not be dissolved that way. Also, the Solidarity Pact included an express provision banning adoption,[79] while civil unions did not have such prohibition.

After these changes, Mexico City Assembly reformed its Civil Code to allow sex changes.[80] The sex change did not require individuals to undergo surgery or

[73]"Decreto por el que se aprueba el diverso por el que se adicionan un Segundo y tercer párrafos al artículo 1o. [. . .]" *Diario Oficial de la Federación*, August 14, 2001. Emphasis added.

[74]Ley Federal para Prevenir y Eliminar la Discriminación, articles 1, 4, 5, 9 (June 11, 2003).

[75]*Ibid.*, articles 17, p. 20.

[76]Ley de Sociedad de Convivencia para el Distrito Federal (November 16, 2006).

[77]Código Penal para el Distrito Federal (2002), article 206 (reformed January 25, 2006).

[78]Genaro Lozano, "The Battle for Marriage Equality in Mexico, 2001–2011", *Same-Sex Marriage in Latin America*. Promise and Resistance, Pierceson, et al., (eds.) 2013, p. 156.

[79]Código Civil para el Estado de Coahuila, article 385–7. This article was just derogated this last February of 2014. Raúl Coronado Garcés, "Aprueban adopción gay en Coahuila", http://www.milenio.com/region/Congreso_de_Coahuila-adopcion_gay-PAN_contra_adopcion_gay_0_243576136.html

[80]Código Civil . . . (1928), article 135-Bis (reformed October 10, 2008).

hormonal treatment. A few months after the law was passed, the Supreme Court issued the *Amparo Directo Civil 6/2008*, in which it established that not allowing people to have a sex change was a violation of the right to the free development of the personality. This was the first time ever that the Court spoke about this right. Interestingly, the Court based its decision mostly on international treaties and their diverse articulation of the right to liberty and privacy, reinterpreted under the paradigm of dignity and non-discrimination.[81] In plain terms, the Court established that the right to the free development of the personality implied that the person was free to be who he or she was. This included deciding whether or not to get married, whether or not to have children, what profession to pursue, and, also, it included deciding over one's "sexual options" and "sexual identity."[82] In this decision, the Supreme Court basically protected gender identity, sexual orientation *and* marriage as part of the right to the free development of the personality.

Less than 1 year after this decision, Mexico City's Assembly approved same-sex marriage and same-sex *concubinato*.[83] The Attorney General challenged the reform.

Parallel to these developments, in 2007, Mexico City decriminalized abortion during the first trimester of the pregnancy. This reform was challenged before the Supreme Court as well. Among the many points that the Court was asked to rule on, one regarded the fact that the man "responsible" for the pregnancy did not have a power to veto the pregnant woman's decision to have an abortion. For those pushing this point, the right to choose was a right that had to be *jointly* exercised by the woman and the man. The Court responded that "the right to be a father or a mother" was not a right that was exercised jointly. Adoption, it argued, was a way to exercise the right to be a father or a mother and it was exercised individually.[84] The Court also affirmed that "sexual liberty and reproductive liberty" were separate liberties; and that reducing sexual liberty to reproductive liberty "ignored that the protection of the basic rights of people includes dimensions of sexuality that have nothing to do with those destined to protect a space for a decision related to the question of whether or not to have children."[85]

---

[81] Articles 1, 2, 3, 6, 7, 12, and 25 of the Universal Declaration of Human Rights; 1, 2, 3, 5, 11, 18, and 24 of the American Convention on Human Rights; 2, 3, 6, 16, 17, and 26 of the International Covenant on Civil and Political Rights; and 2, 4, and 12 of the International Covenant on Economic, Social, and Cultural Rights.

Amparo Directo Civil 6/2008, pp. 75–83.

[82] *Ibid.*, pp. 85–86, 89–90.

[83] Although it did not come up during the Mexico City case (Acción de Inconstitucionalidad 2/2010), in January of 2010, the Supreme Court solved a case related to tax law, in which it established the "purpose" of the right to non-discrimination. In explaining this right, the Court ended up clarifying that when the Constitution spoke of "preferences" as a suspect category, it meant *sexual* preferences. This because of the logic of the right to non-discrimination, which was *not* designed to protect *any* preference, but those that have been a cause for discrimination for certain groups. *See* Amparo en revisión 2199/2009, p. 45.

[84] Acción de Inconstitucionalidad 146/2007 y su acumulada, p. 187.

[85] *Ibid.*

3.2.1 The Mexico City Ruling

The statutes on same-sex marriage and *concubinato* passed by Mexico City's legislature were challenged through an *acción de inconstitucionalidad* (action of unconstitutionality), a judicial mechanism of abstract review that requires a supra-majority of 8 Justices –out of 11– to strike down the challenged law. Nine Justices voted in favor of upholding same-sex marriage and upholding same-sex couples accessing the adoption procedures.

The *acción de inconstitucionalidad* was initiated by the Attorney General of Mexico. It was not the only challenge against the reform. Six other States challenged it through a mechanism known as the *controversia constitucional* (constitutional controversy), which is designed to protect the constitutional division of powers and federalism, by allowing each level and power of government to challenge what they perceive to be an infringement on their own powers by other levels and powers of government.[86] These States argued that the Mexico City reform would force them to recognize a type of marriage that their legislation either did not recognize or explicitly prohibited. All six of these challenges were ultimately dismissed. The reason was simple: it was the Federal Constitution, in its article 121, clause IV, that forced them to recognize Mexico City's marriages.

Within the *Acción de Inconstitucionalidad 2/2010,* three main briefs were filed. The first was the General Attorney's. The second was filed by Mexico City Assembly explaining why it approved the reform and why the Court should uphold it. The third brief was filed by Mexico City's government, in which it too explained why it published –and thus, implicitly approved– the reform.

The Attorney General's brief challenged same-sex *marriage*, but not same-sex *concubinato*. He argued that he was not against legal recognition of same sex relationships but only against their recognition through marriage. Same-sex couples, he sustained, should be regulated through civil unions, an institution more "appropriate" for them. The brief did not argue that sexual preference or orientation should not be treated as a suspect class when arguing discrimination. His position was that not allowing same-sex couples to marry was an authorized differentiation, even within the doctrine of the right to non-discrimination. The law, the Attorney General argued, should treat equally those who are equal and unequally those who are unequal. Homosexuals and heterosexuals, for the purposes of marriage, were *not* equal. The brief also argued that marriage was *designed* for procreation, which he understood in strict (hetero)sexual terms. Thus, same-sex couples could not "fit" into marriage, since same-sex couples could not sexually reproduce with each other. The brief also argued that this understanding of marriage was reflected in article 4, paragraph 1 of the Federal Constitution, which states that the "law must protect

[86]The States were Morelos (controversia constitucional 6/2010), Guanajuato (7/2010), Tlaxcala (9/2010), Sonora (12/2010), Baja California (13/2010) and Jalisco (14/2010). For a review of the arguments used in these *controversias*, see Omar Feliciano, "Corta, pega, litiga: impotencia y vaginitis", *Animal Político*.

the development and organization of the family." He also argued that this was the concept of marriage included in international treaties such as the Universal Declaration of Human Rights, the American Convention on Human Rights and CEDAW. Finally, he argued against same-sex couples having access to adoption based on the suffering these children would endure from social discrimination.

The Mexico City Assembly and Government ended up writing different, yet complimenting briefs. The Assembly focused, mainly, on homophobia, making the case fundamentally about discrimination against people that were not heterosexual. It included a section in which it casted the history of LGBT persecution. Whether they were criminally prosecuted for the sex they had or whether they were denied recognition for their family life, State action against these people amounted to a violation of their rights. Given that the issue was marriage, specifically, they focused on two rights: the right to the protection of the family and the right to freedom of expression. The latter was more thoroughly developed: allowing same-sex couples to access marriage granted them access to a State-created form of expression. This was important because it was connected to the right to the development of one's personality: these couples were now free to (live and) express their love in *this* form.

The Mexico City Government, on the other hand, made the case about family diversity. This was not, the City argued, just about LGBT families, but about all families that did not conform to the husband/father-wife/mother-(sexually produced) offspring model of the family. Its brief focused on three things: (1) tracking the sociological development of the family in Mexico and showing how today, family diversity is a *fact*; (2) holding that article 4, paragraph 1 of the Federal Constitution protected *all* types of families: straight, gay, two-parent, one-parent, no children, adopted children, etcetera; (3) and holding that the Universal Declaration of Human Rights, the American Convention on Human Rights, and CEDAW did not *limit* marriage to opposite-sex couples.

The Supreme Court's ruling is a mixture of the Assembly and Government's briefs, with its own innovations. The first thing that must be noted is that it is a decision both about LGBT discrimination *and* family diversity. The Court used mainly the narrative of family diversity to resolve the issue around marriage; while it was the narrative around discrimination that helped solve the issue of adoption.

3.2.1.1 Why Is Same-Sex Marriage Constitutional?

The first question the Court answered was whether same-sex marriage was constitutional. Since the Attorney General argued that article 4, paragraph 1 of the Federal Constitution prohibited expanding marriage to same-sex couples, the Court focused its first efforts on showing why this was not the case. For the Court, article 4, paragraph 1 of the Federal Constitution mandated the protection of all families. In spite of the Constitution using the singular *the* family ("*la familia*"), the Court established that this meant *families*. And it understood this concept as implying not only couples, but filial relationships as well such as parents and their offspring, partners, grandparents, and their grandchildren. These were all examples of constitutionally and, most importantly, *independently* protected family relationships.

In addition to understanding "the family" to mean relationships that went beyond the couple, the Court then established that the law had to recognize socially relevant family relationships. "The family," the Court reasoned, "rather than being a legal creation, spawns from human relationships, and corresponds to a social design that [...] is different in each culture [...]."[87] What a family was depended on the social context. And since social contexts change over time, so did family structures.

> Social phenomena like the incorporation of women to the workforce; reduced birth rates; divorce rates and, thus, remarriages [...]; the increase in the number of single parents; common-law marriages [...]; [the development of] assisted reproductive technology; [... new patterns and waves of] immigration and the economy, among other factors, have [resulted] in the traditional organization of the family changing.[88]

The Court stated that Article 4, paragraph 1 protected *families* and it was up to the legislator to determine how it would protect them. In this determination, the legislator had to acknowledge social change, if the Constitution was to be a "living document."[89] In this scheme, marriage appeared as one of the legislative – as opposed to constitutional– designs which had been used to protect family ties. And there was no reason for it to be the only one or for it to have any content in particular; other, of course, than that required by other rights. This is where international treaties came into play.

For the Court, international treaties led to two conclusions: the first was that marriage was not exclusively heterosexual. A simple reading of the articles that regulate the family and marriage in these documents did not lead to the conclusion that marriage had to be between a man and a woman[90]; but rather that both men and women had an individual right to get married. Second: these provisions did not ban States from expanding marriage. And third: even if one was to accept that international treaties assumed the heterosexual paradigm, this could not to be construed in a way that impeded recognition of same-sex marriage.

> It is an undeniable fact that in previous times –not too long ago–, homosexual persons remained hidden, didn't show themselves as such, given the social disapproval of them; this condition until recently was even considered a "pathology" [...] [For this reason,] evidently, in such documents –the Federal Constitution and international treaties–, their existence wasn't even conceivable or recognizable, let alone the relationships or unions that they established according to their sexual orientation.[91]

[87] Acción de Inconstitucionalidad 2/2010, par. 238, p. 88.

[88] *Ibid.*, par. 239.

[89] *Ibid.*, par. 240.

[90] *Ibid.*, par. 255.

[91] *Ibid.*, par. 252.

"Homosexual persons" became a new reality that the law had to recognize just like the incorporation of women to the workforce or the decrease in birthrates became a reality that had to be contemplated in the regulation of the family. The law, for the Court, had to be read in accordance to these new realities, and not just within the historical context in which it came to be. The law was what people, today, demanded it to be.

Regarding marriage specifically, the Court held that it too was "not an immutable or 'petrified' concept"[92] that the legislator could not touch. The review of the history of marriage, the Court explained, showed that the legislator had been changing it, as social transformations had been taking place.

> [I]t is an undeniable fact that the secularization of society and of marriage itself, [as well as] other social transformations, have led to different sexual [and] affective relationships, and other ways in which people help each other out [. . .]. [This, in turn, has lead] to legal transformations to the institution of marriage, [which has included no longer considering procreation as one of its ends.][93]

The Court connected the many marriage modifications that have occurred with time, focusing particularly on its dissociation with reproduction. Divorce, it argued, had been one of the most fundamental changes to marriage; divorce proved how a couple could split without necessarily affecting children in a negative way. With this, the Court separated the protection of the couple from the protection of the offspring. It also argued that the will of the parties to remain together had become the most important factor in the regulation of marriage.[94] The Court even cited the reform that allowed sex reassignment surgery as relevant to marriage, specifically for the purposes of procreation: if transsexual people, who generally underwent reassignment surgery that resulted in infertility,[95] could access marriage, there was no reason to ban same-sex couples from accessing marriage too.

Marriage, the Court argued, had been changing *de facto*. Today, it is not about reproduction, but about "affection, [. . .] identity, solidarity and mutual commitment between those that want to share a life together."[96]

> A person's decision to be joined with someone else and project a life together, just like the decision to have –or not to have– children, is derived from the self-determination of each person, from the right to the free development of each individual's personality [. . .] [And it is not necessary] for the decision to be joined with someone else to [be tied] to the second one, that is, to have children with each other. [Especially considering that, in this aspect] there are [physiological] factors that might impede a person from having children, which cannot become an obstacle to the free development of the personality, as far as these decisions go.[97]

---

[92] *Ibid.*, par. 242.

[93] *Ibid.*, par. 242.

[94] *Ibid.*, par. 246.

[95] *Ibid.*, par. 248.

[96] *Ibid.*, par. 250.

[97] *Ibid.*, par. 251.

The Court accepted that there are differences between same-sex and opposite-sex couples regarding their ability to have children that were genetically theirs. But this was not a relevant difference for accessing marriage. First, because the decision to have children was a right that could not be conditioned to marriage. Likewise, the decision of being joined with someone was part of a right that could not be conditioned to reproduction. Second: because reproduction was no longer an end of marriage, even for opposite-sex couples, as the evolution of marriage showed. If an opposite-sex couple would not or could not reproduce, they would still have access to marriage.[98]

The Court also understood that along with the right to the development of the personality there were not only decisions regarding reproduction or marriage, but those regarding a person's "sexual options":

> A person's sexual orientation, as part of her personal identity, is a relevant element of her life's project [. . .] It is an element that will undeniably determine [her] affective and/or sexual relationships [. . .] and because of that, with whom she will form a life in common with or have children with, if she wants to.
>
> [. . .] For homosexual persons, just like it happens with people whose sexual orientation is towards those of a different sex, freely and voluntarily establishing affective relationships with persons of the same-sex is part of their full development. [Both types of] relationships, as sociological [studies] show, [are similar] in that they form a community of life built on bonds of affection, sexual attraction, and reciprocal solidarity, with a tendency towards stability and permanence in time.[99]
>
> [. . . In conclusion], if one of the aspects that drives the way in which a person projects her life and her relationships is her sexual orientation, it is a fact that, in full respect of human dignity, a person can demand State recognition both of her sexual orientation [. . .], and of her unions, *under the modalities that, in a given moment, a State decides to adopt* (civil unions, solidarity pacts, common-law marriages, and marriages).[100]

Once again, marriage appears as one of the options the State has for regulating affective relationships. In any case, if the State chooses to regulate these relationships through marriage, it does have to comply with certain rules. Freedom to enter into the marriage contract –for instance– has to be guaranteed. For the Court, women's freedom to enter a marriage is the most relevant protection granted by international treaties' regulation of marriage. Another rule is that it must be open for everybody, unless there is a very good reason for a person or group of persons to be excluded. In this decision, the Court established that a person's sexual orientation was not a good reason to restrict marriage but, on the contrary, it was precisely a reason to open it up.

State recognition and protection of people's affective relationships is at the intersection between the right to the free development of the personality and the right to the protection of the family. The first protects all matters of sex,

[98] *Ibid.*, par. 270.

[99] *Ibid.*, par. 264, p. 266.

[100] *Ibid.*, par. 269. Emphasis added.

reproduction, and love, regardless of whether they take the shape the State offers or not. The second is the right that allows people to demand State recognition and protection of their family bonds.

What is important to note about this decision is how it counters the Attorney General's essentialist and originalist arguments on marriage. While the Attorney General saw in the protection of "the family," the protection of "marriage," the Court saw in this provision the protection of all families. While the Attorney General viewed marriage as an institution with an essence the law cannot alter; the Court viewed marriage as an institution that had been, could be and should be altered by the law. While the Attorney General viewed the "essence" of marriage as reproduction, the Court viewed marriage as important because, *today*, it is *one* way to protect affective bonds. It is not that marriage ceases to be "for" something (it is designed to protect affective bonds); it is that the purpose of marriage changed with time, according to the current realities of society and people's rights.

3.2.1.2 Why Is Same-Sex-Parent Adoption Constitutional?

The second fundamental question the Court had to solve was regarding same-sex couples adoption. The Attorney General's main argument was that opening the process of adoption to same-sex couples was a violation of the "best interest of children," also included in article 4 of the Constitution and in the Convention on the Rights of the Child. By not excluding same-sex couples from the process of adoption, Mexico City's Assembly had privileged the adults' rights vis-á-vis the children's. Specifically, the right to grow up in a constitutionally protected –that is, two opposite-sex parent– household, and the right not to be discriminated against by others, which is what would happen to children adopted by these couples. The Court responded with several arguments.

Homosexuality, according to the Court was "simply one of the options that is present in human nature and, as such, is part of a person's self-determination and her right to the free development of her personality."[101] For this reason, it cannot be argued that being gay makes a person –or a couple– less valuable and should therefore be "considered harmful for the development of a minor." The Court cited "expert testimony" through a brief filed by the National University (*Universidad Nacional Autónoma de México*) sustaining that:

> There is no basis to affirm that homo-parental homes or families possess an anomalous factor that directly results in bad parenting. Whoever believes otherwise has to offer evidence to support the claim. Neither the Attorney General, nor anybody in the world, has presented this evidence in the form of studies that are serious and methodologically sound. [. . .] Those [that believe that homosexual parents damage their children] are making an inconsistent generalization, based on a particular fact or anecdote, elevating

[101] *Ibid.*, par. 314.

it to a characteristic of a whole social group. These inconsistent generalizations are called stereotypes and they are the erroneous cognitive bases of social prejudices and of intolerance.[102]

This is where the Court turns to the issue of out-right discrimination:

[We] cannot tell the constitutional or legal difference between excluding an entire group of people from adoption because of their sexual orientation or excluding them for reasons of race, for example, or because of their ethnic, religious, or economical origins [...] For the same reason that it is not necessary to know the effect for children of living in families that are indigenous or not indigenous, rich or poor, with parents that have a disability or not [...] because, in any case, it would be constitutionally prohibited to not consider them a family protected by the Constitution or to consider them a "threatening" or "dysfunctional" family for children: the Constitution makes this inquiry unnecessary.[103]

"Heterosexuality," the Court wrote, "does not guarantee that the adopted child will live in optimal conditions for her development: this has nothing to do with heterosexuality-homosexuality. Every family model has advantages and disadvantages and every family must be analyzed in particular, not from a statistical point."[104] What "the best interest of the child" requires, the Court reasoned, is a legal structure that allows administrative authorities to limit potential adoptive parents on account of *other* factors that specifically relate to their ability to offer the adopted child the necessary conditions for her development and care.[105] This principle does *not* force the State to guarantee the "best possible parents," in the sense that the Attorney General implies. Understanding the "best interest of the child" in his terms would render the adoption regime "absolutely inoperative"[106] and it "would probably also result in grave violations of"[107] the right to non-discrimination.

At this point, the Court turned to the issue of children being discriminated against on the basis of their parents.

In a democratic State, the legislator must eliminate the diverse ways of discrimination and intolerance present in society, [a feat that] is accomplished through the recognition and protection of all families [...], not through their "exclusion" or "denial."

[A]s we said when we referenced the family and marriage: societies are always dynamical. At some point, in other countries, interracial couples were discriminated and an object of criticism, which no longer happens today. Interracial adoptions were also frowned-upon and today are completely accepted. Likewise, children of single mothers or divorced parents, at some point, were discriminated. Adoption itself, for some time, was kept a secret, because adopted children could be discriminated against [...].[108]

---

[102] *Ibid.*, p. 131, footnote 3.

[103] *Ibid.*, par. 317.

[104] *Ibid.*, par. 338.

[105] *Ibid.*, par. 318.

[106] *Ibid.*, par. 319.

[107] *Ibid.*

[108] *Ibid.*, par. 329–330.

Last but not least, the Court referred to the possibility of children already living with their "biological father or mother and their homosexual partner. What happens if the biological father is missing, if he is not there physically at some point or dies? Who is going to be responsible for that child?"[109] The challenged law also remedies these situations, the Court argues. And for this reason, it does *not* violate the best interest of children, but rather guarantees it.

> [. . .] Law must be part of social change. If this Supreme Court established that the challenged law was unconstitutional, because society would discriminate against children adopted by homosexual couples, [the Supreme Court itself would be discriminating against] these children.[110]

In this decision the Court did not get tangled up in the debate regarding the existence of a fundamental right to parenthood *per se*, which covers adoption. In its view, adoption is a legal option "for those persons that, for whatever reason, cannot or do not want to have biological children," and it is also an optimal way to "satisfy the right of every boy and girl –that, for whatever reason, are not with their biological mother or father or both–, to have a family that will provide assistance, care, and love, with all that this implies: education, housing, clothes, food, etcetera."[111] The regulation of adoption should be judged, thus, from these two perspectives: does it guarantee for children what it should guarantee? And, regarding adults, does it discriminate in any way?

Although the Court affirmed that the right to non-discrimination bars us from even questioning whether children should grow up in certain types of families (those that fall under a suspect class), it did offer a response to the question of whether same-sex couples were impaired –in some way– of fulfilling the duties that spawn from a filial relationship. For the Court, the answer was that they were not. Same-sex couples are capable of offering what parenthood, ultimately, entails: both material goods and emotional care. This is the core of the Court's argument. If adoption exists, it must be opened to all of those that are able to give children what they need. Unless there is proof that same-sex couples cannot give children what they need, they cannot be barred from accessing the process of adoption.

Finally, the Court went as far as to affirm that, if people were genuinely concerned with the best interest of children, their efforts should rather be focused on improving the process of adoption. The focus should be on guaranteeing that "thousands of children, that today remain in shelters or orphanages, have a family" and that "thousands of couples that want children" are actually able to get them "in ways that are safe for those boys and girls."[112]

---

[109] *Ibid.*, par. 334.

[110] *Ibid.*, par. 331.

[111] *Ibid.*, par. 325.

[112] *Ibid.*, par. 328.

3.2.2 The Oaxaca Ruling

The First Chamber of the Supreme Court solved, in December of 2012, three different *amparo* suits brought against the Oaxaca Civil Code for *excluding* same-sex marriage. In Mexican law, the *amparo* suit is a mechanism of judicial review designed for individual persons to combat laws or governmental acts that infringe on their rights. The most important feature of this mechanism is that, if the case is won, it only benefits the parties to the suit. Ultimately, if five separate cases are won on the same issue, with the approval of 4 –out of 5– Justices (in cases solved by the First Chamber), a *jurisprudencia* will be formed. The *jurisprudencia* is a normative criterion that, in the case of the First Chamber, must be followed by all inferior *judges*, federal and local. As of recently, the Constitution established that when this *jurisprudencia* gets formed, the Supreme Court must notify the legislature so it modifies the law at hand. If in 90 days the law is not modified, the Supreme Court will issue –if it is approved by 8 out of 11 Justices–, a "declaration of unconstitutionality" of the law.[113] This means that it will no longer be applicable, for *anybody*. Now, for the case of same-sex marriage, this still implies that *each* civil code –out of the 31 states– must be challenged at least on five different occasions for a change within that legislature to happen.

In this section, I want to focus on what the First Chamber of the Court solved in one of these *amparos*. I am not going to focus on what the defendants claimed, since they did not really innovate on the arguments, but just replicated the Mexico City ruling; nor am I going to focus on what the Oaxaca authorities, defending the Code, argued, since they didn't, either, present novel arguments against same-sex marriage. For instance, the Governor of Oaxaca, one of the authorities that opposed same-sex marriage, argued that marriage could not be reduced to the will of the parties; that, by virtue of its "historical, natural, social, cultural, and axiological formation" it was a legal institution with one purpose and specific elements: (i) it was a contract; (ii) that required a man and a woman; (iii) with the purpose of procreating and (iv) mutually aiding each other. "Marriage's own teleology essentially entails [that it be considered an] alliance between a man and a woman, that set out to procreate, educate those children and aid each other."[114] Essentialism in all its glory, even after the Supreme Court's Mexico City ruling.

The first thing that must be noted about the Oaxaca ruling is how it frames the problem and understands the Mexico City ruling. For the First Chamber of the Supreme Court, this new case differed from the previous, since in the latter, the Court had to establish if *expanding* same-sex marriage was "allowed," while in the former, it had to decide if *excluding* same-sex marriage was "prohibited". In the first case, the question was, according to the Oaxaca ruling, whether there is something

---

[113]Article 107, fractions (I) and (II) of the Federal Constitution; Articles 216, 217, 218, 223, 232 of the *Ley de Amparo* (Law of Amparo).

[114]Amparo en revisión 581/2012, pp. 19–20.

about the constitutional regulation of the family that prohibits expanding marriage; in the second case, the question is whether the traditional definition of marriage as the union of a man and a woman violates equality.[115]

This is a curious distinction, given how the Mexico City decision is *actually* written: same-sex marriage is not *allowed*, it is *required* given the right to the protection of the family and the right to the free development of the personality. However, the Court, 2 years later, considers it is deciding a new problem. A problem it chooses to decide according to the logic of the right to non-discrimination.[116]

3.2.2.1 The Right to Non-discrimination

Analyzing the case according to the right to non-discrimination, implies two things, according to the Court: (1) first, determining whether the Oaxaca Civil Code, when defining marriage, draws a distinction based on a suspect class, prohibited by the right to non-discrimination; and (2) second, determining whether this distinction is constitutional. Establishing the first point is important, because it determines the "test" the Court must use to determine the second point: if the distinction was based on a suspect class, the Court had to use a strict scrutiny test to analyze it.[117]

The Court determined that "sexual preference" was a suspect class, according to article 1 of the Federal Constitution. It thus proceeded to establish why the definition of marriage contained in the Oaxaca Civil Code was drawn based on a distinction on sexual preference.

For the Court, although every "person" could get married, "a homosexual could only access [marriage] if she denied her sexual orientation, which was precisely the characteristic that defined her as a homosexual."[118] "Sexual preference," the Court wrote, "is not a status that a person holds, but something that is shown through concrete conducts like the choice of a partner."[119] If a person could not choose to marry a partner of the same sex, the definition of marriage was "implicitly" drawing a distinction based on sexual preference.

3.2.2.2 Is the Distinction Constitutional?

Given that the Oaxaca Civil Code established access to marriage based on sexual preference, the Court had to determine whether this distinction: (a) pursued a constitutionally *compelling* interest; (b) whether it was a measure that was narrowly tailored to this end; and (c) whether it was the least restrictive means to pursue this end.[120]

---

[115] *Ibid.*, pp. 27–28.

[116] *Ibid.*, p. 29.

[117] *Ibid.*, pp. 30–32.

[118] *Ibid.*, p. 33.

[119] *Ibid.*

[120] *Ibid.*, pp. 34–35.

The Court determined that the definition of marriage pursued a constitutionally compelling interest: to protect the family, in compliance with article 4, paragraph 1 of the Federal Constitution. The question was really whether defining marriage as the union between a man and a woman with the purpose of procreating was tailored to that end. The Court's response was that it was not.

This was where the Court connected the Oaxaca ruling with the Mexico City ruling. How could it determine whether defining marriage in such terms complied with article 4, paragraph 1? By determining what article 4, paragraph 1 protects: all families –including couples and filial relationships; and couples, specifically, through marriage, without it being tied to procreation. Under this scheme, the Court argued, Oaxaca's definition of marriage was both over-inclusive and under-inclusive. It was over-inclusive because, if it aimed to connect marriage to procreation, it failed to do so by allowing opposite-sex couples that could not or did not want to have children to marry. It was under-inclusive, because same-sex couples that were similarly situated –that is, that wanted to and had children– could not access the norm.

> For all relevant effects, homosexual couples are in an equivalent situation as heterosexual couples [. . .] [Following] the European Court of Human Rights [in] *Schalk & Kopf v. Austria*, [. . .] the relationship two homosexual persons who form a life as a couple constitutes *family life* under the European Convention of Human Rights. But the family life of two homosexual persons is not limited to life as a couple. Procreating and raising children is not a phenomenon that is incompatible with homosexual preferences. There are same-sex couples that make a family life with minors procreated or adopted by one of them, or homosexual couples that use means derived from scientific progress to procreate, regardless of having access to the normative power of marriage.[121]

Given that the definition of marriage contained in the Oaxaca Civil Code was not directly connected to the end it pursued, the Court concluded that validating it in such terms could only perpetuate "a decision based on prejudices that historically have existed against homosexuals."[122] Their exclusion from marriage was not a "legislative over-sight", "but the legacy" of these "severe prejudices."[123]

In this point, the Court referred to the "historical disadvantages" suffered by homosexuals, which had been "widely recognized and documented: public harassment, verbal violence, employment and access to health discrimination, besides the exclusion of some aspects of their public life."[124] Citing *Loving v. Virginia*, it drew on the analogy between race and sexual orientation discrimination and concluded: "the normative power to get married does little if it does not grant a person the possibility of marrying the person of her choice."[125]

Next, the Court proceeded to establish why marriage was important. "The right to marry did not only include the right to access the expressive benefits associated

[121] *Ibid.*, pp. 39–40.

[122] *Ibid.*, p. 41.

[123] *Ibid.*

[124] *Ibid.*

[125] *Ibid.*, p. 42.

to marriage" –benefits that were never individually referred to–, "but also the right to the material benefits that the laws ascribe to the institution."[126] "In this sense," it wrote, "marriage is really 'a right to other rights'."[127] Then it affirmed: "the rights that civil marriage grants increase considerably the quality of life for people."[128] "In Mexican law there are a great amount of economic and non-economic benefits associated to marriage ...."[129] After citing some concrete examples of these benefits, the Court concluded that denying them for homosexuals was treating them like "second class citizens."[130] The Court then stated that excluding same-sex couples from marriage, also "translates into a differentiated treatment towards the children of homosexual couples, placing them in a disadvantage vis-à-vis the children of heterosexual couples."[131]

3.2.2.3 Would a Different Distinction Be Constitutional?

The Court took up one of the arguments made by the Oaxaca government: that marriage is for heterosexual couples and that same-sex couples should have access to a different institution. Technically, this was not part of the problem, especially since Oaxaca didn't even have a different regime for same-sex couples. However, the Court took it upon itself to answer this problem.

In this point too, the Mexican Supreme Court decided to make an analogy between the discrimination suffered on account of sexual orientation and racial discrimination in the United States. "Even if [same-sex couples could access a different regime with the exact same rights as marriage, such a regime] evokes the measures validated by the doctrine known as 'separate but equal' that developed in the United States in the context of racial segregation at the end of the nineteenth century."[132] After briefly recapping *Plessy v. Ferguson* and *Brown v. Board of Education*, the Mexican Court concluded:

> The models for the recognition of same-sex couples, even if their only difference with marriage is the name they get, are inherently discriminatory because they constitute a "separate but equal" regime. Just like racial segregation was based on the unacceptable idea of white supremacy, the exclusion of homosexual couples from marriage is too based on the historical prejudices that have existed against homosexuals. Their exclusion from marriage perpetuates the notion that same-sex couples are less worthy of recognition than heterosexuals, thus offending their dignity as persons.[133]

---

[126] *Ibid.*, p. 41.

[127] *Ibid.*, p. 42.

[128] *Ibid.*

[129] *Ibid.*

[130] *Ibid.*, p. 46.

[131] *Ibid.*, p. 47.

[132] *Ibid.*, p. 48.

[133] *Ibid.*, p. 49.

3.3 Conclusion

The Supreme Court rulings on marriage are a result of changes to family law and those brought about by the LGBT movement.

First, the rulings represent the defeat of the essentialist thrust of the original doctrine of marriage. These rulings were not, as I showed, the first time the Court countered this logic. It had been doing it for some years, in many issues that involved marriage. What the Mexico City ruling did was to expose and counter-argue this logic to its full extent. It showed the prominence of text versus doctrine, which is another way of saying that it showed that what is important is *who* determines the content of marriage: today's legislature –through the Constitution, international treaties and the law– and not those that created the original doctrine of marriage. The Court uncovered marriage for what it was: an institution actually created by people that must always be able to respond *why* they chose a certain design.

Second: the rulings upheld a conception of marriage that has been evolving in the law through time. Marriage is *one* type of family relationship. The Court inverts the logic of marriage: before, marriage was the path that people had to conform to; today, marriage can be a path people conform to, if they want to. Constitutionally, family relationships are protected, unless there's a constitutional reason for them not to be.

Third: same-sex relationships have no reason to be excluded from family arrangements. They have no reason to be excluded from marriage –and thus, from *concubinato*–, nor can they be excluded from parenthood. Regarding marriage, the Court was clear: even if marriage was understood as tied to reproduction, same-sex couples would be able to access it because same-sex couples can and do, actually, "reproduce." The Court did not restrict reproduction to the genetic reproduction of the couple; it understood reproduction as the ability to "have" children, legally speaking. If marriage is understood as a "community of life," in which people help each other out, same-sex couples are perfectly capable of complying with it.

Fourth: regarding social discrimination suffered by children of LGBT parents, the Court was clear to state that the law must recognize same-sex families as a reality, in order to better protect these children and their parents from this discrimination.

Since the Supreme Court rulings the victories for the LGBT community have spread beyond Mexico City. The only real pushback since the 2010 ruling came from the Federal Government. The two institutions in charge of social security (IMSS, for workers in private companies, and ISSSTE, for government employees) refused to recognize same-sex marriages, thus denying them social security benefits. The strategy was clear: if the Federal Government could not control *who* would *marry*, it would try to control what being married, in terms of access to rights vis-à-vis the State, implied. It would empty marriage of its content.[134] The citizenry, however,

[134]The Defense of Marriage Act of the United States, for instance, did this by redefining marriage. The Federation did this by denying rights that *federal laws* attached to state marriages. The distinction is not minor, especially if one considers the ideas that bounced around in the U.S.

pushed back. Couples that were denied access to these rights challenged these administrative decisions before the federal judiciary. Every single case that was brought forth was won. The Supreme Court Mexico City precedent started being used in all these cases to challenge the denial of social security benefits as a violation of rights.[135] Ultimately, the ISSSTE started recognizing these marriages.[136] The IMSS, however, refused to do so until the Supreme Court ruled that denying these benefits amounted to discrimination.[137]

Other than the pushback from these two institutions, the battle has been concentrated in getting marriage in other Mexican States. First, there was a wave of individual challenges to several state civil and family codes for their exclusion of same-sex couples from marriage. Until this day, suits have been brought and won in at least 8 of the 31 states.[138] And the numbers are growing. The Supreme Court has been called to rule on several of them.

In addition to judicial challenges, changes also happened in the legislative and administrative arenas. In the State of Colima, "conjugal unions" (*enlaces conyugales*) were approved by the legislature exclusively for same-sex couples.[139] These unions have the exact same rights and obligations as marriage; they even grant access, as couples, to adoption.[140] The members that comprise the couple, once married, are even considered "spouses."But the name of the institution that

---

Supreme Court, for example, with DOMA. The Federation may not have the power to define marriage; but the Federation does have the power to determine what protections it offers to the family –within its powers–. The Federation could choose not to give Access to citizenship for marriage, for example. The problem is that this got lost, when the federation denied access to a whole group of families, with criteria that were not sound.

[135]The Supreme Court has not ruled on the merits, yet, only regarding the admissibility of the suit brought against one of these decisiones (*see* Amparo en Revisión 86/2012); the National Council to Prevent Discrimination issued a resolution in which it condemned the authorities for denying these benefits. *See* CONAPRED, Resolución por disposición 2/2011, July 6, 2011.

[136]CONAPRED, "Registra ISSSTE a matrimonios igualitarios en cumplimiento a Resolución del Conapred", May 13, 2013. Several news outlets, including CONAPRED's own note, talk about a press release done by ISSSTE in which it communicates its change in policy. I have not been able to find this release.

[137]Amparo en Revisión 485/2013, decided on January 30, 2014; IMSS, "Comunicado de prensa no. 009", February 17, 2014, http://www.imss.gob.mx/prensa/archivo/201402/009

[138]Oaxaca, Colima, Yucatán, Sinaloa, Chihuahua, Estado de México, Jalisco, and Nuevo León.

[139]"Congreso de Colima aprueba unions civiles entre personas del mismo sexo", *CNN México*, July 4, 2012; Código Civil del Estado de Colima, articles 139 on.

[140]Coahuila in 2007 created "solidarity pacts" (*pactos de solidaridad*) for same-sex couples and opposite-sex couples. Unlike the conjugal unions in Colima, whoever, these pacts, when it comes to same-sex couples, do not grant access to adoption; nor is it clear if they grant access to social security and other federal benefits (since the laws in which these benefits are established are for "spouses"). Código Civil para el Estado de Coahuila, articles 385–1 on.

these couples say "yes" to is named differently: *matrimonio* for opposite-sex couples, *enlace conyugal* for same-sex couples. The reform has been challenged for establishing a "separate-but-equal" regime.[141]

The State of Jalisco passed a law regulating civil unions (*sociedades de convivencia*), for two *or more* persons living in the same household, regardless of their sex.[142] Unlike the conjugal unions approved in Colima, this new figure offers far less rights and obligations for the contracting parties (just like the civil unions that were approved in Mexico City in 2007). Prominently, it does not grant access to social security benefits. However, it is being supported by major LGBT organizations as a victory in what is considered to be a very conservative State. It has also been challenged by the new Attorney General for establishing a "separate-but-equal" regime.[143]

In the State of Quintana Roo, local authorities started marrying same-sex couples after one of them argued that since the Quintana Roo Civil Code did not even include a definition of marriage (such as the widely reproduced "marriage is the union of a man and a woman . . . "),[144] there was not any legal impediment for them to get married.[145] Without any formal –be it legislative or judicial– change, the Code was transformed. Following the same logic of administrative reinterpretation, authorities in Mexico City started issuing new birth certificates for children that were born *prior* to the 2009 reform that had been registered as sons and daughters of single parents, thus recognizing *both* of their same-sex parents.[146] This change was done not by using second parent adoption, but through the process originally established to force "irresponsible men" to *recognize* their children (a processed dubbed "the recognition of children").[147] The advantage of this strategy –besides not having to adopt one's own child– is that the process is done directly before the Civil Registry without the need to go to court. This is another novel use of an existing law.

In the middle of all these changes, in June of 2011, the Federal Constitution was reformed to include the right to non-discrimination specifically on account

[141]Pedro Zamora Briseño, "Se amparan contra figura de 'enlace conyugal' en Colima", *Proceso*, September 30, 2013, http://www.proceso.com.mx/?p=354188

[142]Ley de Libre Convivencia del Estado de Jalisco, *El Estado de Jalisco. Periódico Oficial*, 1 de noviembre de 2013, núm. 27 bis. http://app.jalisco.gob.mx/PeriodicoOficial.nsf/BusquedaAvanzada/EE03503DDBE546E786257C16007AAB33/$FILE/11-01-13-BIS.pdf

[143]The Attorney General –incredibly so– has challenged it through an *Acción de Inconstitucionalidad* (number 36/2012), so the Supreme Court will have to solve the case.

[144]Código Civil para el Estado de Quintana Roo, articles 680–704.

[145]Adriana Varillas, "Revocan anulación de bodas gay en QRoo", *El Universal*, May 3, 2012, http://www.eluniversal.com.mx/notas/845171.html; Estefanía Vela Barba, "Derecho y ciudadanía: el caso del matrimonio gay en México", *Nexos: El Juego de la Corte*, March 20, 2013, http://eljuegodelacorte.nexos.com.mx/?p=2501

[146]Valentina Pérez Botero, "Familias homoparentales logran reconocimiento jurídico de su composición", *Revolución. Tres punto cero*, August 21, 2013. http://revoluciontrespuntocero.com/familias-homoparentales-logran-reconocimiento-juridico-de-su-composicion/

[147]Código Civil para el Distrito Federal, articles 78–8 (1928).

of *sexual* preference (before, it only established a generic "preference"). Also, it determined that *every* authority, within its own powers, had to respect, protect, guarantee and promote human rights, established both in the Constitution *and* in international treaties subscribed by Mexico. With this new norm, a Civil Registry in one of the State of Colima's towns began marrying couples arguing that, as an authority with the power to marry people, it had to respect, protect and guarantee human rights when doing so. Colima is a State in which three separate strategies have been tried: the legislative one (resulting in conjugal unions), the judicial one (at least one *amparo* –an individual suit– has been won) and the "administrative" one (directly before the Civil Registry, couples are getting married).

It seems that the issue of same-sex unions is legally solved in Mexico. All that is left to do is to continue pushing the transformation of *all* legal codes. Two notes, though: in the rest of the states, people have not been pushing for the recognition of same-sex *concubinato*, only of marriage. Although this thrust is understandable –especially if the way to push change is through the judiciary–, it would be lamentable to see the LGBT movement reinstate the prominence of marriage, especially in a country with an important history of alternative family arrangements.[148] And particularly when it was the protection of *all* families what rendered same-sex marriage a *must*. Second: same-sex unions in Mexico show how successful lobbying and litigation can bring about change. Also: it shows how change in one area of law can "spark" change in other areas. However, I am not sure if the path and tools that were used to fight for same-sex unions are useful to fight other types of exclusion, such as those suffered when class is added to the mix. Although the first prominent LGBT case that was won before the Supreme Court was related to trans rights, it has been noticeable how, unlike the same-sex marriage case, there have been no other cases related to trans rights. The barriers to effectively access justice cannot be forgotten.[149] Remembering the original Homosexual Revolutionary Action Front: "no one is free until we are all free."[150]

[148] See, for example, Nancy D. Polikoff, *Beyond (Straight and Gay) Marriage: Valuing All Families Under the Law*, Beacon Press, 2009; Janet Halley, "Behind the Law of Marriage (I): From Status/Contract to the Marriage System", *Unbound*, 2010, vol. 6, no. 1; Brook J. Sadler, "Re-Thinking Civil Unions and Same-Sex Marriage", *The Monist,* vol. 91, no. 3/4, 2008; and Libby Adler, "The Gay Agenda", *Michigan Journal of Gender & Law*, 2009, vol. 16, no. 1.

[149] See, for example, Libby Adler in "Gay Rights and Lefts: Rights Critique and the Distributive Analysis", *Harvard Civil Rights-Civil Liberties Law Review* (Amicus Online Supplement), Vol. 46, No. 1, 2011; and Dean Spade, "Trans Law Reform Strategies, Co-Optation, and the Potential for Transformative Change", *Rutgers School of Law Newark*, vol. 30, 2009.

[150] Rodrigo Parrini, "Sujeto, tiempo y nación. La emergencia de un sujeto politico minoritario", *supra*, p. 8.

Bibliography

1. Aquinas, Thomas. 1920. *Summa Theologica. Supplement to the third part (Supplementum Tertiae Partis)*. Second and Revised Edition, Question 64, Article 3. Available at: http://www.newadvent.org/summa/5.htm.
2. Blanco, Mercedes, and Edith Pacheco. 2009. Aging and the family-work link: A comparative analysis of two generations of Mexican women (1936–1938 and 1951–1953). *Journal of Comparative Family Studies* 40(2).
3. Censida. 2006. *Manual de organización específico del Centro Ambulatorio Para la Prevención y Atención del SIDA e Infecciones de Transmisión Sexual,* noviembre. http://www.censida.salud.gob.mx/descargas/man_org_capasits.pdf.
4. Collier, Jane. *Cambio y continuidad en los procedimientos legales zinacantecos,* Haciendo justicia. Interlegalidad, derecho y género en regiones indígenas, ed. María Teresa Sierra. (CIESAS 2004).
5. Cosme, Granados, José Arturo, and Luis Ortiz Hernández. 2003. Descentralización sanitaria en México: transformaciones en una estructura de poder. *Revista Mexicana de Sociología* 65(3): 591–627.
6. De la Dehesa, Rafael. 2010. *Queering the public sphere in Mexico and Brazil*. Durham: Duke University Press.
7. Gavito, Barrón, and Miguel Ángel. 2010. El baile de los 41: la representación de lo afeminado en la prensa porfiriana. *Historia y Grafía* 34: 62–64.
8. George, Robert P., Sherif Girgis, and Ryan T. Anderson. 2010. What is marriage?. *Harvard Journal of Law & Public Policy* 34(1).
9. Gordley, James. 1991. *The philosophical foundations of modern contract doctrine*. Oxford: Clarendon.
10. Gordley, James. 2013. The method of the roman jurists. *Tulane Law Review* 87: 940, 941, 947, 948.
11. Halley, Janet. 2010. Behind the law of marriage (I): From status/contract to the marriage system. *Unbound* 6(1).
12. Knaul, Felicia, and Susan Parker. Cuidado infantil y empleo femenino en México: evidencia descriptiva y consideraciones sobre las políticas. *Estudios demográficos y urbanos* 11(3).
13. Libby, Adler. 2009. The gay agenda. *Michigan Journal of Gender & Law* 16(1).
14. Libby, Adler. 2011. Gay rights and lefts: Rights critique and the distributive analysis. *Harvard Civil Rights-Civil Liberties Law Review* (Amicus Online Supplement) 46(1).
15. Lopez-Acuña, Daniel. 1980. Health services in Mexico. *Journal of Public Health Policy* 1(1): 83–95.
16. Lozano, Genaro. 2013. The battle for marriage equality in Mexico, 2001-2011. In *Same-sex marriage in Latin America: Promise and resistance*, ed. J. Pierceson et al., 156. Lanham: Lexington Books.
17. Madrazo Lajous, Alejandro. 2012. El formalismo desde el derecho privado. In *Teoría y crítica del derecho civil y comercial*, ed. Martín Hevia, 290–291. Mexico: Fontamara.
18. Madrazo Lajous, Alejandro. 2008. From revelation to creation: The origins of text and doctrine in the civil law tradition. *Mexican Law Journal*, New Series 1(1); *Revelation and creation: The theological foundations of modern legal science in Mexico*, Yale Law School JSD dissertation (directed by Paul Kahn), 2006.
19. Matrimonio, Requisitos del Contrato de. *Semanario Judicial de la Federación*, tomo XLVIII, 3297 (Segunda Sala, Quinta Época, Tesis Aislada, 358723).
20. Mijangos, Pablo. 2014. *Secularization or reformation? The religious origins of civil marriage in Mexico*. Paper presented at the 2014 annual meeting of the American Historical Association, cited with the author's permission.
21. Molyneux, Maxine. 2006. Mothers at the service of the new poverty agenda: Progresa/Oportunidades, México's Conditional Transfer Programme. *Social Policy & Administration* 40(4), August.

22. Moreno, Hortensia. 2010. La construcción cultural de la homosexualidad. *Revista Digital Universitaria* 11(8).
23. Pacheco Escobedo, Alberto. 2006. El matrimonio canónico y el matrimonio natural. *Familia. Naturaleza, derechos y responsabilidades,* Virginia Aspe Armella (comp.), Porrúa-Universidad Panamericana, México, 57.
24. Pérez Botero, Valentina. 2013. Familias homoparentales logran reconocimiento jurídico de su composición, *Revolución. Tres punto cero*, August 21.
25. Polikoff, Nancy D. 2009. *Beyond (straight and gay) marriage: Valuing all families under the law*. Boston: Beacon.
26. Rojina Villegas, Rafael. *Derecho civil mexicano*, tomo II, ed. 2006 (1962), 250–253.
27. Sadler, Brook J. 2008. Re-thinking civil unions and same-sex marriage. *The Monist* 91(3/4).
28. Spade, Dean. 2009. Trans law reform strategies, Co-optation, and the potential for transformative change. *Rutgers School of Law Newark* 30.
29. Vela Barba, Estefanía. 2013. La evolución del divorcio en clave de derechos y libertades. *Nexos: El Juego de la Corte*, August 20. http://eljuegodelacorte.nexos.com.mx/?p=3004.

Statutes

30. American Convention on Human Rights.
31. Circular del Ministerio de Justicia. Remite la ley del matrimonio civil.
32. Código Civil de Mexico (1928).
33. Código Civil ... (1928), article 291-Bis. (reformed May 25, 2000).
34. Código Civil para el Distrito y Territorios Federales en Materia Común y para toda la República en Materia Federal (1928), (reformed October 3, 2000).
35. Código Penal para el Distrito Federal (2002).
36. Constitución Política de los Estados Unidos Mexicanos 4 (reformed December 31, 1974).
37. International Covenant on Civil and Political Rights.
38. Ley de 14 de Diciembre de 1874, reglamentaria de las adiciones y reformas de la Constitución Federal, article 23, section IX (reformed December 29, 1914).
39. Ley de Sociedad de Convivencia para el Distrito Federal.
40. Ley de Sociedad de Convivencia para el Distrito Federal, November 16, 2006.
41. Ley de Vivienda (June 27, 2006).
42. Ley del Matrimonio Civil (1859).
43. Ley del Instituto del Fondo Nacional de la Vivienda para los Trabajadores (April 24, 1972).
44. Ley del Seguro Social (1973).
45. Ley Federal para Prevenir y Eliminar la Discriminación, June 11, 2003.
46. Ley General de Salud (February 7, 1984).
47. Ley General de Salud (May 15, 2003), Articles 77-Bis-1, 77-Bis-4.
48. Ley Sobre Relaciones Familiares (1917).

Cases

49. Acción de Inconstitucionalidad 146/2007 y su acumulada, p. 187.
50. Acción de Inconstitucionalidad 2/2010, par. 238, p. 88.
51. Amparo Directo Civil 6/2008, pp. 75–83.
52. Amparo Directo en Revisión 917/2009, p. 22.
53. Amparo en revisión 581/2012, pp. 19–20.
54. Amparo en Revisión 485/2013.

55. Amparo en Revisión 93/92, Primer Tribunal Colegiado del Sexto Circuito, *cited in* Contradicción de Tesis 5/92, Primera Sala de la Suprema Corte de Justicia de la Nación.
56. Contradicción de Tesis 21/2006, pp. 15–16.
57. Contradicción de Tesis 5/92, Primera Sala de la Suprema Corte de Justicia de la Nación.
58. *Corbett v. Corbett* (UK, 1970).
59. Solicitud de Modificación de Jurisprudencia 9/2005, Primera Sala de la Suprema Corte de Justicia de la Nación, p. 12.

Chapter 4
Same-Sex Marriage in the United States

Macarena Sáez

Abstract This Chapter gives a brief analysis of the status of same-sex marriage in the United States prior to the US Supreme Court decisions of 2013 and the status of litigation and political reforms triggered in part by these court decisions. It shows that marriage is a central institution in the country's rationale of family law in ways that separate it from other western countries that have allowed same-sex marriage.

4.1 The Value of Marriage

The link between marriage and the family has historical roots. Since Aristotle, political science has linked family and nation building. In his Politics I, Aristotle referred to the family (*oikos*) as the first relationship to arise between man and woman. He thought that when several families unite aiming at fulfilling not only their daily needs, "the first society to be formed is the village."[1] The *Politics* follows by saying that "the most natural form of the village appears to be that of a colony from the family ..."[2] and then states that "When several villages are united in a single complete community, large enough to be nearly or quite self-sufficing, the state comes to existence ..."[3] they form a village and then a *polis*. Cicero also made the connection between marriage and government: "[T]he first bond of union is that between husband and wife; the next, that between parents and children;

[1] Aristotle "The Politics of Aristotle, trans. into English with introduction, marginal analysis, essays, notes and indices by B. Jowett. Oxford, Clarendon Press, 1885. 2 vols, Book 1, 3.

[2] *Ibid.*

[3] *Ibid.*

M. Sáez (✉)
Washington College of Law, American University, Massachusetts Ave. N.W. 4801, Washington, DC 20016, USA
e-mail: msaez@wcl.american.edu

M. Sáez (ed.), *Same Sex Couples - Comparative Insights on Marriage and Cohabitation*, Ius Gentium: Comparative Perspectives on Law and Justice 42,
DOI 10.1007/978-94-017-9774-0_4

then we find one home, with everything in common. And this is the foundation of civil government, the nursery, as it were, of the state."[4]

The English historian Peter Laslett states that "the intellectual tradition of patriarchalism" that placed the family "at the centre of all social institutions" was widespread among sixteen and seventeen century European thinkers.[5] For these thinkers the relationship between family and the political state was obvious and the analogies recurrent.[6] The war against Mormon polygamy was partly based on a discourse of monogamy as essential to the construction of the United States.[7] Nancy Cott argues that the founding fathers had "a political theory of marriage."[8] Influenced by Montesquieu, the founders would have "tied the institution of Christian-modeled monogamy to the kind of polity they envisioned."[9] This thinking propelled the analogy between the two forms of consensual union –marriage and government—into the republican nation's self-understanding and identity.[10]

Marriage is linked to family as citizenship has been linked to the state. Cohabitation outside of marriage has been to family what illegal immigration has been to the state. In different periods, countries have been forced to redefine citizenship or include as citizens individuals that originally were not welcomed as such. The same has happened with families; countries have been forced by reality to recognize as family members individuals that were unwelcomed in the acceptable family structure. Recognition of family members outside the realm of marriage has been slow and within a limited scope. In the United States many social welfare benefits are attached to marriage.[11] Marriage is still today the equivalent to voting rights for citizenship. Married individuals have access to benefits and special treatment within family law, social welfare policy, immigration law, torts, tax law, among others. *Ceteris paribus,* unmarried individuals who function as families may not have access to those benefits and special treatment. Unmarried families are to married families what illegal aliens are to citizens. Sometimes states decide to grant limited benefits to illegal aliens or even grant them a window of opportunity to legalize their status, become legal residents and, eventually, citizens.[12] Sometimes

---

[4]Cicero, De Oficiis, Book I, 57 (Walter Miller trans., 1913).

[5]Robert Filmer, Patriarcha and Other Political Works, Introduction by Peter Laslett 24 (2009).

[6]*Ibid.*, p. 27.

[7]Nancy Cott, Public Vows: A History of Marriage and the Nation, 10, (2002); Sara Barringer Gordon, The Mormon question: polygamy and constitutional conflict in nineteenth-century America 222 (2002).

[8]*Id.* at 9.

[9]*Id.* at 10.

[10]*Ibid.*

[11]The Personal Responsibility and Work Opportunity Reform Act (PRWORA) Pub. L. No 104–193 includes several provisions to promote marriage.

[12]Undocumented immigration is a serious issue in the United States. "Estimates based on the March Supplement of the U.S. Census Bureau's Current Population Survey (CPS) indicate that the unauthorized resident alien population rose from 3.2 million in 1986 to 12.4 million

states decide to grant certain benefits to unmarried couples, and in rare opportunities, grant a group of them full and equal access to marriage. Most of the time, however, states fall short of doing that and create differentiated status, just as citizens and foreign immigrants under a visa or permit may be able to reside in a country and enjoy limited benefits. By the beginning of the 21st century, several states granted same-sex couples limited rights and, in some cases a broad array of rights through registered partnership arrangements.[13]

The link between marriage and citizenship is not a metaphor. Marriage is treated as an essential gateway to citizenship. Thus, marriage can pave the way to citizenship in a manner that no other relationship between two individuals not connected by blood or adoption can. This may be the strongest signal of differentiation between families that start through marriage and families that start through cohabitation. In 2010, 82,449 individuals obtained legal permanent resident status as spouses of U.S. citizens coming from abroad.[14] This is the largest category of new arrivals, followed by parents of U.S. citizens.[15] Immigration policies can say a great deal

in 2007, before leveling off at 11.1 million in 2011." Ruth Ellen Wasem, U.S. Immigration Policy: Chart Book of Key Trends, Congressional Research Service, Report for Congress R42988, March 7, 2013. Among the several problems that undocumented immigration creates, what to do with children who came to the U.S. at young age with undocumented parents and have lived most of their lives here is highly controversial. A possible solution has been the passing of the DREAM Act (acronym for Development, Relief, and Education for Alien Minors) but several forms of this bill have been in Congress since 2001. On June 15, 2012 President Barak Obama's administration issued a memorandum known as the Deferred Action for Childhood Arrivals (DACA). "Individuals who demonstrate that they meet the guidelines below may request consideration of deferred action for childhood arrivals (DACA) for a period of 2 years, subject to renewal for a period of 2 years, and may be eligible for employment authorization." U.S. Citizens and Immigration Services, Consideration of Deferred Action for Childhood Arrivals Process, Frequently Asked Questions List at http://www.uscis.gov/humanitarian/consideration-deferred-action-childhood-arrivals-process/frequently-asked-questions#what is DACA. For information on the DREAM Act see Mariela Olivares, *Renewing the Dream: Dream Act Redux and Immigration Reform,* 16 Harv. Latino L. Rev. 79, (2013).

[13]Benefits in these systems vary greatly. For example, in *Lewis v. Harris* the Supreme Court of New Jersey decided that same-sex couples had a right to enjoy the same rights and benefits of different-sex couples under civil marriage in New Jersey. See *Lewis v. Harris,* 188 *N.J.* 415, 908 *A.*2d 196 (2006). The New Jersey Legislature enacted the Civil Union Act creating a parallel system of civil unions for same-sex couples. Same-sex couples in civil unions were entitled to all of the rights, benefits, and responsibilities of marriage. See N.J.S.A. 37:1–33. A more limited system was enacted in Wisconsin, where in 2009 the Wisconsin legislature created a domestic partnership for same-sex couples that would allow them to access to limited benefits such as the right to make decisions on behalf of the ill partner, visit partners in hospitals, insurance benefits, among others. See, Wisconsin Legislative Reference Bureau, Domestic Partnership, Budget Brief 09–2, September 2009.

[14]Office Of Immigration Statistics, 2010 Yearbook Of Immigration Statistics 19 tbl. 6, (2011).

[15]*Ibid.*

about the types of families a country value and the associations it excludes. Through immigration law, countries can limit those associations that reject.[16]

The United States has traditionally protected marriage, and in the era of same-sex couples' recognition, it is still protecting the married family.[17] What is changing is the composition of the married couple, but not the composition of the legal family. Despite uncontestable statistics showing that marriage is on decline,[18] U.S. courts still value the married family more than any other type of family association. This emphasis on marriage distances the United States from most countries where marriage equality has gained ground. Brazil, Portugal, Mexico, South Africa, Spain, and Canada are only a few of the countries that have accepted same-sex marriage while, at the same time, providing more rights to unmarried families or at least basing their decisions on arguments that reinforce the legal recognition of social constructions of the family.

In the United States, marriage is still treated as the main gateway to family formation, deserving constitutional protection.[19] Before recognition of a right to family, comes the recognition of a right to marry. This right is presented to the community as an individual right, but one that makes a community function as such.[20] Statistics, however, show that an increasing number of families are formed outside the realm of marriage.[21] Many of them repeat the pattern of a sexual family that has replaced the marriage certificate for an informal agreement that resembles marriage in all aspects of familial life, but in the formality of marriage itself. Proof of marriage is, however, simpler than proof of companionship. It only requires applicants to show the actual marriage certificate. Regardless of whether a married couple hates each other, actually supports each other, or does not speak to each

[16]For an account on the restrictions imposed by US immigration laws on interracial marriages between a white American citizen and a non-white foreigner until the 1960s, see Rose Cuison Villazor, *The Other Loving: Uncovering the Federal Government's Racial Regulation on Marriage,* 86 NYU L. Rev. 1361–1439 (2011).

[17]In the United States marriage is a fundamental right within the right to privacy protected by the 14th and 5th amendments of the U.S. Constitution. Although several decisions pointed into this direction, the 1978 U.S. Supreme Court decision *Zablocki v. Redhail* leaves no doubt that marriage is a fundamental right: "[I]t would make little sense to recognize a right to privacy with respect to other matters of family life and not with respect to the decision to enter the relationship that is the foundation of the family in our society . . . " *Zablocki v. Redhail,* 434 U.S. 374 (1978).

[18]According to the Pew Research Center, in 2011 only 51 % of Americans 18 years and older were married, compared to 72 % in 1960. See Richard Fry, "No Reversal in Decline of Marriage," *Pew Research Social & Demographic Trends*, November 20, 2012 at http://www.pewsocialtrends.org/2012/11/20/no-reversal-in-decline-of-marriage/ and D'vera Cohn, Jeffrey S. Passel, Wendy Wang And Gretchen Livingston, "Barely Half of U.S. Adults Are Married – A Record Low," *Pew Research Social & Demographic Trends,* December 14, 2011 at http://www.pewsocialtrends.org/2011/12/14/barely-half-of-u-s-adults-are-married-a-record-low/

[19]See Zablocki, *supra* note 17.

[20]The U.S. Supreme Court has said that "[m]arriage is one of the 'basic civil rights of man,' fundamental to our very existence and survival. *Loving v. Virginia* 388 U.S. 1, 87 S.Ct. 1824 (1967).

[21]See *Pew Research Social & Demographic Trends*, *supra,* note 18.

other, a marriage certificate will be enough to treat that couple as a family. Despite its procedural benefits, focusing on the formality of marriage as the paramount evidence of family ties is problematic.

In the case of immigration, for example, using a marriage certificate as proof of family tie may allow the entrance of people who did not really have family ties with the sponsor,[22] and it may leave out real families with individuals who support and care for each other.[23]

4.2 A Dialogue Between Politics and Rights

The United States is experiencing a transitioning period on marriage regulation. Same-sex marriage has become a common topic for scholarly discussions,[24] a cause for litigation in many states,[25] and a source of legislation reform in many others.[26] On June 26, 2013 the Supreme Court issued its first two decisions on same-sex marriage. *Hollingsworth v. Perry (Perry)*[27] and *United States v. Windsor (Windsor).*[28] In *Perry* the Supreme Court did not advance any substantive opinions on whether same-sex marriage was constitutionally protected, allowed or prohibited. It did, however, have the effect of allowing same-sex marriage in California.[29] The *Windsor* case was not about legalizing same-sex marriage but about challenging the restriction of marriage as a union between a man and a woman for federal purposes.

[22]Linda Kelly, *Marriage for Sale: The Mail-Order Bride Industry and the Changing Value of Marriage*, 5 J. Gender Race & Just. 175 (2001).

[23]Aubry Holland, *The Modern Family Unit: Toward A More Inclusive Vision of the Family in Immigration Law*, 96 Cal. L. Rev. 1049, 1059 (2008).

[24]Scholarly literature on same-sex marriage was almost nonexistent until the 1980s. A limited search in the United States Library of Congress catalog showed 13 books with the word "same-sex marriage" in the title between 1900 and 1989, 42 between 1990 and 1999 and 450 since the year 2000. The Worldcat database showed 5 entries between 1900 and 1989 that contain "same-sex" in the title, and the word "marriage" as a subject when searching for books in English, excluding juvenile and fiction categories. The same search showed 160 hits from 1990 to 2000, and 974 from 2001 to 2013.

[25]Prior to the decisions from the U.S. Supreme Court *Perry* and *Windsor*, same-sex marriage had been gained by court decisions in the states of Massachusetts, Connecticut, Iowa, California, New Mexico, and New Jersey.

[26]New Hampshire, Vermont, New York, Maine, Maryland, Washington, Rhode Island, Delaware, Minnesota, Hawaii, Illinois, and the District of Columbia.

[27]*Hollingsworth v. Perry*, 133 S. Ct. 2652, 186 L. Ed. 2d 768 (U.S. 2013).

[28]*United States v. Windsor*, 133 S. Ct. 2675, 2682, 186 L. Ed. 2d 808 (2013).

[29]The U.S. Supreme Court decided that the official sponsors of the California ballot initiative "Proposition 8" did not have standing to challenge the decision of the District Court that had declared Proposition 8 unconstitutional. Proposition 8 had limited marriage to the union of one man and one woman. *Perry* made the District Court decision final, allowing same-sex marriage in California.

In this decision the Supreme Court could have refrained from providing arguments in favor or against same-sex marriage. It chose, however, to advance arguments that, while working well in the narrow field of restricting the power of the federal government to define marriage for federal purposes, also paved the way for broader challenges to the constitutionality of same-sex marriage in general.

Perry and *Windsor* were not about making same-sex marriage available in each of the United States. Both decisions, however, have changed the landscape of same-sex marriage. For the first time in history same-sex marriage is perceived by many as an actual possibility in the foreseeable future of the United States. These decisions were the first but certainly will not be the last on same-sex marriage that the Supreme Court will issue.[30] On October 6, 2014, the Supreme Court denied review of five cases, which left as final decisions striking down bans to same-sex marriages in Indiana, Wisconsin, Utah, Oklahoma, and Virginia.[31] This decision also opened the door for other states to open same-sex marriage as well.

An important component of the debate on same-sex marriage relates to the proper forum to address marriage and family. Whether same-sex marriage is a matter of rights or of politics defines the proper forum to address the issue. Some courts have denied same-sex marriage not because the institution would be bad for society but because the majorities should decide on this issue. In the United States we find decisions that gave the legislature the role of deciding on same-sex marriage, and courts that considered the issue a matter of rights that was outside the scope of the majorities.[32]

Over the last century, western societies including the United States, have slowly accepted that citizens cannot use their political power to discriminate on the basis of race. Western societies have also accepted, albeit at an even slower pace, that political majorities cannot discriminate on the basis of gender. The same-sex marriage debate shows that sexual orientation is gradually becoming a protected category such as gender and race. As Justice Jackson stated more than 60 years ago:

> The very purpose of a Bill of Rights was to withdraw certain subjects from the vicissitudes of political controversy, to place them beyond the reach of majorities and officials and to establish them as legal principles to be applied by the courts. One's right to life, liberty, and property, to free speech, a free press, freedom of worship and assembly, and other fundamental rights may not be submitted to vote; they depend on the outcome of no elections.[33]

[30] The Supreme Court decided in January of 2015 to hear four new cases on same-sex marriage in 2015.

[31] *Baskin v. Bogan* (7th Cir. Sep. 4, 2014); *Kitchen v. Herbert*, 755 F.3d 1193, 1201 (10th Cir. 2014); *Bishop v. Smith*, 760 F.3d 1070, 1074 (10th Cir. 2014); *Bostic v. Schaefer*, 760 F.3d 352, 368 (4th Cir. 2014); *Wolf v. Walker*, 986 F. Supp. 2d 982, 988 (W.D. Wis. 2014), judgment entered (June 13, 2014), *aff'd sub nom. Baskin v. Bogan*, 14–2386, 2014 WL 4359059 (7th Cir. Sept. 4, 2014).

[32] *Goodridge v. Dep't of Pub. Health*, 798 N.E.2d 941, 948 (Mass. 2003), *Kerrigan v. Comm'r of Pub. Health*, 289 Conn. 135, 156–57, 957 A.2d 407, 420–21 (2008), *Varnum v. Brien*, 763 N.W.2d 862, 882 (Iowa 2009), and *Griego v. Oliver*, 2014-NMSC-003, 316 P.3d 865.

[33] *W.Va. State Bd. Of Educ. v. Barnette*, 319 US 624, 638.

Not all courts agree that same-sex marriage is one of those "certain subjects" that must be withdrawn from the "vicissitudes of political controversy." The same-sex marriage debate, therefore, opens a broader debate about the role of courts in deciding issues related to same-sex marriage. If what is at stake is a modification of the concept of marriage, and marriage is an essential democratic concept, then it is a political issue subject to political definitions. The political branches of each nation shape immigration policies. Citizens vote for representatives who will enact statutes that will have an impact on who can be admitted into the country. Congress, as representing the desires of the majority, passes statutes on budget, housing, health, national security, among many other areas. This power, however, is limited by fundamental rights as set in the Constitution of a country/state and international conventions subscribed by a state. Constitutions and international law thus limit the political power of citizens. Once a particular issue is defined as protected or affecting fundamental rights, that issue no longer belongs to the political realm.

In the United States, once the Supreme Court declared racial segregation unconstitutional, it shielded it from the majority's views.[34] Once it decided that marriage was a fundamental right, it reduced the space for political intervention on such right. These decisions provoked political disagreement[35] but once claims of substantive due process or equal treatment were set, opposing groups had to accept that they would no longer decide to build a society where children would be divided by race in schools, or that marriage would be limited to people of the same race. These are no longer political decisions because they touch on fundamental rights.

4.2.1 From Courts to Political Processes and Vice Versa

Marriage equality activists have used different strategies to achieve same-sex marriage. For advocates, however, there is no question that marriage equality is a matter of rights. Challenges to marriage statutes, however, have not always triggered a positive outcome because of the position by some courts that same-sex marriage is a matter for legislatures to decide. For example, the New York Court of Appeals stated in 2006 that "the New York Constitution does not compel recognition of marriages between members of the same sex. Whether such marriages should be recognized is a question to be addressed by the Legislature."[36] This decision triggered a political process that ended, after much back and forth between the

---

[34]*Brown v. Board of Education*, 347 U.S. 483 (1954).

[35]For an account of the immediate backlash of Brown v. Board of Education see Waldo E. Martin Jr., Brown v. Board of Education: A Brief History with Documents 199–222 (1998); For examples of opposition to *Loving v. Virginia* see Peggy Pascoe, What comes naturally: Miscegenation law and the making of race in America 287 (2009).

[36]*Hernandez v. Robles*, 7 N.Y.3d 338, 356, 855 N.E.2d 1, 5 (2006).

New York State Assembly and the Senate, with the Marriage Equality Act that recognized same-sex marriage and became effective on July 24, 2011.[37]

Courts, at other times, have recognized that marriage entails rights and benefits that non-married couples may also deserve. These courts have considered, however, that it is the role of legislatures to determine the specific institution or method of distribution of those rights. A decision by the Supreme Court of New Jersey illustrates this rationale:

> To comply with this constitutional mandate, the Legislature must either amend the marriage statutes to include same-sex couples or create a parallel statutory structure, which will provide for, on equal terms, the rights and benefits enjoyed and burdens and obligations borne by married couples. We will not presume that a separate statutory scheme, which uses a title other than marriage, contravenes equal protection principles, so long as the rights and benefits of civil marriage are made equally available to same-sex couples. The name to be given to the statutory scheme that provides full rights and benefits to same-sex couples, whether marriage or some other term, is a matter left to the democratic process.[38]

The New Jersey court gave the legislature six months to enact legislation giving some sort of recognition to same-sex couples. The court did not mandate the legislature to recognize same-sex marriage. It gave the political branch the option of either expanding marriage or creating a different institution that would grant equal benefits and rights to same-sex couples outside the scope of marriage. The legislature took the second option enacting on December of 2006 a Civil Union Act.[39] The Bill stated:

> It is the intent of the Legislature to comply with the constitutional mandate set forth by the New Jersey Supreme Court in the recent landmark decision of Lewis v. Harris, 188 N.J. 415, (October 25, 2006) wherein the Court held that the equal protection guarantee of Article I, paragraph 1 of the State Constitution was violated by denying rights and benefits to committed same-sex couples which were statutorily given to their heterosexual counterparts. The Court stated that the 'State can fulfill that constitutional requirement in one of two ways. It can either amend the marriage statutes to include same-sex couples or enact a parallel statutory structure by another name, in which same-sex couples would not only enjoy the rights and benefits, but also bear the burdens and obligations of civil marriage.' ...
>
> The Legislature has chosen to establish civil unions by amending the current marriage statute to include same-sex couples.[40]

New Jersey provided same-sex couples the same rights and obligations afforded to married heterosexual couples but it refused to grant them access to the brand marriage. As shown below, New Jersey's system did not last that long. After *Windsor* another decision declared New Jersey's dual system unconstitutional.[41]

[37] Assem. 8354, 2011 Leg., 234th Reg. Sess. (N.Y. 2011), in Bill Jacket, L. 2011 c. 95.

[38] *Lewis v. Harris, supra* note 13, 200 (2006).

[39] N.J. Stat. Ann. § 37:1–28 (West).

[40] *Ibid.*

[41] Garden State Equality et al. v. Dow et al., 434 N.J.Super. 163 (2013). See below Sect. 4.2.2.

Hawaii was the first of these "dialogues" going wrong in the United States. In 1993 the Hawaii Supreme Court rejected the claim that the Hawaii constitution provided a fundamental right to same-sex marriage.[42] It considered, however, that requiring marriage to be between a man and a woman constituted sex discrimination and remanded the case to a state court to determine whether the state could prove that it had a "compelling" state interest that would overcome such sex discrimination.[43] Later, a trial court ruled that the state marriage law was unconstitutional but before a final decision was issued on appeal, Hawaii citizens, through a referendum, amended Hawaii's constitution, giving the legislature the power to reserve marriage to opposite-sex couples.[44] As this Chapter will show later, *Windsor* contributed—and it still does—to a shift towards same-sex marriage in several states, including Hawaii.

Same-sex marriage creates, therefore, a sort of "dialogue" between courts and legislatures. Outside the United States, the case of South Africa[45] and Colombia illustrate the connections and disconnections these dialogues can produce.[46]

4.2.2 California: From a Mayor's Decision to a Court's Decision

The "dialogue" between courts and legislatures comes in part as a reaction of either a court or a legislature to what the other branch has stated. California's process to same-sex marriage illustrates very well this action-reaction "dialogue" between courts and political processes because it involved not only courts and legislature, but also the citizens of California.

On February 12 of 2004, the Mayor of San Francisco authorized officials of the city and county of San Francisco to issue marriage licenses. In a period of a month, around 4,000 marriage licenses were issued. The weddings stopped on March 11,

[42] *Baehr v. Lewin*, 852 P.2d 44 (Haw. 1993).

[43] *Ibid.*

[44] "The legislature shall have the power to reserve marriage to opposite-sex couples." Haw. Const. art. 1, § 23 (ratified Nov. 3, 1998).

[45] In *Minister of Home Affairs and Another v. Fourie and another* the South African Constitutional Court mandated the legislature to provide a scheme of protection to same-sex couples similar to the one already afforded to opposite-sex couples. The result was the Civil Union Act of 2006, which allows same-sex marriage, as well as opposite sex marriage, with the same rights and protections afforded to individuals of opposite sex marrying under the Marriage Act of 1961. *Minister of Home Affairs and Another v. Fourie and another* [CC] [Constitutional Court] (CCT 60/04) [2005] ZACC 19; 2006 (3) BCRL 355(CC); 2006(1) SA524(CC) (1 December 2005) (S. Afr.). See Civil Union Act, 2006, Government Gazzette, Republic of South Africa, Vol. 497 Cape Town 17 November 2006.

[46] For a thorough account of Colombia's situation with same-sex marriage, see Chap. 5 of this book.

2004 when the California Supreme Court issued an interim stay directing officials to stop issuing marriage licenses.[47] On August of the same year, the Supreme Court stated that "local executive officials lacked authority to issue marriage licenses to, solemnize marriages of, or register certificates of marriage for same-sex couples."[48] It also stated that "marriages conducted between same-sex couples in violation of the applicable statutes [were] void and of no legal effect."[49]

Parallel to the debates on same-sex marriage, California had afforded same-sex couples the same rights and benefits enjoyed by married opposite-sex couples, through a civil partnership regime. In other words, the debate on same-sex marriage was not about legal recognition of same-sex couples, or about accessing benefits or rights afforded to married couples. It was about accessing marriage and its branding:

> Accordingly, the legal issue we must resolve is not whether it would be constitutionally permissible under the California Constitution for the state to limit marriage only to opposite-sex couples while denying same-sex couples any opportunity to enter into an official relationship with all or virtually all of the same substantive attributes, but rather whether our state Constitution prohibits the state from establishing a statutory scheme in which both opposite-sex and same-sex couples are granted the right to enter into an officially recognized family relationship that affords all of the significant legal rights and obligations traditionally associated under state law with the institution of marriage, but under which the union of an opposite-sex couple is officially designated a 'marriage' whereas the union of a same-sex couple is officially designated a 'domestic partnership.'[50]

The Supreme Court concluded that California's Constitution guaranteed "the same substantive constitutional rights as opposite-sex couples to choose one's life partner and enter with that person into a committed, officially recognized, and protected family relationship that enjoys all of the constitutionally based incidents of marriage."[51]

After this decision state voters passed a ballot initiative known as Proposition 8 (Prop 8), amending the State Constitution to define marriage as a union between a man and a woman**.** The proponents of the ballot were not only against same-sex marriage, but against courts being the right forum to decide on the issue. In the voter's guide informing citizens on the ballot, proponents of Prop 8 stated that

> CALIFORNIANS HAVE NEVER VOTED FOR SAME-SEX MARRIAGE. If gay activists want to legalize gay marriage, they should put it on the ballot. Instead, they have gone behind the backs of voters and convinced four activist judges in San Francisco to redefine marriage for the rest of society. That is the wrong approach.[52]

---

[47] *Lockyer v. City & Cnty. of San Francisco*, S122923, 2004 WL 473257 (Cal. Mar. 11, 2004).

[48] *Lockyer v. City & Cnty. of San Francisco*, 33 Cal. 4th 1055, 1069, 95 P.3d 459, 464 (2004).

[49] *Ibid.*

[50] *In re Marriage Cases*, 43 Cal. 4th 757, 779–80, 183 P.3d 384, 398 (2008).

[51] *Ibid., pp.* 433–434.

[52] California, General Election, Tuesday November 8, 2008, Official Voter Information Guide. Arguments in Favor of Proposition 8. Available at http://voterguide.sos.ca.gov/past/2008/general/argu-rebut/argu-rebutt8.htm

Proposition 8 prevailed with the support of 52 % of the votes. Advocates of same-sex marriage challenged the constitutional amendment. The opinion of California's Attorney General was that the amendment was unconstitutional because it took away a fundamental right that had already been granted to a minority group.[53] The "dialogue" between courts and political processes continued with the Supreme Court of California deciding whether the amendment was constitutional or not. In *Strauss v. Horton* it decided that, precisely because same-sex couples already enjoyed similar rights and benefits afforded to married opposite-sex couples, the amendment was narrow enough to be constitutional.[54] The court, however, maintained as valid all marriages celebrated before its decision.[55]

This back and forth between judicial and political processes, as it is well documented by now, did not end there. Two couples filed suit in federal court and started the litigation that ended in 2013 with the first of the two U.S. Supreme Court decisions issued the same day.[56] California's Attorney General decided not to defend Proposition 8. That left the challenge with plaintiffs and no official defendants. The official proponents of Prop 8 decided to act as defendants, which let the issue of legal standing open. At the end, the U.S. Supreme Court decided *Perry* on procedural grounds, declaring a lack of standing of a private party to defend the constitutionality of a statute when state officials had chosen not to defend it.[57] Defendants of Prop 8 before the U.S. Supreme Court repeated in their brief the argument they had used to justify Proposition 8 in the first place, regarding the right forum to decide issues on same-sex marriage:

> Our Constitution does not mandate the traditional gendered definition of marriage, but neither does our Constitution condemn it. This Court, accordingly, should allow the public debate regarding marriage to continue through the democratic process, both in California and throughout the Nation.[58]

Whether courts or political actors have the final word on same-sex marriage is not yet defined. It is, however, clear, that the practical effects of *Perry,* and the substantive reasons provided by the U.S. Supreme Court in *Windsor* have moved same-sex marriage closer to substantive due process or equal protection issues and further away from political processes subject to majoritarian decisions.

---

[53]Attorney General's Response to Amicus Curiae Briefs, January 21, 2009, p. 4.

[54]*Strauss v. Horton*, 46 Cal. 4th 364, 411, 207 P.3d 48, 77 (2009).

[55]*Ibid.*

[56]For a thorough account on the legal strategies behind California's same-sex marriage litigation see Scott L. Cummings & Douglas NeJaime, *Lawyering for Marriage Equality*, 57 UCLA L. Rev. 1235, 1330 (2010).

[57]*Perry supra* note 27 at 2668.

[58]Brief for Petitioners at 8, *Hollingsworth et al. v. Perry* 570 US–(2013) (No. 12–144).

4.3 *Windsor*: The Game Changer

In 1996 the U.S. Congress passed the Defense of Marriage Act (DOMA). Section 3 of the DOMA stated that for federal purposes:

> In determining the meaning of any Act of Congress, or of any ruling, regulation, or interpretation of the various administrative bureaus and agencies of the United States, the word 'marriage' means only a legal union between one man and one woman as husband and wife, and the word 'spouse' refers only to a person of the opposite sex who is a husband or a wife.[59]

Since 2008 the State of New York recognized same-sex marriages legally performed outside the State. Edith Windsor and Thea Spyer lived in New York and married in Ontario, Canada, in 2007. Thea Spyer died in 2009 leaving her entire estate to Edith Windsor. Although her marriage was recognized by the State of New York, Section 3 of DOMA barred her from claiming the federal estate tax exemption for surviving spouses. Edith Windsor brought a refund suit arguing that DOMA violated her equal protection rights. Similarly to the Attorney General of California in the *Perry* case, the United States Attorney General notified the Speaker of the House of Representatives that the Department of Justice would no longer defend Section 3's constitutionality.[60] A Bipartisan Legal Advisory Group (BLAG) of the House of Representatives voted to intervene in the case defending the constitutionality of Section 3 of DOMA. The District Court permitted the intervention and found Section 3 unconstitutional, ordering the Treasury to refund Ms. Windsor's tax payments. The Court of Appeal for the Second Circuit affirmed the decision but the United States still did not enforce the judgment. The U.S. Supreme Court granted *certiorari*.

The decision in *Windsor* changed the landscape of same-sex marriage litigation because it provided reasons based on dignity and on equality to affirm the lower courts decisions. The Court had other options that would have kept the outcome intact but would have provided less fuel for future litigation. One of the main issues with Section 3 of DOMA was whether it interfered with the states' power to regulate family law matters: "The definition of marriage is the foundation of the State's broader authority to regulate the subject of domestic relations with respect to the '[p]rotection of offspring, property interests, and the enforcement of marital responsibilities.'"[61] The court further argued that "[c]onsistent with this allocation of authority, the Federal Government, through our history, has deferred to state-law

---

[59] Defense of Marriage Act, Section 3.

[60] For an analysis of the Supreme Court reasoning on both *Perry* and *Windsor* cases on the issue of standing see Ryan W. Scott, *Standing to Appeal and Executive Non-Defense of Federal Law After the Marriage Cases*, 89 Ind. L.J. 67 (2014).

[61] *Windsor supra,* note 28, p. 2691.

policy decisions with respect to domestic relations."[62] Despite this recognition of state power, the Court decided that the issue at hand on substantive grounds beyond federalism:

> Despite these considerations, it is unnecessary to decide whether this federal intrusion on state power is a violation of the Constitution because it disrupts the federal balance. The State's power in defining the marital relation is of central relevance in this case quite apart from principles of federalism.[63]

4.3.1 Windsor and Dignity: A Lost Opportunity

Many courts around the world have based their decisions for granting same-sex marriage on the value of dignity. South Africa's Constitutional Court is famous for its use of dignity as a pillar of constitutional review.[64] It was not a surprise, therefore, that in *Minister of Home Affairs and Another v. Fourie* the South African Constitutional Court justified the constitutionality of same-sex marriage on dignity as linked to equality.[65] Other countries have also heavily relied on dignity to justify their shifts from opposite-sex marriage to marriage equality. Mexico, for example, has issued several decisions on same-sex marriage. The first one is worth noticing for its use of dignity as autonomy. For the Mexican Supreme Court, dignity was the basis for which each individual had the right to choose her own family.[66] The rationale of the Court was that marriage between individuals of the same sex was constitutional not because *marriage* was important, but because dignity led to the free development of one's personality. What was important, therefore, was that every individual had to be respected in her choices about family formation.[67]

Of all uses of dignity, when it comes to same-sex marriage courts have used it to reinforce concepts of equality and autonomy. Dignity is not a foreign concept to U.S. courts.[68] It has not, however, used it consistently. A few courts did use dignity as autonomy in their state decisions on same sex marriage. In *Goodridge* v. *Department of Public Health* Justice Marshall used dignity as equality, stating that

---

[62] *Ibid.*

[63] *Ibid.*, p. 2692.

[64] Stu Woolman, *The Architecture of Dignity,* in The Dignity Jurisprudence of the Constitutional Court of South Africa: Cases and Materials 76 (Drucilla Cornell et al. eds., 2013).

[65] *Fourie, supra* note 45.

[66] Acción de inconstitucionalidad 2/2010, Pleno de la Suprema Corte de Justicia [SCJN] [Supreme Court], Novena Época, 10 de Agosto de 2010, Par. 275 (Mex.)

[67] *Ibid.*

[68] Neomi Rao, *On the Use and Abuse of Dignity in Constitutional Law*, 14 Colum. J. Eur. L. 238 (2008); Erin Daly, *Human Dignity in the Roberts Court: A Story of Inchoate Institutions, Autonomous Individuals, and the Reluctant Recognition of A Right*, 37 Ohio N.U. L. Rev. 381 (2011).

"The Massachusetts Constitution affirms the dignity and equality of all individuals. It forbids the creation of second-class citizens."[69] This approach was also used by the 9th Circuit in *Perry v. Brown*.[70]

The U.S. Supreme Court used the term dignity several times in *Lawrence v. Texas*[71] and it again went back to dignity in *Windsor*. Although in *Lawrence* dignity was rightly linked to autonomy, *Windsor* gave another use of dignity that narrows its ability to be used outside the scope of marriage. Instead of reinforcing the idea of dignity as autonomy, it used dignity as status: marriage became the focus of dignity rather than individuals and their families. The decision referred 22 times to the idea of dignity. The most important references to dignity as status derived from marriage are illustrated below:

- "Here the State's decision to give this class of persons the right to marry conferred upon them a *dignity* and status of immense import. When the State used its historic and essential authority to define the marital relation in this way, its role and its power in making the decision enhanced the recognition, dignity, and protection of the class in their own community."[72]
- "It seems fair to conclude that, until recent years, many citizens had not even considered the possibility that two persons of the same sex might aspire to occupy the same status and *dignity* as that of a man and woman in lawful marriage."[73]
- "By its recognition of the validity of same-sex marriages performed in other jurisdictions and then by authorizing same-sex unions and same-sex marriages, New York sought to give further protection and *dignity* to that bond."[74]

Windsor sought a protection to same-sex couples based on their recognition as worth of marriage. It was, undoubtedly, a statement on equality. This equality, however, is not for all families and all individuals. It is only for same-sex couples worth of being granted the dignity of marriage. The decision argued that the federal definition of marriage as the union between a man and a woman "places same-sex couples in an unstable position of being in a second-tier marriage. The differentiation demeans the couple, whose moral and sexual choices the Constitution protects, . . . and whose relationship the State has sought to dignify. *And it humiliates tens of thousands of children now being raised by same-sex couples*."[75]

---

[69] See *Goodridge v. Dep't of Pub. Health*, *supra* note 32, at 312, 313, 337,392, and 395.

[70] "The designation of 'marriage' is the status that we recognize. It is the principal manner in which the State attaches respect and dignity to the highest form of a committed relationship and to the individuals who have entered into it." *Perry v. Brown*, 671 F.3d 1052, 1079 (9th Cir. 2012) vacated and remanded sub nom. *Hollingsworth v. Perry*, 133 S. Ct. 2652, 186 L. Ed. 2d 768 (U.S. 2013).

[71] *Lawrence v. Texas* 539 U.S. 571 (2003).

[72] *Windsor*, *supra* note 28, p. 2692. Emphasis added.

[73] *Ibid.*, p. 2689. Emphasis added.

[74] *Ibid.*, p. 2692. Emphasis added.

[75] *Ibid.*, p. 2694. Emphasis added.

The reference to children makes it clear that the Supreme Court had no intention of recognizing the same dignity to families of married and unmarried parents. The issue, for this court, was marriage and not equality and even less, autonomy to choose one's family. It may be precisely the narrative on institutional dignity, along with the image of children being humiliated by their parents' impossibility to be married what ignited so many decisions favorable to same-sex marriage. *Windsor* provided same-sex couples with the best assimilation argument: they were worth of marrying and not having access to marriage was an affront to their dignity. This insult affected innocent children. The couples the *Windsor* decision seemed to speak about do not resemble at all the individuals that gathered outside the Stonewall Inn in 1969.[76] They did not resemble the individuals that brought constitutional challenges to the sodomy statutes in the past.[77]

The decision showed the plaintiff as selfless as possible. *Windsor* was a case of a tax credit and yet the decision barely talked about money and tangible benefits. It referred to the institution of marriage as something bigger than its benefits and obligations. This was also the narrative chosen by the plaintiff and its legal team. The ACLU produced several videos showing the love story of Ms. Windsor and Mr. Spyer. They got engaged in 1967 and were together until 2009, when Ms. Spyer passed away. In one of the videos Ms. Windsor reflects on the day after their marriage in Canada in 2007. She talks about how marriage is special. She can't point out to what it is but she thinks that marriage is different.[78]

Ms. Windsor and Ms. Spyer's story is beautiful and marriage should have been available to them in 1967. Their decision to marry, however, could have been protected by the Supreme Court on the basis of their right to have the family of their choice. Treating individuals with dignity, as it was the idea developed by the Supreme Court in *Lawrence v. Texas* requires allowing individuals to make the most intimate decisions without government interference. *Windsor*, instead, is not a decision on autonomy, but on marriage and the dignity that comes from it.

[76]For an account of the role of the Stonewall riots in the rise of the LGBT movement see David Carter, Stonewall: The Riots that Sparked the Gay Revolution, New York, 2010.

[77]The plaintiff in *Bowers v. Hardwick*, the case in which the Supreme Court upheld the constitutionality of anti sodomy statutes, was a gay man who was arrested by a police officer who entered into Hardwick's apartment and found him engaged in consensual oral sex with another male. *Bowers v. Hardwick*, 478 U.S. 186 (1986). In *Lawrence v. Texas* the Supreme Court overturned *Bowers*. The plaintiff was also a gay man who had been arrested by a police officer who entered Lawrence's bedroom and saw him engaged in consensual oral sex with another man. *Lawrence v Texas*, *supra* note 71 at 558.

[78]Time, *Edith and Thea: A Love Story*, December 20, 2013.

4.3.2 *After Windsor: The Dialogue Between Rights and Politics Revisited*

The *Windsor* decision made more than ordering the federal government to reimburse Ms. Windsor the estate taxes she had paid. Although the decision was limited to declaring Section 3 of DOMA unconstitutional, the impact it has had on state decisions is unmistakable. Less than 2 years after *Windsor* more than 80 cases were being litigated in state courts and more than 40 decisions were issued.[79] Likewise, most circuit courts had issued at least one decision on same-sex marriage.[80] Between November of 2013 and June of 2014 same-sex marriage became legal trough court decisions in several States.[81]

In Michigan, a District Court decided on March 2014 that the Michigan Marriage Amendment violated equal protection under Michigan's Constitution.[82] The U.S. Court of Appeal for the 6th Circuit issued a halt on same-sex marriage decisions until an appeal was decided. The decision by the District Court, however, cited *Windsor* several times. Defendants claimed that the ban on same-sex marriage was justified because the best environment to raise children was a married father and mother.[83] The District Court, following *Windsor*, harshly criticized this argument:

> In attempting to define this case as a challenge to "the will of the people," state defendants lost sight of what this case is truly about: people. No court record of this proceeding could ever fully convey the personal sacrifice of these two plaintiffs who seek to ensure that the state may no longer impair the rights of their children and the thousands of others now being raised by same-sex couples. It is the Court's fervent hope that these children will grow up "to understand the integrity and closeness of their own family and its concord with other families in their community and in their daily lives." Windsor, 133 S. Ct. at 2694.[84]

Some of the states in which same-sex marriage statutes are being challenged are the most conservative of the United States. Virginia, for example, until recently not only did not recognize same-sex marriage but a 2006 constitutional amendment denied the recognition of any type of same-sex association.[85] *Bostic v. Rainey*,

---

[79]For an accurate account of same-sex marriage litigation in the United States, see Freedom to Marry's website at www.freedomtomarry.org/litigation

[80]*Id.*

[81]In New Jersey, Garden State Equality et al. v. Dow et al., *supra* note 41; in New Mexico, *Griego v. Oliver*, *supra* note 32, 865; in Oregon, *Geiger v. Kitzhaber*, 6:13-CV-01834-MC, 2014 WL 2054264 (D. Or. 2014); in Pennsylvania, *Whitewood v. Wolf*, 1:13-CV-1861, 2014 WL 2058105 (M.D. Pa. 2014); in Illinois the legislature had already passed a marriage equality statute that had deferred its implementation to June 2014. A court decision ordered the immediate implementation of the statute. *Lee v. Orr*, Dist. Court, ND, Illinois 2014.

[82]*DeBoer v. Snyder*, Civil Action No. 12-CV-10285.

[83]*DeBoer*, *Id.*

[84]*Ibid.*

[85]Chris Jenkins, *Ban on Same-sex Unions Added to Virginia Constitution*, The Washington Post, Nov. 8, 2006.

however, changed family law for gays and lesbians in Virginia. In a 41 page decision, the District Court rejected the rationale of protecting heterosexual marriage as the best framework for raising children. Using arguments from *Windsor,* as well as other U.S. Supreme Court decisions, it declared the ban on same-sex marriage in Virginia a violation of the U.S. Constitution.[86]

In addition to a flow of cases pending all around the United States, several legislatures have also amended their state constitutions, also citing *Windsor* as one of the reasons for the change. In Hawaii, it was the legislature itself that revised its former stance on marriage. On October of 2013, Hawaii's Attorney General issued Formal Opinion 13–1 stating that "the plain language of article I section 23 [of the Hawaii Constitution] does not compel the legislature to limit marriages to one man and one woman; it gives the legislature the option to do so."[87] On November of 2013 the Hawaii State Legislature passed the Hawaii Marriage Equality Act of 2013. The Bill stated in its first paragraphs the link between this new legislation and the Supreme Court's decision in Windsor:

> The legislature acknowledges the recent decision of the United States Supreme Court in United States v. Windsor, 133 S.Ct. 2675 (2013), which held that Section 3 of the Defense of Marriage Act, Public Law 104–199, unlawfully discriminated against married same-sex couples by prohibiting the federal government from recognizing those marriages and by denying federal rights, benefits, protections, and responsibilities to those couples.[88]

4.4 Before and After Windsor: A Narrow Concept of the Family

The value of marriage in the U.S. seems to trump the value of equality and autonomy combined. *Windsor* is, no doubt, a game changer because it is triggering marriage equality at a speed that would have not been predicted ten years ago. What *Windsor* has not, however, done, is to shift the focus from marriage to equality. Married and unmarried couples will still be treated differently in most states. The Massachusetts decision on same-sex marriage of 2003 illustrates this commitment to marriage:

> Here, the plaintiffs seek only to be married, not to undermine the institution of civil marriage. They do not want marriage abolished. They do not attack the binary nature of marriage, the consanguinity provisions, or any of the other gate-keeping provisions of the marriage licensing law. Recognizing the right of an individual to marry a person of the same sex will not diminish the validity or dignity of opposite-sex marriage, any more than recognizing the right of an individual to marry a person of a different race devalues the marriage of a person who marries someone of her own race. If anything, extending civil marriage to same-sex couples reinforces the importance of marriage to individuals and

[86] *Bostic v. Rainey*, Case 2:13-cv-00395-AWA-LRL.

[87] State of Hawaii, Office of the Attorney General, October 14, 2013, Op. No 13–1.

[88] Hawaii State Legislature, Senate Bill 1 (SB1).
Available at http://www.capitol.hawaii.gov/splsession2013b/SB1_HD1_.pdf

communities. That same-sex couples are willing to embrace marriage's solemn obligations of exclusivity, mutual support, and commitment to one another is a testament to the enduring place of marriage in our laws and in the human spirit.[89]

The California decision of 2008 is also centered on an idea of the married family:

The family is the basic unit of our society, the center of the personal affections that ennoble and enrich human life. It channels biological drives that might otherwise become socially destructive; it ensures the care and education of children in a stable environment; it establishes continuity from one generation to another; it nurtures and develops the individual initiative that distinguishes a free people. Since the family is the core of our society, the law seeks to foster and preserve marriage.[90]

Recognizing same-sex marriage is a positive outcome, but it could have been a real "game changer" if the Supreme Court, and the decisions that have followed, would have focused on dignity as autonomy and the role of family law to afford protection to families regardless of their marital status.

The Supreme Court will have more opportunities to define the scope of marriage as a fundamental right. It is still possible that the Supreme Court will use new cases to strengthen the protection of the family, and will focus on the right of same-sex couples to enjoy the benefits of marriage because they chose to do so. There is, however, a real possibility that the Supreme Court will continue focusing on the right to enter into a marriage and lose the opportunity to talk about the family as a reality beyond marriage. It may focus on the dignity that marriage, according to their prior opinions, gives individuals, rather than the dignity of each individual regardless of their marital status. This would be unfortunate. It is through the respect of autonomy that the dignity of each individual is recognized.

Bibliography

1. Aristotle. Politics, book I, part II, Benjamin Jowett Transl. Electronic version available at http://classics.mit.edu/Aristotle/politics.1.one.html
2. Barringer Gordon, Sara. 2002. *The Mormon question: Polygamy and constitutional conflict in nineteenth-century America*. Chapel Hill: The University of North Carolina Press.
3. Carter, David. 2010. *Stonewall: The riots that sparked the gay revolution*. New York: St Martin's Press.
4. Cicero. 1913. *De Oficiis*, Book I. Trans. Walter Miller.
5. Cott, Nancy. 2002. *Public Vows: A History of Marriage and the Nation*. Cambridge: Harvard University Press.
6. Cummings, Scott L., and Douglas NeJaime. 2010. Lawyering for marriage equality. *UCLA Law Review* 57: 1235–1330.
7. Daly, Erin. 2011. Human dignity in the Roberts court: A story of Inchoate Institutions, autonomous individuals, and the reluctant recognition of a right. *Ohio Northern University Law Review* 37: 381.

---

[89] *Goodridge, supra* note 7, 965.

[90] *Ibid; In re Marriage Cases supra* note 50, 813.

8. Filmer, Robert. 2009. *Patriarcha and other political works*. New Brunswick: Transaction Publishers.
9. Kelly, Linda. 2001. Marriage for sale: The mail-order bride industry and the changing value of marriage. *The Journal of Gender Race & Justice* 175.
10. Martin Jr., Waldo E. 1998. *Brown v. Board of Education: A brief history with documents*, 1st ed. Boston: Bedford/St. Martin's.
11. Office of Immigration Statistics. 2011. *2010 yearbook of immigration statistics*. Washington, DC: Office of Immigration Statistics.
12. Pascoe, Peggy. 2009. *What comes naturally: Miscegenation law and the making of race in America*. Oxford: Oxford University Press.
13. Rao, Neomi. 2008. On the use and abuse of dignity in constitutional law. *Columbia Journal of European Law* 14: 238.
14. Scott, Ryan W. 2014. Standing to appeal and executive non-defense of federal law after the marriage cases. *Indiana Law Journal* 67.
15. Villazor, Rose Cuison. 2011. The other Loving: Uncovering the federal government's racial regulation on marriage. *NYU Law Review* 86: 1361–1439.
16. Woolman, Stu, et al. 2013. The architecture of dignity. In *The dignity jurisprudence of the Constitutional Court of South Africa: Cases and Materials*, vol. 76, ed. Drucilla Cornell. New York: Fordham University Press.

Cases and Documents

17. *Hollingsworth v. Perry*, 133 S. Ct. 2652, 186 L. Ed. 2d 768 (U.S. 2013).
18. *United States v. Windsor*, 133 S. Ct. 2675, 2682, 186 L. Ed. 2d 808 (2013).
19. *Goodridge v. Dep't of Pub. Health*, 798 N.E.2d 941, 948 (Mass. 2003).
20. *Kerrigan v. Comm'r of Pub. Health*, 289 Conn. 135, 156–57, 957 A.2d 407, 420–21 (2008).
21. *In re Marriage Cases*, 43 Cal. 4th 757, 779–80, 183 P.3d 384, 398 (2008).
22. *Varnum v. Brien*, 763 N.W.2d 862, 882 (Iowa 2009).
23. *Griego v. Oliver*, 2014-NMSC-003, 316 P.3d 865.
24. *W.Va. State Bd. Of Educ. v. Barnette*, 319 US 624, 638.
25. *Brown v. Board of Education*, 347 U.S. 483 (1954).
26. *Hernandez v. Robles*, 7 N.Y.3d 338, 356, 855 N.E.2d 1, 5 (2006).
27. *Lewis v. Harris,* 188 N.J. 415, 423, 908 A.2d 196, 200 (2006).
28. N.J. Stat. Ann. § 37:1–28 (West).
29. *Baehr v. Lewin,* 852 P.2d 44 (Haw. 1993).
30. *Lockyer v. City & Cnty. of San Francisco*, S122923, 2004 WL 473257 (Cal. Mar. 11, 2004).
31. *Strauss v. Horton*, 46 Cal. 4th 364, 411, 207 P.3d 48, 77 (2009).
32. *Perry v. Brown*, 671 F.3d 1052, 1079 (9th Cir. 2012) vacated and remanded sub nom.
33. *Hollingsworth v. Perry,* 133 S. Ct. 2652, 186 L. Ed. 2d 768 (U.S. 2013).
34. *Lawrence v. Texas* 539 U.S. 571 (2003).
35. *Bowers v. Hardwick*, 478 U.S. 186 (1986).
36. *DeBoer v. Snyder,* Civil Action No. 12-CV-10285.
37. *Bostic v. Rainey*, Case 2:13-cv-00395-AWA-LRL.
38. *Loving v. Virginia* 388 U.S. 1, 87 S.Ct. 1824 (1967).
39. *Minister of Home Affairs and Another v. Fourie and another* [CC] [Constitutional Court] (CCT 60/04) [2005] ZACC 19; 2006 (3) BCRL 355(CC); 2006(1) SA524(CC) (1 December 2005) (S. Afr.).
40. Attorney General's Response to Amicus Curiae Briefs, January 21, 2009, 4.
41. Acción de inconstitucionalidad 2/2010, Pleno de la Suprema Corte de Justicia [SCJN] [Supreme Court], Novena Época, 10 de Agosto de 2010, Par. 275 (Mex.).

Statutes

42. Assem. 8354, 2011 Leg., 234th Reg. Sess. (N.Y. 2011), in Bill Jacket, L. 2011 c. 95.
43. Civil Union Act, 2006, Government Gazzette, Republic of South Africa, Vol. 497 Cape Town 17 November 2006.
44. Haw. Const. art. 1, § 23 (ratified Nov. 3, 1998).
45. Defense of Marriage Act, Section 3.
46. State of Hawaii, Office of the Attorney General, October 14, 2013, Op. No 13–1.
47. Hawaii State Legislature, Senate Bill 1 (SB1).

Chapter 5
Marriage Between Two. Changing and Unchanging Concepts of Family: The Case of LGBTI Rights Litigation on Family Issues in Colombia

Natalia Ramírez-Bustamante

Abstract The article tracks the paradigmatic cases of LGBTI rights litigation in Colombian Constitutional Court that impacted family law in the domestic legal system. Issues brought to Court, such as cohabitation rights, the concept of family and adoption of LGBTI couples, show the changing and unchanging characteristics that family issues have under the Colombian constitutional system. It also invites a critical appraisal of the LGBTI campaign for marriage equality.

Colombia's legal order underwent fundamental changes after the enactment of the Political Constitution of 1991. The Constitutional Assembly provided a space of confluence for liberals, conservatives, indigenous peoples, and ex members of the Movimiento 19 de abril (M-19) [9th of April Movement] and Ejército Popular de Liberación (EPL) [People's Liberation Army] popular fronts to discuss and reach agreements on the design of a new social pact. This diverse group of individuals embraced a wide array of political visions and political commitments, which translated into an ideologically inclusive democratic project. As a result, the new Constitution was meant to provide a new basis for a society fragmented by political violence, drug trafficking, armed conflict, poverty and profound social inequality. The end promise was social peace, achieved, in part, by the political inclusion of voices that had been silenced or marginalized in the past.[1]

[1]For Julieta Lemaitre: "The 1991 Constitution appeared at the time, and so entitled *Semana* magazine as the "magic wand," that powerful object whose influence would achieve the end of violence. Even for many who did not believe it was an immediate and magical end to violence, it was the beginning of the end, the foundation to build it, the right track to achieve it." Julieta

N. Ramírez-Bustamante (✉)
Harvard Law School, Harvard University, 2 Peabody Terrace, 514, 2138 Cambridge, MA, USA
e-mail: nramirez@sjd.harvard.law.edu

M. Sáez (ed.), *Same Sex Couples - Comparative Insights on Marriage and Cohabitation*, Ius Gentium: Comparative Perspectives on Law and Justice 42,
DOI 10.1007/978-94-017-9774-0_5

Contrasting the Constitutional Chart of 1886, -which was for the most part a document of institutional design and ascription of legal duties for public servants and citizens, 1991s Constitutional Chart was designed to include a wide charter of rights ranging from first generation rights (i.e. rights of freedom and participation); second generation rights (i.e. equality rights and economic, social and cultural rights); and third generation rights (i.e. collective rights as well as rights to a safe environment). In particular, first and second generation rights serve individuals, activists and public interest law groups, to activate judicial proceedings in order to defend, promote and advance the LGBTI (lesbian, gay, bisexual, transexual and intersexed) rights agenda. As will be evident in the sections to come, a particular characteristic of the LGBTI rights movement in Colombia is its focus on high impact litigation as a vehicle for social change almost to the exclusion of the legislature due to the latter's majoritarian conservatism on social issues. In the judicial process that took place at the Constitutional Court, the rights of self-determination, free development of personality, and equality and non-discrimination, as well as the supremacy clause of the Constitution, have provided fertile ground to push the limits of interpretation to include those of LGBTI community members.[2]

This push through the judiciary, however, would not have been possible absent two central mechanisms of constitutional control included in the 1991 Charter. First, the "acción de tutela" a type of claim that obligates a judge to decide a case in a maximum period of 10 days calendar in order to protect the fundamental rights of citizens against actions or omissions of the state or, in some cases, private individuals. Second, the "acción pública de inconstitucionalidad," a type of claim that can be made by any individual who finds that a law issued by Congress violates the rights or duties established in the Constitution.[3] Because neither the Constitution, nor any law enacted by Congress thus far includes express provisions of rights to LGBTI community members, LGBTI activists and community members have progressively gained access to similar rights as heterosexual citizens and couples through the use of these two actions, as well as a creative use of legal interpretation and judicial precedent.

Lemaitre, *El derecho como conjuro. Fetichismo legal, violencia y movimientos sociales*, (Bogotá: Siglo del Hombre Editores, 2009).

[2]The constitutional supremacy clause included in article 4 of the Constitution states that "[t]he Constitution is the supreme law. In any case of incompatibility between the Constitution and any other law or legal norm, the constitutional provisions shall be applied."

[3]These two actions give way to two different kinds of decisions. An "acción de tutela" is decided by a type "T" decision in which the Constitutional Court decides whether or not there has been an infringement of the fundamental constitutional rights of the claimant and provides a resolution reinstating or not, the rights whose violation has been requested. The effect of these decisions is restricted to the case at hand, but the precedent set by the decision binds other judges and the Constitutional Court in later analogous cases. An "acción pública de inconstitucionalidad" is decided by a type "C" decision. In this case, the Court reviews whether a challenged law fits the constitutional mandates and if it can be harmoniously interpreted in accordance with the rights, values and principles of the Chart. Any citizen can present this challenge to the Court.

The early years of the Constitutional Court's decisions on LGBT issues focused on individuals who challenged legal rules and social practices that were discriminatory against the LGBTI community. The Court's decisions from that early stage (1994–2007)[4] start recognizing the individual rights of persons with alternative sexual orientations. In such decisions, the Court emphasized that "homosexuals cannot be subject to discrimination because of their condition [...] the fact that their sexual behavior is not the same as that of the majority of the population does not justify an unequal treatment [...] A fair treatment of homosexuals has to be based on respect, consideration and tolerance, since they are human beings who, in conditions of whole equality, are entitled to the same fundamental rights as other citizens, even if their mores are not exactly the same as those of everyone else."[5]

Consequently, the Court declared as unconstitutional a diverse set of practices and laws that established an unequal, and adverse treatment of gay and lesbian citizens. Among them the Court declared unconstitutional the State censorship of TV commercials featuring a gay couple kissing in public,[6] the discrimination of members of the military because of their sexual orientation,[7] the ban on homosexuals to be members of the Boy Scout society,[8] and the inclusion of homosexuality as a disciplinary contravention for notary public servants.[9] However, during this same period the Court dismissed other challenges that sought to provide same-sex couples with the same legal recognition given to *de facto* civil unions.[10] Additionally, the Court dismissed cases that involved granting equal access to same-sex couples seeking social security benefits for their partner's as granted in *de facto* civil unions,[11] and the right of same-sex couples to adopt.[12] The diverse outcomes of these cases show that the justices of the Constitutional Court were willing to recognize the rights of individuals with non-normative sexualities in so far as such entitlements only reached them as individuals, not as couples.

The second stage of Constitutional Court decisions (from 2007 and ongoing) started with the constitutional challenge of Law 54 of 1994, which established the legal recognition of *de facto* marital unions between heterosexual couples, the requisites for its legal recognition, and the derivative consequences for members of *de facto* unions during the relationship and after its dissolution. In this case,

[4]This periodization has been proposed by Daniel Bonilla "Parejas del mismo sexo en Colombia: tres modelos para su reconocimiento jurídico y político", *Anuario de Derechos Humanos* Universidad de Chile, (2010); as well as by Julieta Lemaitre, "El amor en los tiempos del cólera: Derechos LGBT en Colombia" *Sur: Revista Internacional de Derechos Humanos*, v. 6, n. 11 (2009).

[5]Colombia, Constitutional Court, Decision T-539/1994.

[6]*Ibid.*, Decision T-539/1994.

[7]*Ibid.*, Decision C-481/1998.

[8]*Ibid.*, Decision T-808/2003.

[9]*Ibid.*, Decision C-373/2002.

[10]*Ibid.*, Decision C-098/1996.

[11]*Ibid.*, Decisions T-999/2000 and SU-623/2001.

[12]*Ibid.*, Decision C-814/2001.

as well as in others that the Court has analyzed since, a change in the constitutional precedent took place regarding the rights of members of same-sex couples to include property rights, social security provisions and rights to alimony. This second stage is the most prolific in the recognition of legal entitlements and one in which the Court has re-conceptualized the notion of family that deserves legal protection and recognition in the Colombian legal system.

This text is divided in two parts. The first part, which is descriptive in nature, answers the question: What has changed in the Family Law regime in Colombia through the judicial recognition of rights for LGBTI couples? This part provides a general view of the litigation processes that have concluded in the recognition of same-sex couples' rights and how these decisions have reshaped family law in the Colombian legal and constitutional order in issues ranging from cohabitation rights to marriage and adoption rights. To accomplish that purpose, I will focus on the decisions that have been central in such effort. I will show, as well, that the evolution of this line of precedent has not been a pacific matter between Constitutional Court justices and that competing visions of morality and human dignity have played a central role in the constitutional interpretation of this issue. The detailed description I provide from the Court's arguments in each case is thought to allow a close track of the constitutional rationality in each of them, and to provide a meticulous map of the advancement of the LGBTI agenda through the judiciary.

The second part is analytic, and critical. I argue that one of the implications of the campaign for the rights of LGBTI community members, in particular the marriage equality campaign, engenders an entrenchment of the concept of family as embodied by a monogamous couple, and that such entrenchment limits the recognition, or at least defers the possibilities of other family formations to be recognized and covered by the legal system. Furthermore, I argue that the crisis that marriage is facing in Colombia, but also in the world at large, together with an understanding of the family's purpose as not centrally revolving around sex or procreation, may be used to trigger reconsideration of the kind of bonds that unite people and the possibility of furthering a distinction between relationships based on care, commitment, companionship and friendship, and others specialized on sex as different entities with different legal implications and possibly different legal regimes. While more in tune with current social practices, this ample understanding of social relations furthers a progressive sexual movement that enhances the rights of freedom of individuals by providing a wider array of social arrangements covered by the legal order.

5.1 Changing Conceptions of the Family. The Family Protected Under 1991 Constitution and Its Multiple Meanings

The Constitutional transit from the 1886 Chart to 1991s, and the latter's freedom and equality rights, provided a new forum of discussion and new testing standards of laws at the Colombian Constitutional Court. After 1991, the supremacy clause of the Constitution imposed an interpretation of law through the guise of the new rights, principles and values included in the Charter. This proved to be an invaluable opportunity for strategic LGBTI activism, and in fact, rights regarding cohabiting same-sex couples as a family formation underwent the most substantive changes. Adoption rights by same sex couples has more recently turned into the hot topic of contention, and one facing rapid changes. Although the first attempts at judicial change of these issues through the Constitutional Court were unsuccessful, activists returned to the Court after failed initiatives in Congress. They fared better the second time around.

5.1.1 Step One: Cohabitation Rights. De facto Marital Unions

In the period 1994–2007, the Colombian Constitutional Court was open to the recognition of individual rights to LGBTI community members, but not their right to form legally covered unions. When confronted during that period with the first constitutional challenge of Law 54 of 1990 – a law that recognizes legal effects to *de facto* marital unions of heterosexual couples- under the charge that it infringed their constitutional rights because it discriminated against homosexual couples by excluding them from its coverage,[13] the Court declared that the law's sole recognition of legal entitlements to heterosexual couples and the exclusion of same sex ones was in agreement with the Constitution.

The Court based its decision on the constitutionality of the law in three main arguments. First, it used a teleological argument to indicate that with the enactment of Law 54 the legislature attempted to grant legal recognition to natural families. This meant families formed by a man and a woman who were not legally married but that had shared their lives for a period of 2 years or more. Furthermore, the legislature established the rights and duties that the parties were entitled to as a consequence of such family formation. As same-sex couples did not fall under the legal structure of heterosexual unions, same-sex couples' exclusion from the law's scope of protection was justified. Second, after arguing that from a constitutional point of view homosexual behaviors were valid and legitimate options of individuals which the State could not forbid or limit, the Court indicated that the exclusion of same-sex couples from this statute did not impinge on the exercise of their constitutional rights. If this was proven to be the case, then a more thorough examination of the constitutionality of the law should take place.[14] Third, the Court

[13]The constitutional challenge identified five fundamental rights that were allegedly violated by Ley 54 of 1990: the right to human dignity (art. 1); the right to equality (art. 13); the right of free development of personality (art. 16); the right to freedom of conscience (art. 18) and the right to have one's honor respected (art. 21). Colombia, Constitutional Court, Decision C-098/1996.

[14]As will be seen in the following paragraphs, this is one of the arguments used by the Court to revive the exam of the constitutionality of Law 54 in a later constitutional challenge to the same law. In the terms of the Court: "[t]he omission of the legislature [alleged in the constitutional challenge], could be subject to a more thorough and rigorous review of constitutionality if it should be found

claimed that the constitutional mandate that established the protection of natural families included in article 42 of the Chart[15] was linked to the heterosexual character of the union, a condition left unfulfilled by same-sex couples and further justified their exclusion of its scope of protection.[16]

Two of the nine constitutional justices took the opportunity to clarify their vote for the constitutionality of the law arguing that it would be "fair and appropriate that the law established a property regime to benefit same-sex couples (. . .) regardless of whether they are considered a family formation or not," but that such an endeavor should be carried out through Congress after a public deliberation on the matter.[17] Two more of the justices seized the opportunity to clarify that "homosexuality could hardly be accepted as a valid, lawful and constitutional source of the family, which, by its very nature is based on procreation, which is possible only between heterosexual couples."[18]

Despite the defeat that this as well as other decisions[19] meant to the gay and lesbian rights agenda, two important outcomes followed from them. First, the legal processes that led to these decisions and the public debate after them, generated mass media coverage. This visibility allowed gay and lesbians to voice publicly their concerns. Furthermore, the LGBTI community demonstrated the ways in which society discriminated against them. The news coverage may have created more tolerances in the public's perception perspective on sexual diversity.[20] Second, LGBTI rights activists started to organize, create new associations[21] and formulate

---

that it purposively harms homosexuals or if its enforcement might create a negative impact against them. However, the purpose of the law was limited to protect heterosexual marital unions without undermining others and without [homosexual couples] suffering any detriment or grief, as indeed it has not happened." Colombia, Constitutional Court, Decision C-098/1996.

[15]In its relevant part, article 42 of the Constitution states: "The family is the fundamental unit of society. It is constituted by natural or legal ties, by the free decision of a man and a woman to marry or the responsible desire to form."

[16]In the terms used by the Court: "The *de facto* marital unions of heterosexual character, as long as they conform a family, are taken into account by the law in order to ensure "comprehensive protection" and in particular, that "women and men" have equal rights and duties, which [. . .] is absent in homosexual couples." Colombia, Constitutional Court, Decision C-098/1996.

[17]Concurring opinion to Decision C-098/1996.

[18]Dissenting opinion to decision C-098/1996, signed by Justices José Gregorio Hernández y Aclaración de voto Hernando Herrera Vergara.

[19]Other decisions that denied the rights of lesbian and gay couples were: T-999/00, T-1426/00 and SU-623/01 in which the Court denied the right of members of same-sex couples to be beneficiaries of social security and the obligatory health services plan; and C-814/01 in which the Court denied the right to adoption of children to same sex couples.

[20]Esteban Restrepo "Reforma Constitucional y progreso social: la constitucionalización de la vida cotidiana en Colombia" in: *El derecho como objeto e instrumento de transformación,* ed. Roberto Saba (Buenos Aires: Editores del Puerto, 2002) pp. 73–88.

[21]Lemaitre, "El amor en los tiempos del cólera", pp. 80–82.

new strategies or refurnish earlier ones (grassroots work with community members, legislative initiatives, and litigation) to accomplish the social and legal inclusion of homosexual community members.[22]

The task of resorting to the legislature, however proved futile. Sponsored by a member of the Liberal party and supported by the leftist party *Polo Democrático*, activists introduced a bill in 2001 to recognize the unions of same sex couples. Moreover, the bill recognized same sex couples' entitlements in terms of property regime and other rights and duties. The proposed bill faced criticism from the Catholic Church and from conservative leaders who warned that the bill would permit the acceptance of same-sex couples as a family formation and even possibly grant them adoption rights which, in their opinion, was unacceptable.[23] The same result occurred two more times with the same proposal. The defeats in the legislature and the lack of both political momentum and legislative majorities to turn the proposal into law forced LGBTI activists to turn again to the Constitutional Court.[24]

Colombia Diversa (an NGO working for the rights of the LGBTI community) and the Public Interest Law Group (G-DIP) formed an alliance in 2006 at Universidad de los Andes, with the purpose of trying a new constitutional challenge against Law 54 of 1990. In this opportunity, the task was to show to the Court that the law violated the rights to live with dignity, freedom of association, and equality of same-sex couples, and that a considerable detriment could effectively be shown as derived from their exclusion from the scope of protection of Law 54. Accordingly, the arguments presented in the case depicted several ways in which Law 54 curtailed the rights of same sex couples, in areas such as criminal law (a lack of protection in cases of domestic violence and the right not to incriminate the permanent partner), family law (lack of right to alimony), and labor law (lack to the right of social security benefits and the right to pension transfer when one of the members of the couple passed away).

In a strategic move, G-DIP and Colombia Diversa distinguished the concepts of "couple" and "family" from one another in the document delivered to the Court. The alliance argued that the concept of "couple" regardless of the sexual orientation of its members, refers to an associative form that is different from the "family," and that a life lived in a couple persists independently from the family. Therefore, the legislature may subject the concepts of "family" and "couples" to diverse legal regulation. The way in which the alliance framed the issue possibly relieved the Court from considering Law 54 under article 42 of the Chart which in the standing precedent defined the family as the union formed by "a man and a woman." The Court instead focused on the property regime applicable to heterosexual couples

[22]Mauricio García and Rodrigo Uprimny, "Corte Constitucional y Emancipación Social en Colombia" in: eds. Boaventura de Sousa Santos and Mauricio García *Emancipación social y Violencia en Colombia*, (Bogotá: Norma, 2004).

[23]Lemaitre, "El amor en los tiempos del cólera", p. 84.

[24]See footnote 16 in Daniel Bonilla and Natalia Ramírez, "National Report: Colombia", *American University Journal of Gender and Social Policy*,(2011), p. 19.

and its extension to same sex ones. Also, the thoughtful and well-crafted argument potentially persuaded the most conservative justices in the Court that this was not an issue that concerned or would imply a change in the concept of the heterosexual family protected by the Constitution.

The argument was successful. In this case (C-075/07), the Court declared the same property regime established for heterosexual couples was also applicable to homosexual ones.[25] In the words of the Court:

> [t]he legislative decision not to include homosexual couples in the property regime provided for *de facto* marital unions actually entails an unjustified restriction on the autonomy of the members of such couples and can have harmful effects, not only because it impedes the realization of their life project together, but because it does not offer an adequate response to conflictual situations that may arise when for any reason the cohabitation ceases.[26]

The Court explained that the change in the constitutional precedent resulted from the efficacy of the challenge in demonstrating the harmful effects suffered by members of same-sex couples due to the inapplicability of the property regime established under Law 54. Notably, however, the Court cautiously crafted the arguments that support the holding in terms of the rights to human dignity and autonomy of individuals with non-normative sexualities, and restricted the discussion of its decision's effect to the patrimonial rights of same sex couples. Any consideration about how this judgment could change the family regime in the legal or constitutional context is completely absent. In fact, in the whole decision there is not a single sentence in which the concept of family is related in any way to same sex couples. Henceforth, gay and lesbian couples whose members shared a continuous and monogamous cohabitation for a minimum period of 2 years were entitled, thereafter, to a regime of marital property[27] identical to the property regime for marriages. In all other areas, same-sex couples had no rights.

The decision, narrowly tailored to provide same-sex couples property rights but not their recognition as a form of family, allowed for eight of the nine justices to agree on its holding. As some scholars have pointed out, this decision is indicative of the change that has taken place in the popular perception of sexual diversity in Colombia, which reached even traditionally conservative justices whose morality and world view is closely intertwined with catholic religious beliefs.[28] The dissenting judge voted against the majority decision because he found that it fell short in the recognition of same sex couples' rights and that the decision to restrict its

---

[25] Colombia, Constitutional Court, Decision C-075/2007.

[26] *Ibid.,* Decision C-075/2007.

[27] In a regime of community or marital property most assets or debts acquired by any of the partners is owned jointly by both members of the couple. Under Colombian law, all marriages and *de facto* marital unions are covered by such regime. In the case of marriage, marital property exists from the day of the marriage; in the case of *de facto* marital unions, such regime only comes into existence after the 2 year period of cohabitation required by law.

[28] Daniel Bonilla, "Parejas del mismo sexo en Colombia: tres modelos para su reconocimiento jurídico y político", pp. 192–193.

effects to the patrimonial rights of *de facto* marital unions left out other civil effects, also derived from the harmonious interpretation of the law in the context of the complex family effects of Law 54. According to this dissenting justice, if the Court had analyzed these effects, its decision should have extended the rights to marriage, adoption and child custody regime to same sex couples.[29] In a separate document, three conservative justices clarified their vote for the conditional constitutionality of Law 54 arguing that they decided to support that decision only after making sure that it did not require or imply a change in the constitutional precedent with regards to the heterosexual family, which, in their understanding, was the only family protected by the Chart.[30]

Conservative justices seemed confident that their decision in this case solidified the Court's precedent against the recognition of other rights for same sex couples, in particular their right to be recognized as family. By doing so, the Court included gay and lesbian couples under a fragmentary regime of the civil and family rights to which heterosexual couples were entitled, but it seemed, out of the Court's consensus, that was as far as they would get.

Based on the precedent set by decision C-075/07, advocates brought before the Court legal rules and factual situations that involved same-sex couple's rights that the Court had previously denied. Advocates expected that the rulings under the new precedent would lead to grant other sets of rights. In the 2 years following the decision on *de facto* marital unions, the Court extended to members of same-sex couples the right to affiliate their partners to mandatory health programs,[31] the right to receive pension survivor annuities when one of the partners passed away,[32] and the right of the party in need to receive alimony after the cohabitation ceased under penalty of prison.[33]

C 029/2009 was the last important decision from this period regarding same sex couples. In this decision, the Court declared the conditional constitutionality of 26 laws that established rights and duties for heterosexual couples. Moreover, the Court declared that the clauses "family," "family group," "spouse," and "permanent partner" should be understood as also covering same sex couples. Five categories group the challenged rules in the case: (i) civil and political rights; (ii) sanctions and contingencies regarding crimes and misdemeanors; (iii) rights of victims of heinous crimes; (iv) access to and exercise of public office and eligibility for government contracts and (v) subsidies and social benefits.[34]

---

[29]Colombia, Constitutional Court, Dissenting opinion to Decision C-075/2007, signed by Justice Jaime Araujo Rentería.

[30]*Ibid.*, Concurring opinion to Decision C-075/2007, signed by Justices Marco Gerardo Monroy Cabra, Rodrigo Escobar Gil and Nilson Pinilla Pinilla.

[31]*Ibid.*, Decision C-811/2007.

[32]*Ibid.*, Decision C-336/2008.

[33]*Ibid.*, Decision C-798/2008.

[34]For a complete list and explanation of all the challenged rules, see: Daniel Bonilla, Natalia Ramírez, "National Report: Colombia", pp. 105–109.

One of the rules challenged in this case broadened the fragmentary family regime that covered same sex couples. As a matter of family law, the decision provided that same-sex couples were also obligated to provide child support and alimony under the applicable rules of the Civil Code. The Court declared that other rules that have a material impact on family relations because they distribute power between family members but, that were not included in the traditional area of Family law because they did not pertain to the Civil Code also covered same sex couples. These new entitlements included the right to constitute marital property and housing as "family property," which implied that these assets were withdrawn from the market and they could not be attached or used as collateral. Moreover, the Court extended the protection to same-sex couples against embezzlement and squandering of family property.[35] Additionally, the Court extended the same protections heterosexual couples had against domestic violence to same sex couples, as well as the right to access family subsidies for social services and housing,[36] and the right to be beneficiaries of compensation under the Mandatory Driver Insurance (SOAT) for death due to traffic accidents.

Although in this case the Court's ruling extended the expression "family" to reach same-sex couples, the Court made clear that it did not change the concept of family protected under the Constitution, which was traditionally interpreted as monogamous and heterosexual. The Court, moreover, could not have changed the concept of family because the constitutional challenges did not include an argument asking to broaden the concept. Two years later, however, LGBTI activists asked the Court to examine the concept of family protected under the Constitution when they turned their focus to "the marriage issue."

5.1.2 Step Two: Marriage

LGBTI activists presented a new constitutional challenge to the Court regarding a group of laws that described the concepts of marriage and family as those constituted by a *man* and a *woman* who unite through legal or natural ties with the objective of *procreation*. The content of the challenged rules reproduced, at least partially, the text of article 42 of the Charter, which in the relevant part states: "The family is the fundamental unit of society. It is constituted by natural or legal ties, by the free decision of a man or a woman to marry, or by the conscious desire to create one."

---

[35]The rule "establishes a greater criminal penalty to those who squander or embezzle the assets they manage as legal guardians due to their status as the permanent partner of an individual who was declared incompetent." Daniel Bonilla, Natalia Ramírez, "National Report: Colombia", p. 107.

[36]"The challenged rules establish the right of a worker's permanent partner to access family subsidies paid in cash, in kind, or in services to middle and lower-income workers, as well as family housing subsidies granted to households that lack sufficient resources to acquire, repair, or obtain title to a home." Daniel Bonilla, Natalia Ramírez, "National Report: Colombia", pp. 108–109.

The issue presented to the Court had three subsections. First, activists asked the Court to interpret harmoniously the challenged laws with Colombian constitutional rights and principles. Second, activists requested a re-interpretation of article 42 of the Charter, which meant that the Court should rule on the constitutionality of marriage between same sex couples. Finally, if the court found that same sex marriage is constitutionally mandated, it should change the standing precedent that restricted the concept of family to heterosexual and monogamous relationships.

The impeached laws allegedly violated the rights to equality, free development of personality, to a life with dignity, recognition of the marital status, intimacy and reproductive autonomy of same sex couples. According to the arguments that supported the challenge, a harmonious interpretation of these constitutional rights recognized the right to marriage for same sex couples. Furthermore, the challenge stated that sexual orientation caused a deficit in protection, which, in essence, was a discriminatory treatment against gays and lesbians. Consequently, the Court identified five different issues that it had to evaluate regarding the constitutional definition of the family as stated in article 42: "(i) to determine the constitutional scope with regard to the family and marriage, (ii) to ascertain whether different types of families were included under the constitutional protection, (iii) to establish whether the union of same-sex couples was consistent with the notion of family, if so, (iv) to determine whether it is subject to constitutional protection, and, if so, (v) what was the scope of this protection and who was entitled to provide it."[37]

Thus far, the traditional understanding of the majority of the Court was that the literal interpretation of the constitutional provision yielded two forms of family: first, one united by legal ties and conformed by "the free decision of a man and a woman to marry;" and second, another one united by natural ties and formed by "the conscious desire to create one," that is, the *de facto* marital unions. The Court said that this interpretation seemed to mandate the constitutional protection as an exclusive prerogative to the family formed by a man and a woman.[38] However, dissenting justices in earlier cases had provided a competing interpretation of the wording in article 4.[39] For those justices, the two propositions considered in article 42 were alternatives, and although the institution of marriage was associated with the heterosexual couple, evidenced in the "man and a woman" clause, the "conscious desire to create one" was not equally determined. Instead, the justices argued that this last clause could work as recognition that both heterosexual and same-sex couples may unite through a conscious decision to do so, and, under this understanding this was an institution different from marriage. Moreover the

[37] *Ibid.*, Decision C-577/2011.

[38] *Ibid.*, Decision T-725/2004.

[39] The first examples of this broader understanding are the dissenting opinions of Justice Jaime Araujo Rentería in C-811/2007 in which the court extended the coverture of *de facto* marital unions to same-sex couples, and Justice Catalina Botero Mariño in C-811/2007 in which the Court extended to members of same-sex couples the right to affiliate their partners to mandatory health programs.

argument went, the framers did not have the intention to limit the concept of family to the heterosexual couple because the Charter did not contain a provision that banned same sex unions. This interpretation, as considered by the dissenting justices in those earlier cases, was more plausible and respectful of the rights and principles included in the Constitution, and was the outcome of a harmonious interpretation of its tenets. Despite the fact that these arguments had been debated in Court since 2007, and included in dissenting opinions since then, the majority decision in earlier cases had sided with a literal interpretation of the wording of article 42. However, this interpretation was about to change.

Using a realistic approach, the Court acknowledged that there was a paradox in the confrontation of the literal content of article 42 which seemed to determine once and for all the concept of family, and the fact that the concept was essentially variable and deeply sensitive to the influences of changing social mores. Using the precedents set in earlier decisions, the Court recognized that its own interpretation of what constituted a family was not mandated centrally or exclusively by the constitutional phrasing, but, instead, by the relationships that citizens naturally build between each other. Examples of this broader interpretation of the family included the recognition of single parents and their children as a family; the recognition of foster families as family; cases in which grandparents are in charge of their grandchildren, or elder brothers in charge of their siblings. The concept of family, then, encompassed not only the natural community formed by parents, siblings and close relatives, but it even incorporated persons that were not related to each other through ties of consanguinity.[40] The Court explained that the particular characteristics of a social, participatory and pluralistic state[41] which includes between its aims the protection of the liberties, beliefs and rights of citizens sustain the constitutional protection of these different formations of family. Moreover, the pluralistic nature of the Colombian state was clearly in tension with the imposition of a unique type of family to the exclusion of others that did not conform to the one that was recognized.

The implications of a broader understanding of situations that could be considered a family, that extend beyond the exact phrasing of article 42 led the Court to conclude that "heterosexuality is not a characteristic that is predicable of all kinds of families, neither is the existence of consanguinity ties as a foster family shows."[42] If neither heterosexuality nor consanguinity were essential characteristics of the family, What was essential to it? The Court held that the common denominator of the social formations known as family and whose realities distanced from the characterization of the family under article 42 were "love, respect and solidarity" as well as "a union of life or destiny that intimately links its members."[43] Out of this line of reasoning, the Court concluded:

---

[40]Colombia, Constitutional Court, Decision C-577/11.

[41]*Ibid.*, article 1.

[42]*Ibid.*, Decision C-577/11.

[43]*Ibid.*, Decision C-577/11.

> A couple who freely expresses its consent or joins with long-term expectations, is already a family, both in marriage and in *de facto* marital unions, which traditionally and for different purposes, has been accepted as a family even without descendants. Therefore, the situation cannot be different in the case of homosexuals that form a stable union.[44]

This understanding of the family focused on the particular kinds of relationships that were built between its members which translated into a long term commitment of love, care and solidarity, instead of the earlier focus on the biological sex of the parties. Finding that those conditions were present both between heterosexual and same sex couples, the Court reached the conclusion that same-sex couples were also covered by the family protected under article 42.

The Court explained the change of precedent through the concept of "living constitution," which implies thinking of constitutional rules as dynamic entities whose meaning is not set exclusively by the intention of its drafters or the meaning of its phrasing at the moment of enactment. Instead, according to this school of legal interpretation, the meanings of constitutional rules continue to change with the passage of time, the variation in people's perceptions and the evolving social, political or economic necessities and ideas. Finding that these changes had taken place in the Colombian social context the Court extended with its decision the scope of the rules that define the family.[45]

After concluding that same-sex couples are a form of family that deserves the constitutional protection established in article 42, the Court faced the issue of determining which protections and guarantees given to heterosexual couples had to be extended to same sex couples. Specifically, the Court focused on the right to marriage. According to the challenge, the deficit of protection that same-sex couples faced was due to their discriminatory exclusion from the possibility of entering into a committed and monogamous relationship that legally tied them (through rights and duties) at the time they gave their consent to start a life together. Instead, same-sex couples had to cohabit for 2 years before any legal effects took place between the partners. During the 2-year period of legally unbinding relationship, many situations may occur that leave one or both partners in a vulnerable situation.[46]

The Court answered this issue through a categorical statement: "the specific protection of the family and marriage of heterosexual couples is an unavoidable constitutional mandate."[47] Accordingly the only way to formalize a union between

---

[44] *Ibid.*, Decision C-577/11.

[45] *Ibid.*, Decision C-774/01 quoted in Decision C-577/2012.

[46] The risks the challenge enunciates and that are used by the Court in this section are: "in the absence of a mechanism to formalize the bond between members of the same sex couples, several issues are left pending for legal solution. Between them: the obligatory recognition of the reciprocal duties of cohabitation and mutual aid; other matters such as the maintenance obligation and its persistence on the party who is guilty of the separation; the property regime emerged at the time the link is formalized, the corresponding civil status and its effects, and the rights arising from the formalization of the link concerning the family property as well as the offense of failure to pay alimony, between many other aspects." *Ibid.*, Decision C-577/2012.

[47] *Ibid.*, Decision C-577/2012.

heterosexual partners was through marriage. At the same time, the Charter did not ban same sex marriage in any express way, so it could be concluded that some kind of legal institution that solemnizes the voluntary commitment of same-sex couples was a viable alternative. Moreover, the lack of such institution contravened the Constitutional right to free development of personality because it restricted same sex couple's right to freely decide on the formation of a family with all the legal formalities and protections heterosexual couples enjoyed. This did not mean, the Court argued, that whatever institution was designed for same-sex couples needed to be *the same* as that provided for heterosexual couples. The Court concluded, however, that the decision to include an institution to cover same-sex couples was a decision that pertained to the legislature. It ordered, therefore, that members of Congress undertake to draft and design an institution suitable for same-sex couples that allowed them to formally enter into a family arrangement at the moment in which the couple expressed consent. Moreover, the Court emphasized that the legislature is charged with the responsibility to establish the conditions under which such institution is created and establish its reach. Granting same-sex couples the right to enter a legally recognized family from the time of its formation is the starting point of such an institution. Additionally, legislative debate had to determine any other rights derived from such unions, such as rights of adoption. Due to the recognition that the current deficit of protection that same-sex couples face endangered and in fact hindered the exercise of their constitutional rights, the Court gave the legislature a term of 1 year to provide the legal terms of such institution. The Court stated that if the legislature failed to deliver a law for same-sex couples by the 20 of June 2013, "same-sex couples will be allowed to ask a notary public or a judge to formalize and solemnize a contractual bond that allows them to become a family."[48]

After the Court's decision, proponents presented four different draft bills to Congress for consideration. The "conservative" draft developed the rights and duties derived from a civil union for both different sex as well as same sex couples. The character of the union was a formal contract that bound the parties in a way similar to the way marriage bound a couple, but the bill was silent on the issue of adoption.[49] The "liberal" draft, extended the right to marriage to same-sex couples by rephrasing the wording of a group of rules and changing the clause "a man and a woman" by the clause "two people," and excluding procreation as the end of marriage. However, the bill lacked an express provision for adoption.[50] A third "multi partisan" draft

[48]The order given by the Court literally states: "If by June 20, 2013 the relevant legislation has not been enacted by Congress, same-sex couples may go before a notary or judge to formalize and solemnize a contractual tie that enable them to start a family, according to the scope that, by then, can legally be attributed to such unions". *Ibid.*, Decision C-577/2011.

[49]"Draft bill 29 of 2011", presented by Congressmen Miguel Gómez Martínez, Partido de la U. Accessed August 20, 2012, http://www.matrimonioigualitario.org/p/en-el-congreso.html

[50]Draft bill 37 of 2011, presented by Congressmen Guillermo Rivera, Partido Liberal. Accessed August 20, 2012, http://www.matrimonioigualitario.org/p/en-el-congreso.html

provided a regulation for "civil unions" for same sex couples, and extended the same rights, duties, and privileges of marriage to such unions. As in the liberal draft, no provision considered the issue of adoption.[51] Finally, the "leftist" draft proposed the recognition of the right to marriage and the right to adopt for same sex couples.[52] At the end all projects were rejected, and same sex couples are facing a diverse set of barriers to materialize their right to marry despite the fact that these unions were allowed by the Constitutional Court if by June 20th, 2013 no bill had been passed.[53]

5.1.3 Step Three: Adoption

In 2001, before most of the Constitutional Court decisions granting rights to same-sex couples that have been exposed thus far, the Court analyzed a constitutional challenge against two articles of Law 2737 of 1989, a law that developed children's rights and that included provisions on the process of adoption of minors. The two challenged articles established requirements that potential adopting parents had to fulfill prior to adopting. According to the constitutional challenges, the condition of "moral integrity" established for adopters as well as the law's restriction to benefit only couples formed by a man and a woman infringed constitutional rights of citizens seeking to adopt. First, for the challengers of the law, the "moral integrity" standard was not a requisite of biological parents and therefore included an illegitimate differentiation between biological and adoptive parents. Second, the standard allegedly required a particular moral stance which contravened the pluralistic tenets of the Colombian Charter. As for the heterosexual character of the

[51]Draft bill 47 presented by Congressmen Alfonso Prada and Carlos Amaya (Partido Verde); Gilma Jiménez, Jorge Londoño, Iván Name y Féliz Valera (Partido Verde) and Armando Benedetti (Partido de la U). Accessed August 20, 2012, http://www.matrimonioigualitario.org/p/en-el-congreso.html

[52]Draft bill 58, presented by Congressmen Iván Cepeda and Congresswoman Alba Luz Pinilla (Polo Democrático Alternativo). Accessed August 20, 2012, http://www.matrimonioigualitario.org/p/en-el-congreso.html

[53]After the Legislature failed to pass a law to govern same-sex couples unions, several couples reached notary publics and judges in order to formalize their unions in accordance with the decision of the Constitutional Court. Some couples have been "united" without the use of the noun "marriage" but some others have faced difficulties in finding a public officer who will conduct the union. Currently, the Constitutional Court is reviewing two "acciones de tutela" that aim to protect the right of same sex couples to have a formal union with the same rights and duties of marriages. See: "Carlos, y Gonzálo, la primera pareja gay "civilmenre casada" pero sin matrimonio" Accessed April 1st, 2014 http://www.rcnradio.com/node/79665 and "Corte Constitucional reabre el debate sobre matrimonio entre parejas del mismo sexo" Accessed April 1st, 2014 http://www.rcnradio.com/noticias/corte-constitucional-reabre-el-debate-de-la-union-de-parejas-del-mismo-sexo-118641

adopting couple, the challengers argued that excluding same-sex couples as eligible adoptive parents was discriminatory against them and illegitimately sanctioned their sexual orientation to disqualify them in the process of adoption.

In its analysis, the Court started by pointing out that the constitutional mandates included two references to the concept of "social morality" which the Court understood to be "the [morality] prevailing in each populace in their own circumstances."[54] In an earlier case regarding a homosexual man looking to adopt a child, the Court recalled that the standard of "moral fitness" was used to reject the adoption not because of the sexual orientation of the adopting parent but because of the adopting parent's living conditions and the likelihood that such an environment would prove detrimental to the minor's well-being. The decision to deny the adoption was, according to the Court, based on the best interest of the child.[55] In the following paragraphs of the ruling, the Court tried, unsatisfactorily, to establish the content of such standard of morality. The Court's difficulty in clarifying the concept may be due, in part, to the fact that it is defined, from the outset, as a category with a changing nature. However, in the paragraph cited below the Court described the content of the category by reference to its opposites, that is, the ways in which public morality may be infringed:

> The [adoption] rules aim, through these requirements [moral fitness], to achieve that the individual selected as an adoptive parent is able to offer the child the best guarantees to their harmonious development, (...) a person who has a history of consistent behavior in accordance with social morality ensures the State in an ideal way that the education of the child shall be conducted in accordance with these ethical criteria. (...) By contrast, the delivery of the child to someone who develops his life project in socially ostracized conditions, as is usual in environments where alcoholism, drug addiction, prostitution, crime or disrespect to human dignity in any way, puts the child in danger of not achieving the proper development of his personality and hinder his peaceful and harmonious coexistence within the socio-cultural environment in which he is embedded.[56]

As "social morality" is a changing concept, then general agreements can supplement the content by reference to the wellbeing of the adoptee. According to the Court, this precluded the judge or the administrative official from deciding an adoption case based on his own ethical or religious convictions. Also, this standard eliminated discriminatory intent against adoptive parents because biological parents must comply with this standard in order to maintain their rights to custody and guardianship. This moral integrity was in fact the only way in which the state

---

[54]Colombia, Constitutional Court, Decision C-224/1994.

[55]According to the proofs presented to the Court, the applicant adoptive parent lived in a "tolerance zone" prone to delinquency acts, and the room that he, his mother and the adoptive child inhabited was in poor living conditions. In addition, the adoptive parent's couple was allegedly an alcoholic. For these reasons, the state authority competent to grant adoptions (ICBF) rejected the adoption application. *Ibid.*, Decision T-280/1995.

[56]*Ibid.*, Decision C-814/2001.

could guarantee the prevalence of the principle of the best interest of the child. Finally, the Court emphasized that this standard was not explicitly focused on the sexual orientation of the applicant parent in the sense that a non-normative sexual orientation indicated lack of moral integrity. Instead, the reason why homosexual couples were not eligible for adoption was that they did not conform to the traditional constitutional understanding of family that the Court had elaborated. The Court in this case said that the family protected under the Constitutional Chart was monogamous and heterosexual[57] formed either by marriage or by the consent of the parties. Moreover, this entailed consequences in the structure of the possible legal and kinship relations that took place in adoptive families. Thus, the content of the law under challenge in the case at hand only reproduced the constitutional mandate that recognized the same rights of married couples and *de facto* marital unions to adopt, which was the social formation that the constitutional drafters aimed to protect as well as the most fit to protect the best interest of the child. The Court acknowledged that this case posed a tension between the right to equality and free development of personality of homosexual individuals or other persons looking to adopt who live in affective unions that under this understanding do not constitute a family, and the constitutional right of minors to be a part of a family. However, the Court concluded that such tension between rights was solved by the Charter, which in article 44 indicates peremptorily the prevalence of the rights of children over all other rights.[58] Consequently, the Court based its decision on the harmonic interpretation of article 42 that establishes the heterosexual character of the family, and article 44 which establishes the paramount prevalence of rights of children.

The Court showed to be divided on this issue, and four of the nine judges signed dissenting opinions. The dissenting judges argued that the family protected by the Charter was the heterosexual, monogamous family that the majority decision sustained, and that the general limitation for homosexual couples to adopt because it does not promote the best interest of the child was discriminatory against couples with a diverse sexual orientation and infringed upon their rights to personal autonomy, human dignity and pluralism.[59]

As I have shown in earlier sections, this understanding of the constitutionally protected family changed in decision C-577/11. It's implications on the change on the right of adoption for same-sex couples, however, is still incompletely addressed. Thus far the Court has decided three cases that have addressed issues around same sex couple's adoption rights but has dodged the question of equality in access with heterosexual couples. The first of this cases revolved around the adoption of two

---

[57] See supra §2.2.

[58] In it's relevant fragment, Article 44 of the Constitution states: "The rights of children take precedence over the rights of others."

[59] Dissenting opinion to Decision C-814/2001 signed by Justices Manuel José Cepeda, Eduardo Montealegre, Jaime Córdoba and Jaime Araujo.

children by a gay man, which took over media coverage both nationally and in the U.S.,[60] and brought this debate to the center stage.[61]

In 2012, the Court decided an "acción de tutela" presented by Chandler Burr, an American citizen who, after complying with the requisites and process of adoption of two Colombian minors aged 8 and 13, was denied permission to take the children out of the country. Subsequently the ICBF (Colombian Institute for Family Welfare) physically separated Burr and the children while it conducted a review of the adoption process, arguing that the adoptive parent may have misrepresented his parental qualifications.

According to Mr. Burr, after finalizing the legal and administrative procedures of the adoption process, and a family judge delivered the decision assigning the two children as adoptive sons to Mr. Burr, the only proceeding left was the issuance of the children's American visas in order to leave the country with their father. Before delivering the visas to Mr. Burr's adoptive children, he decided to pay a visit to ICBF's (Colombian Institute for Family Welfare) offices to say good bye to some of the officers involved in the adoption process. During that visit, Mr. Burr talked with the Deputy Director of Adoptions of ICBF. In their brief conversation, Mr. Burr "expressed his concern about the fear that exists in Colombia against adoption by homosexuals and hinted that he, being a gay man, was never considered not suitable for adopting."[62] After finishing the visit, Mr. Burr and the children went to the American Embassy in Bogotá where the Embassy notified them that although the visas had been initially granted, their visas had been "denied without prejudice" due to a recent communication from the ICBF denying permission to the kids to leave the country.

When asked the reason of the withdrawal of permission for the children to leave the country, ICBF officers argued that Mr. Burr omitted information in the administrative and judicial process of adoption by not disclosing his sexual orientation. This led the ICBF to take two actions. First, it accused Mr. Burr's for falseness in public proceedings and reported him to the authorities for his criminal prosecution. Second, regarding the children, ICFB ordered that the children be

---

[60] "Chandler Burr, American Journalist, Describes Colombian Fight For Gay Adoption Rights" *Hufftington Post*, May 27, 2012, http://www.huffingtonpost.com/2012/05/27/chandler-burr-Colombia-gay-adoption-rights-_n_1548477.html accessed July 19th, 2012 "Chandler Burr claims Colombia denied adoption because of his sexual orientation" *CNN* December 1st, 2011, http://am.blogs.cnn.com/2011/12/01/chandler-burrt-claims-Colombia-denied-adoption-because-of-his-sexual-orientation/ accessed July 19th, 2012; "Procuraduría impugnará adopción de niños al periodista Chandler Burr", *Semana*, December 13th, 2011, http://www.semana.com/nacion/procuraduria-impugnara-adopcion-ninos-periodista-chandler-burr/169111-3.aspx, accessed July 19th, 2012.

[61] "Fuertes declaraciones de iglesia sobre adopción al estadounidense gay" *El Tiempo*, December 13th, 2011 http://www.eltiempo.com/gente/ARTICULO-WEB-NEW_NOTA_INTERIOR-10913132.html accessed July 21st, 2012; "Iglesia y academia chocan sobre la adopción de parejas gay" *Semana*, April 26th, 2012 In: http://www.semana.com/nacion/iglesia-academia-chocan-sobre-adopcion-parejas-gay/176188-3.aspx, accessed July 21st, 2012.

[62] Colombia, Constitutional Court, Decision T-276/2012.

taken away from his custody and returned to a foster home, declared their rights endangered, and started a process of restitution of the children's rights which could result in the annulment of the adoption by Mr. Burr and return them to the situation of adoptability by another family. In response, Mr. Burr initiated an *acción de tutela* asking for the protection of his rights to equality, free development of personality and due process, as well as the children's rights to have a family, not being taken away from it, and not to be discriminated because of their family origin.

The Court found that the issue at stake was whether through its actions, the ICBF infringed the rights of Mr. Burr and his children. Additionally the Court divided its analysis in two fronts. First, on the mandated constitutional guarantees in processes of restitution of children's rights, and second, on the rights of children and adolescents to be heard and their opinions taken into consideration in administrative and judicial processes.

After evaluating the case, the Court found that ICBF could not show evidence to suggest a menace to the emotional health of the children when the protective measures were taken, and that even if it could be proven that such a menace existed, ICBF could not prove there was a relation of causality between the absence of notification of Mr. Burr's sexual orientation during the adoption proceedings and such menace. Therefore, the Court decided that the ICBF should stop all administrative and judicial proceedings and return the definitive custody of the children to Mr. Burr as their legitimate adoptive parent.

Despite the fact that national media widely publicized Mr. Burr's case as a case of discrimination against a gay man because of his sexual orientation,[63] the Court examined the issue in a less than a peripheral way. As it was proven by Mr. Burr, and accepted by the Court, he was not obligated to disclose his sexual orientation during the adoption proceedings because part of the process had been carried out through an adoption agency in the state of New York (U.S.) where it is illegal to ask an adoptive parent his or her sexual orientation. Moreover, as the court highlighted, ICBF was unable to provide conclusive proof that the absence of this information endangered the children's right, nor that Mr. Burr's sexual orientation showed a lack of capability to raise a child.

Although the case was as much about due process as it was about children's rights, it was fundamentally about a state agency discriminating against a man because of his sexual orientation, which was the motivating factor for ICBF's measures. Nevertheless, the Court decided not to address this issue. Indeed, the Court's press release that informed its decision stated that it "did not rule on the issue of equality and in any way states that ICBF has discriminated against the plaintiff. Nor does it resolve the controversy over whether same-sex couples can adopt."

[63]"Homosexual recupera a sus hijos adoptados" *El Tiempo,* December 13th, 2011, http://www.eltiempo.com/archivo/documento/MAM-5025080, last accessed 12 July, 2012. "ICBF revisa caso de padre gay" *El Tiempo,* December 9th, 2011, http://www.eltiempo.com/archivo/documento/MAM-5017443, "ICBF tendrá que devolver niños en adopción a estadounidense homosexual", *El Espectador,* December 12, 2011, http://www.elespectador.com/noticias/judicial/articulo-316255-icbf-tendra-devolver-ninos-adopcion-estadounidense-homosexual, last accessed July 12th, 2012.

While the LGBTI activists and mass media cheerfully received the decision,[64] its impact was narrow because it only ratified earlier precedents about due process in adoption procedures and the prevalence of the rights of children therein. The *ratio decidendi* of the decision revolved around due process and children's rights while references to sexual orientation as a possible danger to the children or as an illegitimate reason for excluding a person as a fit adoptive parent were, at the most, *obiter dicta*. Therefore, no fragment of this particular decision serves as future constitutional precedent against the discrimination of an adoptive parent because of his or her sexual orientation.

Trying to explain the reluctance of the Court to examine the charge of discrimination for sexual orientation is speculative. I will, however, try to flesh out what was at stake in this decision and the reasons that may have restrained the Court's analysis. First, this decision came only 9 months after the Court decided to extend the concept of family protected under the Constitution to same sex couples. Second, and most important, in that decision the Court argued that it was the legislature's responsibility to decide the form and extent that this newly recognized protection had, which meant that it deferred to that body the decision on the right to adopt for members of same sex couples. Therefore, if the Court had decided that Mr. Burr had been discriminated because of his sexual orientation, and that such discrimination was illegitimate because it infringed his constitutional rights, such a decision could be understood to concede the right to adopt to individuals regardless of their sexual orientation. Such a pronouncement would have, at least in part, conflicted with the reasoning that gave the legislator the power to decide on these issues. Moreover, it would have invited a clash of powers between the Constitutional Court and the Legislature if the latter had had an interest in denying such adoptions. However, remember that the Court had established a window for Congress to pass a bill until June 20th, 2013, time at which- if no bill had passed- same sex couples could ask notary publics and judges to perform formal unions. Well, by August 2014, the Court seemed ready to discuss the long time pending case of two mothers who challenged an administrative decision that denied the adoption of a child by his non biological mother.[65] In this case, the two women had shared their life together for several years and the non biological mother wanted to adopt the child bore by her

---

[64]"La Familia de Chandler Burr" *El Tiempo,* May 25th 2012 stating that despite the restrictive effect of the Court's decision "the very fact of recognizing a man his right to be a homosexual adoptive parent must be received as an unprecedented news that may well mean a definitive step towards a tolerant and inclusive society in which we can truthfully live amongst difference", http://www.eltiempo.com/opinion/editoriales/ARTICULO-WEB-NEW_NOTA_INTERIOR-11881961.html, accessed 18 July, 2012 "ICBF reconoce adopción de dos niños a estadounidense homosexual" *RCN* December 12, 2012, http://www.rcnradio.com/node/125287, accessed 18 July 2012; "Autorizan adopción de dos niños a estadounidense homosexual" *El País*, http://www.elpais.com.co/elpais/Colombia/noticias/autorizan-adopcion-dos-ninos-estadounidense-homosexual, accessed 18 July 2012.

[65]"Fighting to be a family" *Washington Post*, July 13, 2012, http://www.washingtonpost.com/world/the_americas/battling-for-equal-rights/2012/08/10/08c7b1d0-e279-11e1-98e7-89d659f9c106_gallery.html#photo=1 accessed July 25, 2012.

partner under their union. Also in this case, the Court strictly tailored the decision to fit very closely the particular facts that were presented. The Court affirmed that in cases of adoption by consent (those in which the biological father or mother of a minor assents to his or her adoption by their common law partner) the sexual orientation of the adoptive parent should not be used as a criteria to deny the adoption.[66] This was the standing law for same sex couple's adoption rights by February 2015, but changes may be on the way after the Court examines a new constitutional challenge on the same issue but in which the framing is the protection of "the best interest of the child". The new framing will allow a shift in analysis from the rights to non-discrimination of same sex couples to an emphasis on the right of minors to have a family.

5.2 Unchanging Conceptions of the Family. Marriage Between Two

Paradoxically, while the LGBTI agenda is devoted to pursuing the legal recognition of same sex "marriage" through the legislature, divorce rates are on the rise, and a certain public worry over its increase is building.[67] Indeed, marriage trajectories in Colombia declined from 62 % in 1982 to 35 % in 2006 and the divorce rate increased from 8 to 17 % in the same period. In the meantime, the percentage of cohabiting couples increased from 12 % in 1982 to 25 % in 2006.[68] Just in the first trimester of 2012, divorce rates escalated 26 % more than in the previous year, which, together with a decline in marriage, should invite us to consider seriously the warning that the institution of marriage is facing crisis, and evaluate whether we should be worried at all like social conservatives warn we should be.[69]

At the same time, Constitutional Court's decisions regarding the family veer towards the recognition of family formations not only based on grounds of

[66]Colombia, Constitutional Court, Press Release http://www.corteconstitucional.gov.co/comunicados/No.%2035%20comunicado%2028%20de%20agosto%20de%202014.pdf, accessed February 15th, 2015.

[67]José Manuel Otaolaurruchi, L.C. "Mejor el divorcio que convivir", *El Tiempo,* October 6, 2012, http://www.eltiempo.com/opinion/columnistas/josemanuelotaolaurruchi/mejor-el-divorcio-que-convivir-jose-manuel-otaolaurruchi-l-c-columnista-el-tiempo_12286778-4 last accessed October 6th, 2012, stating that due to the fear of divorce, young couples are increasing the rates of cohabitation.

[68]Diego Amador and Raquel Bernal, "Cohabitation vs Marriage: The effect in children's well-being", Documentos CEDE, (Bogotá: Universidad de los Andes) January 2012: http://economia.uniandes.edu.co/profesores/planta/Bernal_Raquel/documentos_de_trabajo accessed August 20, 2012.

[69]"Divorcios en Colombia crecieron 26,2 % en primer semestre de 2010", *El Espectador*, August 29, 2012 In: http://www.elespectador.com/noticias/politica/articulo-370915-divorcios-Colombia-crecieron-262-primer-semestre-de-2012, accessed August 20, 2012, "Atarofobia: el miedo de los jóvenes al altar" El Universal, Cartagena, September 29, 2012.

consanguinity but on a commitment between its members based on care, respect and tolerance regardless of procreation. This framework, it seems, allows for a more "organic" less stagnant understanding of the family and of personal ties that can become real family formations without the need of procreation as its main end. By "organic understanding" or "organic family" I try to highlight the contextual, changing character of the elements that constitute a family, and the way in which those can and are shaped by the way in which people actually live, who they share their commitments with, who they depend on, and who they want to associate with, regardless of the legal ties that bind them. It is this understanding which led the Court to recognize same-sex couples as family.

Despite the inclusion of same-sex couples as families, under the banner "the same rights with the same name" the LGBTI agenda is committed to the recognition of same sex *marriage* as the only satisfactory way to reach formal equality between same sex and different sex couples. Evidently, then, two forces are in tension. On the one hand the social reality of marriage under siege due to low rates of marriage and high divorce rates as well as a series of constitutional decisions backing a range of family formations that exceed the traditional nuclear family; on the other, a push for marriage in the terms of the traditional biparental unit for LGBTI couples. Another way of understanding this tension is by understanding each side's commitments. The first side is grounded in a pragmatic understanding of the family based on the actual practice of families. Conversely, the second side takes a traditional approach to the concept of family as a legally determined, legally enforced institution that finds its legitimacy in state sanctioned formalities. My interest in this last part is to question the implications of this veer to the traditional, biparental, state sanctioned family towards which the LGBTI agenda pushes current law reform. Specifically, I would like to question the effect of entrenchment of the traditional family that the LGBTI agenda accomplishes through the campaign for marriage equality and the way in which such entrenchment limits the possibilities of alternative family formations, and in the end, alternative understandings of sexuality and association. Rather than being for or against the LGBTI campaign for marriage, I would like to flesh out what is at stake in the debate and identify some of the costs of this line of political engagement.

Why is marriage so important for LGBTI activists? And, why are Colombian LGBTI activists focused not only in the recognition of the bundle of rights associated with legal marriage but, also in conquering the word *marriage* for same sex couples? There are several reasons that can explain this framing, but I will focus on two that are at the center of the current debate in Colombia as elsewhere. First, the enjoyment of the same benefits and burdens ascribed to heterosexual marriage. Second, the principled reason of formal equality and acquisition of legitimacy.

The first, most plain reason that LGBTI activists pursue the recognition of the right to marriage enunciates an interest in enjoying the same benefits that heterosexual marriages enjoy, which, in the current Colombian context, would guarantee their right to adopt. The second principled reason for pursuing marriage is that, for LGBTI activists and community members, the extension of this right for same-sex couples signifies a recognition of the legitimacy of their bonds in the same terms and under the same conditions as heterosexual couples, that is, their equalization with the traditional monogamous heterosexual family under the guise of law. Similarly, couching their bond in the traditional parlance conveys a message of social acceptance and recognition of sexual diversity which is not accomplished by obtaining the same bundle of rights with a different denomination. LGBTI activists find that a different denomination for their unions is still discriminatory because it communicates the message that there is a fundamental difference between heterosexual and homosexual couples, which continues to undermine the genuineness of their bonds.[70] This line of argument is an instance of what Libby Adler identifies as the normalization of the gay family, through which gay rights advocates pursue the portrayal of homosexual unions as "morally indistinct" from the idealized version of the traditional heterosexual family, which is much more about love than about sex, and which seems to "naturally" allow for the extension of marriage from heterosexual to same sex couples.[71]

These are certainly good reasons to advocate for social change in the hope that we will once live in a pluralistic society where sexual orientation, but also every kind of discrimination is a thing of the past. However, the road that leads us in that direction is not necessarily served by entitling same-sex couples to get married. This is, no doubt, a sensitive issue. Because of the hardships that LGBTI community members suffered in the past and continue to suffer today, a critical appraisal of the campaign for marriage equality may seem insensitive to their grief and diminishing of their right to push for a more inclusive society. This is of course, not my interest. Quite on the contrary, taking advantage of this opportunity in the Colombian debate to rethink the bonds that tie us together would be both more inclusive and more sexually liberating for individuals, all individuals, regardless of their sexual orientation, than reducing the issue to marriage.

In the American debate, other scholars have stated reasons to question the emphasis of LGBTI activism around marriage equality and attempted to highlight its costs.[72] Particularly, Judith Butler has argued that the debate over marriage equality is polarized between legitimate and illegitimate unions. Legitimation, which is conferred by the state, has its own molds and establishes its own rules of entry to the exclusion of whatever is different. In terms of social arrangements, hetereosexual couples traditionally monopolize the legitimate field, whose legitimation is in part based on the establishment of formalities that exclude homosexual couples.

[70] Marcela Sánchez' intervention in the first debate on one of the marriage equality legislative drafts. October 1st, 2012, in: http://www.matrimonioigualitario.org/, accessed October 4th, 2012.

[71] Libby Adler, "The gay agenda", *Michigan Journal of Gender & Law* 16 (2009): 17, accessed August 18, 2012, http://papers.ssrn.com/sol3/papers.cfm?abstract_id=1268303

[72] See for example Janet Halley "Recognition, Rights, Regulation, Normalization: Rhetorics of Justification in the Same-Sex Marriage Debate" eds. Robert Wintemute & Mads Andenaes, *Legal Recognition of Same-Sex Partnerships: A Study of National, European, and International Law* (Hart Publishing: 2001); Judith Butler "Is kinship already heterosexual?" and Michael Warner, "Beyond Gay Marriage", both in eds. Wendy Brown and Janet Halley, *Left Legalism/Left Critique*, (Duke University Press: 2002).

Those who cannot comply with established formalities inhabit the illegitimate field. Legitimation, in turn poses the problem that its terms are set by the state, and that to acquire it, one must conform to the preexisting mold. Consequently, sexuality undergoes the same polarization: sexuality is thought in terms of marriage, and marriage is the way to acquire legitimacy, that is, legitimate sexuality is that which happens inside the boundaries of marriage. This dichotomic way of understanding legitimacy and sexuality, is built on the fundamental exclusion of other sexualities and other types of kinship, and forecloses the intelligibility of other kinds of social arrangements different from marriage. The naturalization of these dichotomic thinking bars our possibility of thinking about sexuality and kinship in terms that exceed the dyad legitimate-illegitimate when in fact reality is filled with *in betweens*, and marginal practices that cannot be completely, if at all, described by such limited universe. Because the LGBTI campaign for marriage equality is immerse in this dichotomic thinking, it naturalizes the terms of the debate and becomes unacceptably conservative.[73]

The current debate over marriage equality in Colombia is unnecessarily polarized in the terms described by Butler. The Constitutional Court's understanding of what constitutes a family and the nature of the ties that bind its members gives way to an understanding of kinship that already exceeds heterosexuality as its condition of possibility and procreation as its end. Such understanding, if taken advantage of, and strategically worked around, gives way to the recognition of a range of different social formations. In fact, if marriage, cohabitation, and divorce rates indicate something, it is that the marriage bond lost part of its social function of legitimizing unions and giving couples a certain social status and acceptability, though it is still a way of distributing costs of care and social entitlements such as social security and health care benefits. This way of social organization and of allocating costs is, however, not the only one possible. Other kinds of arrangements between friends, relatives, or lovers, who explicitly agree to form a "family," accomplish a distribution, similar to the French PACS (Pacts of Civil Solidarity) without its restriction on adoption rights, and maybe even without the restriction of encompassing only two individuals. Such unions could allow for some relations to be based on sex and love (lovers), friendship, companionship, and a long term life project (friends); companionship and solidarity (relatives), or different mixes of the above that lead people to conform long-lasting unions in which offspring may or may not be a manifestation of the parties commitment or life projects. Also, some of these unions would avoid the inconveniences of infidelity or romantic love running out as causes for separation because some of them would have other relationships specialized in sex and romantic love. Moreover, they allow some individuals to fulfill their interests of having offspring despite the fact that they have not found a love partner without having to carry all responsibility of childrearing on their own. The aforementioned simply exemplifies a few ways in which broadening the concept of family, without compromising the parties through marriage enhances people's

[73]Butler, J., "Is Kinship already heterosexual?", pp. 228–236.

life projects possibilities. So far, the exercise of deconstruction of the concept of family in the Colombian constitutional context has yielded its understanding as not necessarily heterosexual and not aimed at procreation as its unique end. How about furthering that exercise and initiate thinking of it also not *mainly* about sex and romantic love and not being a formality between two people but maybe three or more?

There is no certainty about which type of social organization serves best the interests of the parties, the child, and a national project, in part because all thinkable possibilities have not been implemented. Before getting married to the idea of "marriage equality," how about opening our minds and our political projects to a more diverse understanding of family, legitimacy, and even human commitment? The Colombian Constitutional Court has taken steps, though still conservative, towards a wider understanding of this issue. The opportunity should be taken to think about enhancing our rights to decide the kinds of commitments we want to be engaged through instead of relinquishing our possibilities to the state's desire of organizing society by coupling people through marriages of two.

Bibliography

1. Adler, Libby. 2009. The gay agenda. *Michigan Journal of Gender & Law* 16(1): 147, 147–266.
2. Bernal, Raquel and Diego Amador. 2012. *Cohabitation vs marriage: The effects on children's wellbeing.* Documentos CEDE, Bogotá: Universidad de los Andes. January 2012. Web. 20 August, 2012.
3. Bonilla, Daniel. 2010. *Parejas del mismo sexo en Colombia: tres modelos para su reconocimiento jurídico y político Anuario de Derechos Humanos*, Universidad de Chile, 2010.
4. Bonilla, Daniel and Natalia Ramírez. 2011. National report: Colombia. *American University Journal of Gender and Social Policy* 19.
5. Butler, Judith. 2002. Is kinship already heterosexual? In *Left legalism/left critique*, ed. Wendy Brown and Janet Halley. Durham: Duke University Press.
6. Cara, A Cara. 2012. Iglesia y academia chocan sobre la adopción de parejas gay. *Semana* 26 April, 2012. Web. July 21, 2012.
7. CNN. Chandler Burr claims Colombia denied adoption because of his sexual orientation. 1 December 2011. Web. 19 July, 2012.
8. Colombia, Constitutional Court, Decision T-539/1994.
9. Colombia, Constitutional Court, Decision T-539/1994.
10. Colombia, Constitutional Court, Decision C-481/1998.
11. Colombia, Constitutional Court, Decision T-808/2003.
12. Colombia, Constitutional Court, Decision C-373/2002.
13. Colombia, Constitutional Court, Decision C-098/1996.
14. Colombia, Constitutional Court, Decisions T-999/2000 and SU-623/2001.
15. Colombia, Constitutional Court, Decision C-814/2001.
16. Colombia, Constitutional Court, Decision C-098/1996. Colombia, Constitutional Court, Decision C-075/2007.
17. Colombia, Constitutional Court, Decision C-811/2007.
18. Colombia, Constitutional Court, Decision C-336/2008.
19. Colombia, Constitutional Court, Decision C-798/2008.
20. Colombia, Constitutional Court, Decision C-577/11.

21. Colombia, Political Constitution, article 1.
22. Colombia, Constitutional Court, Decision C-774/01 quoted in Decision C-577/2012.
23. Colombia, Constitutional Court, Decision T-725/2004.
24. Colombia, Constitutional Court, Decision C-224/1994.
25. Colombia, Constitutional Court, Decision T-280/1995.
26. Colombia, Constitutional Court, Decision C-814/2001.
27. Colombia, Constitutional Court, Decision T-276/2012.
28. Draft bill 29 of 2011, presented by Congressmen Miguel Gómez Martínez, Partido de la U. Matrimonio igualitario. Web. August 20, 2012.
29. Draft bill 37 of 2011, presented by Congressmen Guillermo Rivera, Partido Liberal. Matrimonio igualitario. Web. August 20, 2012.
30. Draft bill 47 presented by Congressmen Alfonso Prada and Carlos Amaya (Partido Verde); Gilma Jiménez, Jorge Londoño, Iván Name y Féliz Valera (Partido Verde) and Armando Benedetti (Partido de la U). Matrimonio igualitario. Web. August 20, 2012.
31. Draft bill 58, presented by Congressmen Iván Cepeda and Congresswoman Alba Luz Pinilla (Polo Democrático Alternativo). Matrimonio igualitario. Web. August 20, 2012.
32. El Espectador. *Divorcios en Colombia crecieron 26.2% en primer semestre de 2012.* 29 August 2012. Web. 20 August, 2013.
33. El Espectador. *ICBF tendrá que devolver niños en adopción a estadounidense homosexual.* 12 December/2011. Web. 12 July, 2012.
34. El País. *Autorizan adopción de dos niños a estadounidense homosexual.* 13 December 2011. Web. 18 July, 2012.
35. El Tiempo. *Fuertes declaraciones de iglesia sobre adopción al estadounidense gay.* 13 December 2011. Web. 21 July, 2012.
36. El Tiempo. *Homosexual recupera a sus hijos adoptados.* 13 December 2011. Web. 12 July, 2012.
37. El Tiempo. *ICBF revisa caso de padre gay El Tiempo,* 9 December 2011. Web. 10 January, 2012.
38. El Tiempo. *La Familia de Chandler Burr.* 25 May 2012. Web. 18 July, 2012.
39. García, Mauricio and Rodrigo Uprimny. 2004. Corte Constitucional y Emancipación Social en Colombia. Boaventura de Sousa Santos and Mauricio García *Emancipación social y Violencia en Colombia*. Bogotá: Norma
40. Halley, Janet. 2001. Recognition, rights, regulation, normalization: Rhetorics of justification in the same-sex marriage debate. In *Legal recognition of same-sex partnerships: A study of national, European, and international law*, eds. Robert Wintemute & Mads Andenaes. Oxford: Hart Publishing.
41. Huffington Post. Chandler Burr, American journalist, describes Colombian fight for gay adoption rights. 27 May 2012. Web. 19 July, 2012.
42. Lemaitre, Julieta. 2009a. *El derecho como conjuro. Fetichismo legal, violencia y movimientos sociales*. Bogotá: Siglo del Hombre Editores.
43. Lemaitre, Julieta. 2009b. *El amor en los tiempos del cólera: Derechos LGBT en Colombia. Sur: Revista Internacional de Derechos Humanos* 6(11): 79–98.
44. Otaolaurruchi, L.C., and José Manuel. 2012. Mejor el divorcio que convivir. *El Tiempo,* 6 October 2012. Web. 6 October, 2012.
45. RCN. *ICBF reconoce adopción de dos niños a estadounidense homosexual*. 12 December 2012. Web. 18 July, 2012.
46. Restrepo, Esteban. 2002. Reforma Constitucional y progreso social: la constitucionalización de la vida cotidiana en Colombia. In *El derecho como objeto e instrumento de transformación*, ed. Roberto Saba. Buenos Aires: Editorial del Puerto.
47. Sánchez, Marcela. 2012. *Intervention in the first debate on one of the marriage equality legislative drafts*. Matrimonio Igualitario. 1 October 2012. Web. 4 October, 2012.
48. Semana. *Procuraduría impugnará adopción de niños al periodista Chandler Burr.* 13 December 2011. Web. 19 July, 2012.

Chapter 6
Same-Sex Relationships and Israeli Law

Ayelet Blecher-Prigat

Abstract Marriage and divorce in Israel is regulated by religious laws. Same-sex marriage, therefore, has no formal place in Israel. The legal system, however, has shown flexibility mainly through Supreme Court decisions recognizing obligations and benefits to same-sex couples. The lack of a religion in Israel that would accept same-sex marriage, and the lack of a secular marriage to fill the void of religious marriage systems has not meant a total invisibility of same-sex couples. On the contrary, in addition to Supreme Court decisions expressly granting rights to same-sex couples, foreign same-sex marriage can be registered as valid marriages performed abroad. More importantly, same-sex parenting has become a possibility through progressive decisions of Israeli courts.

The status of same-sex relationships under Israeli law is somewhat schizophrenic. On one hand, Israeli family law and the formal laws that pertain to marriage and divorce in particular are conservative religious laws. On the other hand, against a traditionalist legal background, the Israeli legal system demonstrates flexibility, especially through the Supreme Court that issued a line of cases recognizing rights, obligations, and benefits that arise from same sex relationships.

This article begins with a general background of Israeli's unique family law system. Given the complexity of this system, knowledge of its basic principles is essential to understand the multifaceted legal rules that pertain to same-sex couples and the process that leads to their formation. Additionally, as many Western legal systems' struggle over legal recognition of same-sex relationships had a dominant constitutional dimension, the following section provides some background of Israel's Constitutional law, especially as it pertains to matters of marriage and divorce. It clarifies why in Israel the constitutional framework provides little or limited recourse for same-sex couples.

The chapter was written in 2013. Since then there have been a number of significant changes and developments, especially regarding legal recognition of the non-biological parent and dissolution of civil same-sex marriage entered into abroad.

A. Blecher-Prigat (✉)
Sha'arei Mishpat Law School, Hod HaSharon, 4510201, Israel
e-mail: ayeletb@mishpat.ac.il

M. Sáez (ed.), *Same Sex Couples - Comparative Insights on Marriage and Cohabitation*, Ius Gentium: Comparative Perspectives on Law and Justice 42,
DOI 10.1007/978-94-017-9774-0_6

Next, this article considers the ways secular courts in Israel have tackled the difficulties and concerns created by conservative religious laws' governance over marriage and divorce. Secular courts first addressed these problems when faced by traditional heterosexual couples and nuclear families. However, the tools developed by the courts in response to the plight of individuals in traditional relationships were subsequently useful to individuals in non-traditional relationships, including same-sex couples. This article focuses on three main avenues developed by secular courts to bypass the religious laws and cope with the difficulties they create, and then considers their application to same-sex relationships. First, this article considers the process Israeli legal system uses to recognize civil marriage entered into abroad. Second, it addresses the recognition of the relationships of unmarried cohabitants years ahead of other Western countries. Third, it considers the narrow interpretation given to "matters of marriage and divorce," to not include the consequences of such relationships, such as property relations and maintenance obligations. As property relations and maintenance obligations were characterized as exogenous to "matters of marriage" or "matters of divorce" over which religious laws holds exclusive sway, the secular courts could develop secular laws pertaining to these issues that apply to relationships not recognized by religious family laws, including same-sex relationships.

Lastly, the article moves from addressing the partnership relationship between same-sex adults to consider parenthood in same-sex families in Israel. It addresses the ways in which same-sex couples can become parents in Israel, including adoption and access to reproductive technologies. Finally, the article considers the ways through which same-sex parents can have their parental status legally recognized.

6.1 Legal Framework

6.1.1 Marriage and Divorce in Israel – Law and Jurisdiction

A split in law as well as a split in jurisdiction characterizes Israeli family law. In terms of law, while civil (territorial) law governs some aspects of family law, other aspects, defined as "matters of personal status" are governed by the "personal law" of the pertinent individual.[1] Marriage and divorce, in the narrow sense, are considered personal status matters, and thus no civil marriage exists in Israel and no uniform territorial law applies to marriage in Israel. Rather, the personal law of the relevant parties governs marriage.

[1] *See* Ariel Rosen-Zvi, *Family and Inheritance Law*, *in* Introduction to the Law of Israel 75, 75–76 (Amos Shapira & Keren C. DeWitt-Arar eds., 1995). The Israeli application of personal laws to "matters of personal status" was inherited from the Ottoman Empire's *millet* (religious community) system, which was preserved by the British Mandatory rule and later adopted by the Israeli legislature with certain amendments. *Ibid.*, p. 75.

The personal law of Israeli citizens and residents is their religious law, provided they belong to a recognized religious community.[2] Israel recognizes various religious communities: Jews, Muslims, Druze, and 10 Christian denominations.[3] No applicable personal law applies to Israeli citizens who do not belong to a recognized religious community, either because they are members of a religious community not recognized under Israeli law, or because they do not belong to any religion.[4] Thus no law applies under which they can get married. The personal law of non-resident foreign citizens is their law of nationality "unless that law imports the law of their domicile, in which case the latter shall be applied."[5]

The split between the civil and religious systems on family law matters is not only in law but in jurisdiction as well. Recognized religious communities under Israeli law operate religious courts.[6] Here again, some aspects of family law are under the exclusive jurisdiction of the relevant religious courts, while others are under a parallel jurisdiction of the civil system of family courts and the religious system.[7] Marriage and divorce are under the exclusive jurisdiction of the relevant religious courts, excluding dissolution of inter-faith marriages or marriages of individuals who do not belong to a recognized religious community.[8] Dissolution of such marriages is generally under the jurisdiction of the civil family courts.[9] Civil family courts also have jurisdiction to decide on matters of marriage and divorce

[2]See Menashe Shava, *Matters of Personal Status of Israeli Citizens not Belonging to a Recognized Religious Community*, 11 YB Hum. Rts. 238 (1981).

[3]The list of recognized religious communities appears in the Second Supplement to the Palestine Order in Council. Rosen-Zvi *supra* note 1, p. 76.

[4]This is when no religious community sees this person as belonging to it based on its religious laws (own definition). See Pinhas Shifman, *Religious Affiliation in Israel Interreligious Law*, 15 Isr. L. Rev. 1, 31 (1980). Such is the case for example when an individual is born to a Muslim mother and a Jewish father, as Orthodox Judaism defines a Jew based on birth to a Jewish mother whereas Islam defines a Muslim based on the father's Islamic affiliation.

[5]Article 64(2) of the Palestinian Order in Council.

[6]Rosen-Zvi *supra* note 1, p. 76. Several religious courts are recognized under Israeli law as having judicial authority over members of their religious communities: Rabbinic Courts (authority over Jews), Shari'a Courts (authority over Muslims), Druze Religious Courts (authority over Druze), and Courts of the Christian Communities (authority over members of the relevant recognized Christian communities). The jurisdiction of each of the religious courts is dependant upon a statutory order instituting such court and determining the scope of its jurisdiction.

[7]Once proceedings are initiated in one of these two systems, however, it assumes jurisdiction and precludes the other's intervention. The result has been the notorious "race for jurisdiction," when each party seeks to precede the other in initiating legal proceedings in order to determine what court will hear a particular case. Ariel Rosen-Zvi, *Forum Shopping between Religious and Secular Courts (and its Impact on the Legal System)*, 9 Tel Aviv U. Stud. L. 347, 348 (1989).

[8]Jurisdiction in the Matter of Dissolution of Marriage Special Cases & International Jurisdiction Act of 1969.

[9]See *infra* note 55 and accompanying text.

of same-faith couples that belong to a recognized religious community when such matters arise incidentally in proceedings before the family court.[10]

Notably, religious affiliation for purposes of law and jurisdiction in Israel is independent from personal beliefs and instead relies on the relevant religious laws.[11] Each recognized religious community, determines whether an individual does or does not belong based on its own religious law. Thus, even those who identify themselves as secular, atheist, or agnostic as a matter of personal belief may still be considered members of a religious community for purposes of law and jurisdiction. Conversely, when the relevant religious law does not recognize individuals who see themselves as affiliated with a particular religion they do not belong to this religion for purposes of personal law.

6.1.2 Marriage, Divorce, and Israeli Constitutional Law

Constitutional rights, such as the right to equality, and the right to marry, played an important part in the struggle of same-sex couples for legal recognition in many countries, especially in obtaining access to the institution of marriage.[12] This section provides an overview of Israeli constitutional law, with a focus on family matters. It explains why Israeli constitutional law can play a very limited role in the struggle for same-sex marriage in Israel, though it can play a role in guaranteeing same-sex couples other legal rights.

When the state of Israel was founded in 1948, it was assumed that the state would adopt a constitution and a bill of rights, as specifically provided in Israel's Declaration of Independence. However, political controversies over the content of the future constitution made it clear that drafting a constitution that would gain

[10]This authority is derived from Section 76 of the Courts Law (Consolidated Version)-1984 that states: "Where a matter has been lawfully brought before any court and a question arises therein the decision of which is necessary for the trial of the matter, the court may decide such question for the purposes of that matter even if the subject of the question is under the exclusive jurisdiction of another court or tribunal." Thus, for example, if while an inheritance case is litigated in the family court, a question arises as to the validity of the marriage between the deceased and a woman who claims to be the widow, the family court may decide on the issue of the marriage validity for purposes of that particular inheritance case. Such a decision does not create res judicata as to the question of the marriage validity.

[11]Rosen-Zvi, *supra* note 1, p. 78.

[12]*See e.g.*, in the U.S.: *Baehr v. Lewin*, 852 P.2d 44 (Haw. 1993); *Goodridge v. Dep't of Pub. Health*, 798 N.E. 2d 941 (Mass. 2003); in Canada: Halpern v. Attorney General of Canada (2002), 60 O.R. (3d) 321 (Div. Gen) (Ontario); Hendricks and Leboeuf v. Quebec (Attorney General), [2002] R.J.Q. 2506 (C.S.) (Quebec); Egale Canada Inc. v. Canada (Attorney General) (2003), 225 D.L.R. (4th) 472 (C.A.); in South Africa: CCT 60/04 Minister of Home Affairs v. Fourie 2006 (3) BCLR (CC) at 27 (S. Afr.), available at http://www.constitutionalcourt.org.za/Archimages/5257. PDF Available at http://www.saflii.org/za/cases/ZACC/2005/19.pdf. Accessed August 23, 2012.

broad-based support was not achievable for the time being.[13] As a result, the state adopted a compromise known as the "Harari Resolution" in 1950, that stated that Israel would gradually enact the future constitution, chapter by chapter in the form of "Basic Laws," so that controversies would be addressed one by one.[14]

Until 1992, the enacted Basic Laws addressed the structure of the State's political and legal system and the powers of its principal institutions, and did not protect human rights.[15] Therefore, they did not provide a safeguard of substantive value. In 1992, the state of affairs changed when the Israeli Knesset enacted two Basic Laws: *Human Dignity and Liberty*[16] and *Freedom of Occupation*.[17] The Knesset designed both of these laws to protect human rights within their respective spheres of influence. As interpreted by the Israeli Supreme Court, these Basic Laws provide for judicial review by any Israeli court, not just the Supreme Court, of Knesset legislation, transforming Israel from a parliament-supremacy democracy to a constitutional democracy.[18] Nonetheless, the so-called Israeli "constitutional revolution" of 1992 had limited impact on family law matters in general and on issues of marriage and divorce in particular.

Basic Law: *Human Dignity and Liberty* contains no express right to marry. Also, the right to equality and freedom of religion are absent from this Basic Law. Legislative history suggests that the omission of these rights from the Basic Law was intentional and motivated by objections expressed by some of Israel's religious political parties. These objections stemmed from the concern that guaranteeing a right to equality, freedom of religion, and certainly an express right to marry, would bring about the eventual invalidation of existing religious family law.[19]

Despite the absence of an express constitutional right to marry in the Basic Law, the Supreme Court interpreted that the right to Human Dignity includes a right to marry.[20] Regarding the right to equality, the Supreme Court includes the right to equality as part of a general right to Human Dignity, but only so far as this right

---

[13]Daphna Barak-Erez, *From an Unwritten to a Written Constitution: the Israeli Challenge in American Perspective*, 26 Colum. Hum. Rts. L. Rev. 309, 312–313 (1995).

[14]*Ibid*., The resolution is named after its author, Yizhar Harari, M.K.

[15]Yoram Rabin & Yuval Shany, *The Israeli Unfinished Constitutional Revolution: Has The Time Come For Protecting Economic And Social Rights*, 37 Isr. L. Rev. 299, 308–309 (2003).

[16]Basic Law: Human Dignity and Liberty, 1992, S.H. 150.

[17]Basic Law: Freedom of Occupation, 1992, S.H. 114, repealed by Basic Law: Freedom of Occupation, 1994, S.H. 90.

[18]CA 6821/93 *Bank Hamizrachi Ltd. v. Migdal et al.* 49(4) P.D. 221 (1995).

[19]See e.g., Yoav Dotan, *The Spillover Effect of Bills of Rights: A Comparative Assessment of the Impact of Bills of Rights in Canada and Israel*, 53 Am. J. Comp. L. 293, 304 (2005); Gidon Sapir, *Religion and State in Israel: The Case for Reevaluation and Constitutional Entrenchment*, 22 Hastings Int'l & Comp. L. Rev. 617, 637–628 (1999).

[20]HCJ 7052/03 *Adalah v. Minister of Interior*, 61(2) P.D. 202 (2006); 2232/03 *Plonit v. The Regional Rabbinical Court Tel Aviv* 61(3) P.D 496 (2006).; F.A. 9607/03, *Ploni v. Plonit,* 61(3) P.D. 726(2006). See also Ayelet Blecher-Prigat *A Basic Right to Marry: Israeli Style*, 47 Isr. L. Rev. 433 (2014).

is closely and objectively connected with human dignity.[21] Under this approach, the law does not recognize the right to equality as an independently implied or non-enumerated constitutional right. Consequently, not all aspects of equality are elevated to the level of constitutional rights, as they would have, had equality been recognized as a self-sustaining constitutional right.[22] The Supreme Court did not decide the issue of whether or not equal access to the institution of marriage is an integral part of the right to human dignity.[23]

In any event, the recognition of a Basic Right to marry and the constitutionality of some aspects of the right to equality with regard to family life have very limited effect on the laws of marriage and divorce, since legislation that predated the Basic Law is immune from judicial review as an additional "safety measure" enshrining religious family law. Article 10 of the Basic Law on *Human Dignity and Liberty* titled "Validity of Laws" states that "this Basic Law shall not affect the validity of any law (*din*) in force prior to the commencement of the Basic Law." The former chief Justice Barak qualified the effect of the Validity of Laws clause, holding that the interpretation of laws that predated the Basic Law is still affected by it because "the freezing of the validity of a law is not tantamount to the freezing of its meaning."[24] Nonetheless, this qualification also has a very limited impact on family law issues because it does not apply to religious laws, which are interpreted according to the relevant religious authorities. Thus, the Basic Law barely affects family law matters governed by religious laws

Another Constitutional issue, relevant for same-sex couples in Israel concerns the recognition of a Basic Right to divorce – a right to exit marriage. Under Jewish law, divorce requires the consent of both husband and wife.[25] Thus, Jewish women and men may find themselves unable to break-free from a marriage when they fail to

[21]HCJ 6427/02 *Movement for Quality Government in Israel v. Knesset* 61(1) P.D. 619 (2006). About the dispute of whether a right to Equality can be derived from Human Dignity see e.g., See e.g., Hillel Sommer, *The Non-Enumerated Rights: On the Scope of the Constitutional Revolution*, 28 Hebrew Univ. L. Rev. (Mishpatim) 257 (1997) (Hebrew); Yehudit Karp, *Basic Law: Human Dignity and Freedom — A Biography of Power Struggles*, 1 Mishpat Umimshal (Law and Government), 323, 347–351(1992) (Hebrew); Amnon Rubinstein & Barak Medina, The Constitutional Law of the State of Israel 921 (Vol I, 5th ed. 1997) (Hebrew); Yehudit Karp, *Several Questions on Human Dignity under the Basic Law: Human Dignity and Liberty*, 25 Hebrew Univ. L. Rev. (Mishpatim) 129, 145 (1995) (Hebrew); Dalia Dorner, *Between Equality and Human Dignity*, Shamgar Book (Articles, vol. 1, 2003) 9.

[22]*Movement for Quality Government in Israel case* at para 30–43 to the former Justice Barak's judgment; *Adalah* case at para 39 to the former Justice Barak's judgment.

[23]Blecher-Prigat, *supra* note 20 at 451–452. In *Adalah*, only two justices of the 11 justices on the panel (President Barak and Justice Procaccia) considered this issue. Both regarded violation of equality in the context of *family life* as constituting a violation of the right to human dignity. Nonetheless, "family life" and "marriage" are not equivalent.

[24]CA 2316/95 *Ganimat v. the State of Israel*, 49(4) P.D. 589 (1995).

[25]For a more detailed discussion see e.g., Ayelet Blecher-Prigat & Benjamin Shmueli, The Interplay Between Tort Law and Religious Family Law: The Israeli Case, 26 Arizona J. of Int'l & Comp. L., (2009) pp. 279, 281–282.

obtain their spouses' consent to divorce.[26] The civil system cannot directly address divorce because divorce is generally under the exclusive jurisdiction and governance of Jewish rabbinical courts and laws. Recently, however, the civil system recognized a civil tort action for Jewish women and men against their recalcitrant spouses, who decline to consent to divorce.[27] Courts recognize such a tort action, *inter alia*, based on the recognition of a Basic Right to exit marriage and divorce as part of the Basic Right to human dignity.[28] As discussed in more detail below, the recognition of a Basic Right to divorce is especially important for Israeli same-sex couples married outside of Israel and may find themselves with no available legal process to dissolve their marital bond.[29]

6.2 Same-Sex Formal Marriage Under Israeli Law

6.2.1 Same-Sex Formal Marriage in Israel

As noted, Israeli law provides no uniform territorial law that applies to marriage and no civil marriage exist in Israel. The personal law of the relevant parties alone governs marriage. Theoretically, if a relevant religious law of a recognized religious community recognizes same-sex marriage, then same-sex couples belonging to this recognized community could get married in Israel. In fact, however, the religious communities recognized in Israel do not recognize same-sex marriage. As a result, same-sex couples cannot marry in Israel.

6.2.2 Same-Sex Formal Marriages Celebrated Abroad

Same-sex couples are not the only couples that cannot get married in Israel due to the complete governance of religious laws on marriage in Israel.[30] Therefore, since

---

[26]For the reasons why women suffer more and have more difficulty to obtain their husbands' consent to divorce see *ibid.*

[27]See Blecher-Prigat & Shmueli, *supra* note 25.

[28]See *e.g.*, FamC (Tel-Aviv) 23849-08-10 *Y.K. v. B. Sh. K.* (Oct. 9, 2011) (unpublished officially); FamC 35371-02-10 (Tel-Aviv) *A.A L. B. v. Ch. B.* (Oct. 11, 2011) (unpublished officially); FamC 9877/02(Rishon Lezion) *P.E. v. P. Y.* (Aug. 17, 2011) (unpublished officially).

[29]See section 3.C *infra*.

[30]Others who cannot get married in Israel are persons who do not belong to a recognized religious community and therefore have no law of marriage applicable to them and inter-faith couples since most recognized religions in Israel do not recognize inter-faith marriages with the exception of marriage between a Muslim man and a Jewish or Christian woman, which the Sharia law recognizes. In addition, various restrictions under the pertinent religious laws may also prevent parties from marrying, as is the limitation under Jewish law on the marriage between a Cohen, a

the early days of the State of Israel, couples that could not marry in Israel or did not want a religious marriage, have looked for ways to bypass the religious restrictions on marriage in Israel. One common practice is to get married abroad. The validity under Israeli law of a civil marriage celebrated abroad between two Israeli citizens and residents was unclear for over 40 years, and still is regarding some of the couples (i.e. inter-faith couples, couples who do not belong to a recognized religious community and same-sex couples).[31]

6.2.2.1 The Registration/Recognition Distinction

Regardless of their validity, civil marriages are registered in the Israeli population registry based on the Supreme Court's landmark decision in *Funk Shlezinger v. Minister of the Interior* handed down almost 50 years ago.[32] According to this decision, the registrar must enter information regarding marital status provided by applicants and accompanied by public record into the population registry. The Court reasoned that the registry merely collects statistical information, which could either be true or false. The records of the population registry do not have the force of evidence or proof as to the veracity of the data they contain, especially regarding marital status.[33] According to the Court, the registration is an administrative, and not a judicial, procedure, and thus, the validity of the marriage is not within the scope of issues considered by the registrar. According to the Court, the registrar may refuse to enter information provided by a party when it is manifestly incorrect. For example, when an individual who is clearly an adult asks to be registered as a 5-year-old child.

While the *Funk-Shlezinger* decision may initially seem merely a formalistic decision, especially given the Court's emphasis that it did not address the question of validity, it provided a practical solution for couples who married in a civil ceremony outside of Israel. Despite the "statistical registry only" declaration of the Court that relies on the formal status of the registry, in reality registration has broader practical implications. As a result of this decision, civilly married couples enjoy practically all

descendant of the priestly clan, and a divorcee. Menachem Elon, THE PRINCIPLES OF JEWISH LAW 361 (1975).

[31] See discussion in part 3.B.(2) *infra*.

[32] HCJ 143/62 *Funk Shlezinger v. Minister of the Interior*, 17 P.D. 225 (1963). The Funk-Shlezinger case involved a Belgian Catholic woman and an Israeli Jewish man who were married in Cyprus and wanted to register as married in the Population Registry in Israel. The Ministry of Interior refused their request based on the argument that civil marriage of Israeli citizens is not recognized under Israeli law. The couple filed a petition against the Minister of the Interior's decision with the Supreme Court sitting as a High Court of Justice, and the Court accepted the petition.

[33] Section 3 of Population Registry Law, 5725–1965, 19 LSI 288 (1964–1965) (Isr.). This section provides that some details registered in the population registry constitute *prima facie* evidence as to their veracity; however, personal status of an individual is not one of them.

economic benefits of the state that couples formally married in religious marriages in Israel enjoy.[34]

In 2006 the Court applied the *Funk-Shlezinger* precedent to same-sex couples married in a civil ceremony outside Israel in the *Ben-Ari* case.[35] This case involved five gay couples married in Canada who requested registration in the Population Registry as married based on *Funk-Shlezinger*. The Ministry of Interior refused to change their registration status from "single" to "married" and they brought an appeal before the Supreme Court. The State did not challenge the *Funk-Shlezinger* decision, despite criticism over this decision in case-law and academic writing focusing on the "statistical registry only" argument that invokes the formal status of the registry but ignores the reality of the far broader implication of it. The State, however, did attempt to distinguish *Funk-Shlezinger*, arguing that same-sex marriage is a legal formation not recognized in Israel. According to the State, "marriage" within the population registry means marriage within the basic "legal formation" in Israeli law, which is marriage between a man and a woman. *Funk-Shlezinger* concerns legal formations recognized under Israeli law (i.e. civil marriages) where only their validity is in question.

The Court rejected the State's argument because providing the registrar with the discretion to consider the existence or lack thereof of "legal formats" under Israeli law stands contrary to current doctrine in which the registrar's role is an administrative and not a judicial one.[36] It thus ordered the registrar to register the couples as married. The Court stated, however, in accordance with the *Funk-Shlezinger* line of reasoning, that the registration is not indicative of whether or not Israeli law recognizes same-sex marriage. The Court also emphasized that its decision did not address the recognition of same-sex marriage in Israel.

The Court's emphasis that its decision does not entail the recognition of same-sex marriage should not cause alarm, as it is in line with the *Funk-Schlezinger* precedent. As noted, the distinction between registration and recognition entailed the de-facto recognition of civil marriage of opposite-sex couples, though the state did not provide a formal recognition. This reality can materialize for same-sex couples married abroad. Following the *Ben-Ari* decision, however, some articulated a concern that certain government agencies and other third parties that ordinarily rely on registration will adhere to the formal status of the registration in the case of

---

[34]Ruth Halperin-Kaddari, Women in Israel: A State of Their Own 244 (2004). This reality triggered criticism over the *Funk-Shlezinger* decision. *See e.g.*, Eitan Levontin, *'Figment of the Imagination: Funk-Schlezinger and Civil Registry Law'* 11 Mishpat Umimshal (Law and Government), (2008), pp. 125, 144–166. Nonetheless, thus far this system was not challenged.

[35]HCJ 3045/05 *Ben-Ari v. Ministry of the Interior*, 61(3) P.D. 537 (2006). Official translation can be found on the Israeli Supreme Court's web-site: http://elyon1.court.gov.il/files_eng/05/450/030/a09/05030450.a09.htm

[36]It should be noted that over the years the *Funk-Schlezinger* precedent has been expanded and applied to various contexts, including to the registration of two mothers of a child, based on a second-parent adoption in California. HCJ 1770/99 *Brener-Kadish v. Minister of the Interior*, 54(2) P.D. 368 (2000). See further discussion of this case *infra* in part 6.B.

same-sex marriages, and maintain that registration does not entail validity.[37] Thus far, this has remained merely a theoretical concern.[38]

Notably, in this respect, the dissent in *Ben-Ari,* Justice Rubinstein based his decision on the reality entailed by registration rather than on its formal status. Justice Rubinstein held that we are no longer talking about a mere statistical tool, but of a social and public symbol that has extensive practical implications for the authorities as well as for the public. The average person, explained Rubinstein, does not distinguish between registration and recognition of status.

6.2.2.2 Validity of Civil Marriage Celebrated Abroad

Regarding validity of civil marriage celebrated outside Israel, the basic distinction under Israeli law has always been between couples who were foreign citizens and residents at the time of the marriage, and couples who were Israeli citizens and residents at the time of the marriage.[39] In the case of civil marriage between two foreign citizens who later immigrated to Israel, where the marriage is valid according to the laws of their previous nationality and residency laws, then this marriage is valid under Israeli law.[40] As for civil marriage between Israeli citizens and residents, it also seems that the Israeli Supreme Court is now moving toward full recognition of such marriages, though it is doing so very slowly and step by step.[41]

For many years, the Court's position, invoked for the first time in *Funk-Shlezinger* and continued for over 40 years, has been that it does not decide the question of validity under Israeli law of civil marriage conducted abroad, when at least one of the parties is an Isareli citizen and resident. Nonetheless, on the same day the Court handed down the *Ben-Ari* decision, it issued an additional decision

---

[37] Aeyal Gross, *Israel's Supreme Court Orders Registration of Same-Sex Marriage Conducted in Canada*, Lesbian/Gay Law Notes (Dec. 2006) p. 226.

[38] If government agencies and other parties adhere to a "statistical tool" only status of the registration in the case of same-sex couples, such couples could theoretically invoke a claim of discrimination vis-à-vis opposite-sex couples who married civilly abroad. Such a claim, however, could challenge the entire registration/recognition distinction and the "statistic registration only" argument that enabled this reality in the first place.

[39] To simplify the discussion, I do not address couples where one of them is a foreign national, and the other is Israeli.

[40] C.A. 191/51 *Skornik v. Skornik*, 8 P.D. 141 (1954).

[41] The law is unclear in the case of couples who were Israeli citizens but foreign residents at the time of the marriage. The *Skornik* decision itself concerns a couple who were both foreign citizens and residents. Most of the Israeli scholarly writing on this issue limits this decision to this specific case, and does not extend its holding to cases of Israeli citizenship but foreign residency. Nevertheless, in HCJ 2232/03 *Plonit v. The Regional Rabbinical Court Tel Aviv*, 61(3) P.D. 496 (2006) Chief Justice Barak refers to *Skornik* as determining the validity of civil marriages conducted abroad by *either* couples who were foreign citizens or foreign residents at the time of the marriage (paragraph 23 to Chief Justice Barak's opinion). This interpretation, however, is disputed.

taking the recognition of civil marriages a step further. In *Plonit v. The Regional Rabbinical Court Tel Aviv*, the Court held that a civil marriage performed abroad between an Israeli Jewish man and an Israeli Jewish woman is valid under Israeli law, although Jewish law does not recognize the civil marriage as creating a valid matrimonial bond.[42] As a general rule, the Court held that when a couple has the capacity to marry in Israel according to their personal law, and the marriage ceremony took place within the framework of a foreign legal system that recognizes it, then the marriage is valid under Israeli law.[43] The Court left open the question of validity of civil marriage conducted abroad when the couple had no capacity to marry under Israeli law.[44] Thus, the Court first addressed the plight of Israeli citizens and residents who can marry in Israel but wish to refrain from a religious marriage,

---

[42]HCJ 2232/03 *Plonit v. The Regional Rabbinical Court Tel Aviv*, 61(3) P.D. 496 (2006). Official English translation is available at http://elyon1.court.gov.il/files_eng/03/320/022/a16/03022320.a16.htm

[43]See Paragraph 26 to Chief Justice Barak's opinion.

[44]The Court's opinion, delivered by President Barak, considered three alternative approaches that were developed in case-law and scholarly writing regarding the validity of such marriages under Israeli law. The first approach ignores the fact that the marriage ceremony was conducted abroad, stating that it does not alter the applicability of religious/personal law in matters concerning marriage, including the determination of a marriage's validity. This approach relies on the following line of reasoning: Article 47 of the Order-in-Council, which determines the application of personal law to questions of personal status, of which marriage and divorce stand at the core, is part of Israeli private international law and establishes an entire arrangement. The applicability of this article does not depend on the nationality of the relevant parties, or on national character in any way. Thus, wherever the parties were married, regardless of their nationality, the validity of their marriage in Israeli courts shall be determined according to their personal law. This approach is identified with Justice Agranat's approach in C.A. 191/51 *Skornik v. Skornik*, 8 P.D. 141 (1954) and with Professor Menashe Shava's approach. Menashe Shava, *Civil Marriage Celebrated Abroad: Validity in Israel*, 9 Tel-Aviv U. Stud. L. 65 (1989). Thus, where the relevant personal law of the parties does not recognize a civil marriage ceremony as creating a valid matrimonial bond, the marriage is not legally valid. The second approach distinguishes between questions of form and questions of capacity to marry. Whereas questions concerning the form of the marriage are governed by the law of the place where the wedding was performed (locus regit actum), questions that concern substance, meaning the capacity of the parties to marry, are governed by the law of their domicile at the time of the marriage, which for Israelis refers to their personal (religious) law. This approach is based on the English rules of private international law, which was incorporated into Israeli law by virtue of article 46 of the Order-in-Council. This approach considers article 47 of the Order-in-Council to be part of Israel's internal municipal law. This approach was introduced by Justice Witkon in the *Skornik* case, as well as in the District Court of Jerusalem in C.C. (Jerusalem) 2/85 *Kleidman v. Kleidman*, 1987(b) P.M. 377. Under this approach a distinction is made between those who have the capacity to marry in Israel in a religious ceremony, but chose a civil ceremony abroad, and those who could not marry in Israel and were forced to marry abroad. The third and final approach does not distinguish between form and capacity but rather considers both issues according to the law of the place where the wedding was performed. According to this approach, subject to limitations of public policy, the law of the country where the marriage ceremony took place governs the validity of the marriage. This approach is associated with Justice Zusman's approach, expressed in obiter dictum in Funk Shlezinger and advocating for the adoption of the American approach to private international law.

so they travel abroad to marry in a civil ceremony. The Court, however, did not address the plight of Israeli citizens and residents who cannot marry in Israel either because they do not have an applicable personal law, or because their personal law does not enable them to marry the person with whom they wish to share their lives.

Until Barak's groundbreaking ruling in the case of *Plonit v. The Regional Rabbinical Court Tel Aviv*, the Israeli Supreme Court had avoided deciding on the validity of civil weddings conducted abroad for over 40 years.[45] Despite situations in which the court had sat in a special extended panel, especially for deciding on this issue, the Court continued to declare that the decision concerning the validity of civil marriage between Israelis conducted abroad was a matter for the legislature to decide.[46] Nonetheless, in 2006 Chief Justice Barak concluded that it was time the Supreme Court started to address the validity of civil marriages conducted abroad, given that the legislator had failed to do so.[47] In recognizing the validity of the marriage, at least where the parties had the capacity to marry in Israel, Chief Justice Barak relied on the constitutionalization of the right to marry as recognized in Supreme Court case law.[48]

In a subsequent case, given just a couple of days later, *Ploni v. Plonit,* the married couple belonged to different religions, the man was Jewish and the woman Christian, and thus had no capacity to marry in Israel.[49] Chief Justice Barak stated that the law of the state in which the couple was married should solely determine the validity of the marriage both regarding issues of capacity to marry and the form of the marriage. Justice Barak also considered as central to argument, the fact that this approach was most compatible with the constitutional right to marry. Nonetheless, this was mere dictum as Justice Barak resolved the case, which dealt with matters of inheritance, without addressing the question of marital validity for all purposes.

It is hard to predict how these decisions will affect the status of same-sex marriages conducted abroad under Israeli law. On one hand, it seems that Justice Barak's position suggests that Courts should recognize same-sex marriages conducted abroad for all purposes under Israeli law. Conversely, even though Justice Barak's position was merely dictum, according to *Ben-Ari,* the question regarding same-sex marriage concerns more than their validity. *Ben-Ari* at least supposedly left open the question of whether Israeli law defines marriage as a relationship between

---

[45]Beginning with *Funk Shlezinger*.

[46]See e.g., HCJ 51/80 *Cohen v. Rabbinical High Court of Appeals,* P.D. 35(2) 8 (1980). The then president of the court, President Landau, created a special panel of seven Justices intending to resolve, among other things, the question of the validity of a foreign marriage in Israel. At that time, when the Israeli Supreme Court sat in an extended panel, it usually sufficed with five justices. The then President Landau explained his unusual decision to expand the panel in the *Cohen* case by the need to resolve a significant question of great import. *Cohen*, 35(2) P.D. at 10. However, he declared that in retrospect the question of the validity of the marriage did not arise. *Ibid.*

[47]Interestingly, this decision was given just a few months prior to Justice Barak's retirement.

[48]See text accompanying *supra* note 20.

[49]F.A. 9607/03, *Ploni v. Plonit*. 61(3) P.D 726 (2006).

a man and a woman or whether it recognizes the legal format of same-sex marriages. In the meantime, same-sex couples who married abroad are registered as married, and enjoy most of the social-economic rights enjoyed by couples who were married in a religious ceremony in Israel.[50]

6.3 Dissolving Same-Sex Marriages Performed Abroad

Here, the discussion refers merely to the narrow question of dissolving the marital bond in the sense of changing the parties' status from "married" to "divorced" or "single." This section does not address substantive issues of property division, spousal support, child custody, if the couple has joint children, child support, and the like. As elaborated in the following sections, given the governance of religious laws over matters of marriage and divorce, courts interpret "matters of divorce" narrowly, so that they apply only to the limited question of dissolution of the marital bond. Courts separate all other issues and consider them as neither "matters of marriage" nor "matters of divorce."[51] Thus, in this section, the discussion addresses the narrow question of dissolution, and other related issues are discussed separately.

The question regarding dissolution of a same-sex marital bond is relevant to same-sex Israeli couples married in a civil ceremony abroad as same-sex couples cannot marry in Israel. While the Supreme Court ordered the registration of same-sex marriage entered into outside Israel, it left open the question regarding the dissolution of such marriages. Though, as noted, registration in the population registry is not indicative of validity or recognition, changes in registration require either a public certificate that testifies to the change or a judicial decision determining such change. A mere statement by the applicant concerning the change is insufficient to serve as basis for a change in registration.[52] The question is, which courts have jurisdiction under Israeli law to dissolve the marriage, at least in terms of ordering the change of status in the population registry. Currently, the law lacks a clear answer – a situation that is incompatible with the recognition of a basic right to exit marriage.

Israeli law makes a distinction regarding dissolution of marriage between same-faith marriages of couples who belong to a recognized legal community in Israel, and marriages that do not fall under this category such as inter-faith marriages, marriages of individuals who do not belong to a recognized legal community, and individuals who have no religion. This issue is complicated when both parties belong to the same religious community, which is a recognized religious

[50]See section 4.B *infra*.

[51]As the Israeli system described these issues as separate and not necessarily related to marriage, these substantive issues are applied irrespective of the marital status of the parties so that similar but not identical rules are applied to cohabitants. See discussion *infra* in section 4.

[52]Sections 16, 17, 19 of the Population Registry Law, 1965, 19 L.S.I., (1964–1965), pp. 288–289.

community. Therefore, although such marriages are more common in Israel, a discussion of their dissolution occurs later.

The question seems simpler regarding inter-faith same-sex couples, couples who are not members of a recognized religious community, or couples who have no religious affiliation.[53] The law governing dissolution of such marriages in Israel is Matters of Dissolution of Marriage Jurisdiction in Special Cases Law,[54] which determines that in principle the civil family court has jurisdiction to dissolve the marriage in such cases.[55]

The Matters of Dissolution of Marriage Law defines "dissolution of marriage" as including "divorce, annulment of marriage, and declaration of a marriage as void *ab initio*."[56] In that manner, the Israeli system sought to provide a practical relief for inter-faith couples, or couples not affiliated with a recognized religious community, while at the same time, avoided endorsing or recognizing such marriages. Regulating the dissolution of the marriage did not depend on recognition of their validity, and a family court can dissolve a marriage bond by declaring it "void."

At the time the legislature enacted the Matters of Dissolution of Marriage (Jurisdiction in Special Cases) Law it did not consider same-sex marriage, however, there is no reason why this law will not apply to same-sex couples, provided they are inter-faith couples, or with no affiliation to a recognized religious community. Especially given that the application of the law does not implicate the validity of same sex marriage, which *Ben-Ari* left open. Also, the application of the Matters of Dissolution of Marriage Law to same-sex couples is compatible with the recognition of a Basic Right to exit marriage.

If the family court recognizes same-sex marriage as valid so that divorce is required to dissolve the marital bond, the Matters of Dissolution of Marriage (Jurisdiction in Special Cases) Law expressly provides only one ground for granting a divorce, which is the consent of both parties to the divorce.[57] In absence of mutual consent, the Law does not provide grounds for divorce. Rather, the law provides choice of law rules listed based on priority. Courts apply the rules considering the

---

[53]Remember that religious affiliation is not based on self-identification of the individual, but is rather by the relevant religious community, if it is a recognized religious community. See *supra* note 11 and accompanying text.

[54]See Matters of Dissolution of Marriage (Jurisdiction in Special Cases) Law, 1969, 23 L.S.I..

[55]In cases where one or both of the parties belong to a recognized religious community, the family court must inquire with the relevant court or courts whether under their religious laws, a religious dissolution of the marital bond is required to enable the relevant party to remarry in Israel. In case the relevant religious law requires a religious dissolution, then the matter shall be referred to the religious court. The religious court will have jurisdiction over dissolving the marriage but not over ancillary matters such as economic consequences of the marital bond. This scenario is irrelevant for same-sex couples, as all the religions recognized in Israel do not recognize same-sex marriage, and thus do not consider whether "dissolution" of the marriage is required for the parties to be able to remarry in Israel, which means marry in a religious ceremony to a partner of the opposite sex.

[56]Section 6 of the Matters of Dissolution of Marriage (Jurisdiction in Special Cases) Law.

[57]Section 5(c) of the Matters of Dissolution of Marriage (Jurisdiction in Special Cases) Law.

following: (a) the substantive law of the common domicile of the spouses; (b) the substantive law of the last common domicile of the spouses; (c) the substantive law of the common state of citizenship of the spouses; (d) the substantive law of the state where the marriage took place.

The Law provides that a court cannot apply any of the aforementioned laws if it applies different laws to the spouses. Such is the case if the spouses are Israeli citizens or domiciled in Israel and they belong to different religions, since the Israeli law applies the relevant personal law to each of them. Indeed, in most cases where the Law is applied the only relevant option is the substantive law of the state where the marriage took place. Furthermore, the Law does not enable the application of a law if the couple cannot obtain a divorce under its provisions.[58]

The question of dissolving the same-sex marital bond is more complicated when both parties belong to the same recognized religion. Allegedly, the relevant religious court has jurisdiction over divorce proceedings between the spouses, as matters of marriage and divorce are under the exclusive jurisdiction of the religious courts in Israel.[59] In the past, some raised doubts regarding the jurisdiction of the rabbinical courts in dissolving civil marriages entered into abroad between Jewish spouses.[60]

However, in *A v. The Regional Rabbinical Court Tel Aviv* the Supreme Court held that the rabbinical court has jurisdiction over dissolution of marriage between two Jewish individuals, even if they married in a civil ceremony.[61] The rabbinical

---

[58] *Ibid.*, section 5(c).

[59] See *supra* note 8 and accompanying text.

[60] The doubts stemmed from the wordings of section 1 of the Rabbinical Courts Jurisdiction Law that determines the jurisdiction of the rabbinical courts over matters of marriage and divorce. The section states: "Matters of marriage and divorce of Jews *in Israel*, being nationals or residents of the State shall be under the exclusive jurisdiction of rabbinical courts". [emphasis added – A.B.P.]. Rabbinical Courts Jurisdiction (Marriage and Divorce) Law-1953, 7 L.S.I 139. The doubts concerned the words "in Israel" – whether they refer only to the Jews that are supposed to be in Israel or whether they relate to matters of marriage and divorce, and the Jews. Even if the latter approach is accepted, once the "matters of divorce" are in Israel, rabbinical courts have jurisdiction, regardless of whether the marriage took place. Nonetheless, this interpretation may affect the rabbinical court's jurisdiction in case it does not recognize the validity of the civil marriage since in such a case no "divorce" is taking place in Israel and the matter of marriage was not done in Israel as well. The Supreme Court did not resolve the interpretation of section 1 of the Rabbinical Courts Jurisdiction Law and the words "in Israel". See HCJ 3/73 *Cahanoff v. the Rabbinical Court*, 29(1) P.D. 449 (1974); HCJ 573/77 *Zak v. the Rabbinical Court*, 32(1) P.D. 281 (1977); Shava, *supra* note 44 at 66–67.

[61] The Court's judgment endorsed the High Rabbinical Court's judgment in this matter and its position on civil marriage. The High Rabbinical Court stated that the Jewish law, the Halakha, contains rules that apply to non-Jews Noahides and they also refer to marriage and divorce. Noahides or *B'nei Noach*, Children of Noah in Hebrew. Noahide Laws refer to the seven laws of Noah, given by God to all mankind. Although Jewish Law does not recognize a civil ceremony of marriage as creating a valid Jewish marital bond, the Noahide rules recognize civil marriage at least for limited purposes, even if it was conducted between a Jewish couple, a man and a woman. Noahide rules enable a rabbinical court to grant a divorce which is different from the Jewish divorce – the Get, to Jewish couples who were married civilly. The divorce regime for

court can either order that a Jewish divorce, a *get*, is required if it finds that the marriage ceremony created a valid Jewish marriage, or as a stringency, or dissolve the marriage by granting a civil divorce. The Supreme Court clarified, nonetheless, that rabbinical courts have jurisdiction only in granting the divorce itself for couples who were married civilly.[62] Civil family courts reserve exclusive jurisdiction over the monetary aspects of civil marital dissolution.

Supposedly, based on *A v. The Regional Rabbinical Court Tel Aviv,* dissolution of a marital bond between same-sex couples who both belong to the same recognized religious community is under the jurisdiction of the relevant religious court. If this is the case, then the relevant religious court will most probably issue a judgment stating the parties are not married and hence their registration should be changed from married to single, as the recognized religious courts in Israel do not recognize same-sex marriage. On one hand, some may argue that such a ruling is not problematic, as the *Ben-Ari* case left open the question whether Israeli law recognizes the legal concept of same-sex marriage. On the other hand, precisely because the relevant religious courts do not recognize the concept of same-sex marriage, but define marriage as a bond between a man and a woman, there are grounds to assume that the Supreme Court will rule that jurisdiction over dissolution of same-sex marriages lies with the civil family courts. Prior precedents of the Supreme Court denied jurisdiction from religious courts when the relevant religious law did not recognize the legal concept or legal format that was under consideration.[63] In fact in *A v. The Regional Rabbinical Court Tel Aviv,* jurisdiction to dissolve a civil marriage between a Jewish couple was granted to the rabbinical courts only after the High Rabbinical Court stated that it recognizes, albeit limitedly, civil marriage between a Jewish man and a Jewish woman.[64] As religious communities will not recognize same sex marriages, rabbinical, and other recognized religious courts, will most probably not have jurisdiction to dissolve same-sex marriages. Civil family courts, which have residual jurisdiction in family matters, will probably exercise jurisdiction over these matters.[65]

Noahide marriages is a no-fault regime, and the ground for the judgment of divorce is a finding that the marriage was irretrievably broken.

[62]Some rabbinical courts challenge this ruling, especially in cases where they find that a Jewish divorce is required. *See e.g.*, Case No. 764411/1 (rabbinical court, Netanya, 3 October 2010).

[63]See e.g., CA 3077/90 *Plonit v. Plonit*, 49(2) P.D. 578 (1995); Ruth Halperin-Kaddari, Towards Concluding Civil Family Law – Israel Style, 17 Mehkarei Mishpat 105, 154 (2001).

[64]Paragraph 29 to Justice Barak's judgment in HCJ 2232/03 *Plonit v. The Regional Rabbinical Court Tel Aviv*, 61(3) P.D. 496 (2006).

[65]Additional reason provided by the Court for deciding that jurisdiction to dissolve a civil marriage between a Jewish man and a Jewish woman lies with the rabbinical courts is also irrelevant regarding same-sex couples. As noted, even a civil marriage ceremony between a Jewish man and a Jewish woman might require a Jewish divorce at least as stringency. Whether or not this is the case can only be done on a case-by-case basis. Since dissolution of the marriage needs to be effective, in the sense that the parties be eligible to remarry in Israel that is, in a religious ceremony, a decision must be made if a *get* is required, and this can only be done by a rabbinical court. Since the religious courts do not recognize the concept of same-sex marriage and see them as void, no religious dissolution might be required.

On August 30, 2012, the first case of same-sex marriage dissolution reached the Israeli court system. The splitting couple, Uzi Even and Amit Kama, both Jewish, first submitted their dissolution application to the rabbinical court.[66] The rabbinical court however, refused to open a file for the case and therefore, at the beginning of September, the couple submitted an application to the civil family court.[67] On November 21, 2012 the family court issued a groundbreaking decision holding that the civil family courts have jurisdiction over dissolution of same-sex divorces in Israel, even when both spouses belong to the same recognized religion. The family court also declared the dissolution of the marriage and based on its decision the parties were registered as divorced in the Population Registry. [68]

6.4 Reputed Spouses

Until 2010 Israeli law provided no establishment of registered civil union. On March 2010, the Israeli Knesset, passed the Covenant Partnership Law. The act, however, provides a very limited option of civil partnership only for Israeli opposite-sex couples in cases where both partners do not belong to a recognized religious community.[69] Until Israel enacted the Covenant Partnership Law, there was no entry in the population registry for civil unions or similar statuses, so same-sex civil unions entered into abroad could not be registered in the population registry. Following the enactment of the Covenant Partnership Law, Israel created a designated entry in the population registry to register covenant partnerships entered into under the law. Yet, it is highly questionable whether the population registry can register same-sex civil unions entered into abroad given the narrow scope of covenant partnerships under the law.

However, as explained in details below, under Israeli law, cohabitants, referred to as "reputed spouses," enjoy most of the rights and benefits and are subject to the obligations as married couples. Consequently, it is possible to assume that registered civil unions entered into abroad will be subject to the rules that apply to reputed spouses. The fact that the couple registered as a civil union will make it easier for them to prove that they fulfill the requirements of "reputed spouses" for purposes of Israeli law.

---

[66]Gay couple turns to rabbis for divorce, Ynet News, available at http://www.ynetnews.com/articles/0,7340,L-4276046,00.html. Joint Application for Divorce by Consent, submitted to the Tel-Aviv rabbinical court [on file with author].

[67]Application for a Declaratory Judgment submitted to the family court in Ramat-Gan [on file with author]. I thank Adv. Judith Meisels, who represents Uzi Even and Amit Kama, for providing me with the court documents.

[68]FamC 11264-09-12 *Plaintiffs v. Ministry of the Interior* (Nov. 21, 2012) (unpublished officially).

[69]Partnership Covenant for the Religionless Law, 2010.

6.4.1 Reputed Spouses Under Israeli Law in General

Despite the lack of a general formal framework for recognizing domestic partnership outside the marital framework, unmarried cohabitants, known under Israeli law as "reputed spouses,"[70] enjoy most of the rights and benefits and are under most of the obligations as married couples. Israeli legislature originally legally recognized "reputed spouses" beginning in the early 1950s, focusing mainly on social rights.[71] Where Israeli legislation is silent, the Israeli Supreme Court continues the trend of equalization, expanding the list of rights, benefits, and obligations accorded to non-married cohabitants to match those of married couples.[72] The extensive legal recognition accorded to unmarried cohabitants under Israeli law is commonly explained as the civil system's reaction to the strict religiously based restrictions on marriage.[73]

Until the case of *Lindorn v. Karnit*, the dominant view held that statutes that do not expressly refer to cohabitants, apply only to married couples. In *Lindorn*, however, the Supreme Court interpreted the term "partner" in the New Version of the Civil Wrongs Ordinance (New Version) and the Road Accident Victims Compensation Law, to include reputed spouses, despite the absence of an express reference to reputed spouses in these statutes. Nonetheless, the Supreme Court made clear that its decision in *Lindorn* did not mean that all acts of legislation that apply to married couples apply to reputed spouses as well. Rather, that decision is made on a case-by-case basis for each and every act that does not expressly refer to reputed spouses. Likewise, the Court should separately examine each right and obligation of married spouses that case law created to determine whether it applies to unmarried cohabitants. Despite these statements of a "case-by-case" evaluation, the accumulated case law suggests that courts afford reputed spouses the vast majority of rights, benefits, and obligations as married couples under Israeli law.[74]

---

[70]The literal translation is "known in the public as spouses."

[71]Rosen-Zvi, *supra* note 1 at 98; Menashe Shava, *The Property Rights of Spouses Cohabiting Without Marriage in Israel – A Comparative Commentary*, 13 Ga. J. Int'l & Comp. L. 465, 468 (1983).

[72]*See e.g.*, C.A. 52/80 *Shachar v. Friedman* P.D. 38(1) 443 (1984) (holding that the then existing presumption of community property applied to married couples should be applied to unmarried cohabitants as well); C.A. 2000/97 *Lindorn v. Karnit*, 55(1) P.D. 12 (1999).

[73]However, by equating the legal status of unmarried cohabitants to that of married couples, the Israeli system ignores the fact that not all the unmarried cohabitants in Israel were barred from marrying under the religious laws of marriage in Israel, or were merely reluctant to form the religious institution of marriage. Israeli law failed to realize that some of these couples chose not to get married, as they rejected the institution of marriage. See e.g., Shahar Lifshitz, *The External Rights Of Cohabiting Couples In Israel*, 37 Isr. L. Rev. 346 (2003–2004).

[74]The Court continued down this path in CA 2622/01 *Manager of Land Betterment Tax v. Levanon*, 37(5) P.D. 309 (2003), holding that tax exemptions for the transfer without remuneration of an asset other than a residential apartment from an individual to his partner should be applied to cohabiting and married couples equally. See also Lifshitz, *Id.*

A very open definition of reputed spouses and flexible criteria accompanied the extensive recognition of the rights, benefits, and obligations of reputed spouses that make it easier for couples to be considered reputed spouses. The essential criteria required by Israeli law are joint cohabitation and the running of a common household. Nonetheless, there is no formal requirement that couples share a common registered address, and in some cases couples are recognized as reputed spouses while not living together in the same residential unit.[75] Additionally, most of the laws applicable to reputed spouses do not stipulate a minimum period of time for them to be recognized as such, and when they do, a relatively short time period is required which is usually 1 year.[76] When legislation does not stipulate a minimum period, courts have sometimes recognized couples as reputed spouses within a very short period of time. Lastly, monogamy is not necessarily required and in several cases the Court recognized couples as reputed spouses, despite additional intimate relations.

6.4.2 *Same-Sex Couples as Reputed Spouses*

In recent years, Israeli case law applied many of the rights, benefits, and obligations of reputed spouses to same-sex couples. However, the Israeli Supreme Court refused to declare that the definition of reputed spouses under Israeli law includes same-sex couples.[77] Instead, each act of legislation that refers to reputed spouses, whether expressly or by way of interpretation, and each right, benefit, and obligation that is accorded to reputed spouses by case-law, is examined separately, on a case-by-case basis, to determine if it applies to same-sex couples. Next, this section addresses specific contexts in which the status of same-sex couples as reputed spouses was addressed under Israeli law.

6.4.2.1 The Family Court

Israel established the family court system between 1995 and 1997 in an attempt to centralize all civil family matters under one roof.[78] The Family Court Law adopts a broad definition of "family members" that includes "reputed spouses."

[75]Lifshitz, *Ibid.*, pp. 409. LCA 3497/09 *Ploni v. Plonit* [unpublished].

[76]Lifshitz, *Ibid.*, pp. 407–408.

[77]HCJ 721/94 *El-Al Israel Airlines Ltd v. Danielowitz* 48(5) P.D. 749 (1994). Official translation can be found on the Israeli Supreme Court's web-site: http://elyon1.court.gov.il/files_eng/94/210/007/Z01/94007210.z01.htm

[78]The Family Courts Law, 1995, S.H. 393. Prior to the establishment of the family court system the District Court exercised jurisdiction over civil family matters.

Nonetheless, family court judges differ on whether the law considers same-sex couples as "reputed spouses" and fall under the jurisdiction of the family court.[79]

These conflicting decisions have not yet been resolved, *inter alia*, due to the paucity of precedents in family matters since the establishment of the Family Court. The family courts' jurisdiction is at the lowest magistrate court level. Individuals have a right to bring appeals on a family court decision to the District Court. A subsequent appeal to the Supreme Court requires permission, which is rarely given.[80]

6.4.2.2 Family Violence

The 1991 Prevention of Violence in Family Law,[81] provides "protective injunctions" aimed to provide immediate protection to family members who suffer from family violence. The Law, phrased in gender-neutral language, adopts a broad definition of "family members" and refers specifically to reputed spouses. Here, again, conflicting decisions exist in family court as to whether the law considers same-sex couples as reputed spouses for purposes of the Prevention of Violence in the Family Law.[82]

6.4.2.3 Family Name

Following Supreme Court cases holding that individuals have the right to change their family names to that of their reputed spouses,[83] the legislature amended Israeli Names Law in 1996 to incorporate this ruling. The rules regarding reputed spouses' surnames applied to same-sex couples who can today change or join their surnames so that they share the same surname.[84]

---

[79]For cases holding same-sex couples as reputed spouses for purposes of the Family Court Law see e.g., FC (Tel-Aviv) 6960/03 *K.Z. v. State of Israel* (2004); FC 3140/03 (Tel-Aviv) *In the matter of R.A. & L.M.F* (2004); FC (Beer-Sheva) 8510/01 *In the matter of A & G* (2002). For cases refusing to recognize same-sex couples as reputed spouses for purposes of the Family Court Law see e.g., FamC (Tel-Aviv) 16610/04 *A v. Attorney-General* (2005).

[80]Prior to the establishment of the Family Court, civil family matters were under the jurisdiction of the District Court, so that an appeal to the Supreme Court was a matter of right.

[81]The Prevention of Family Violence Law, 1991, S.H. 138.

[82]*Cf.* FamC (Haifa) 32520/97, *Plonit v. Almonit* (1997) (holding that the Prevention of Family Violence Law applies to same-sex couples) and FamC (Ramat-Gan) 1630/08 *Ploni v. Almoni* (2008) (holding that same-sex couples are not to be considered as reputed spouses for purposes of the Prevention of Family Violence Law).

[83]HCJ 693/91 *Efrat v. Commissioner of the Population Registry*, 47(1) PD 749 (1993); HCJ 6086/94 *Nizri v. Commissioner of the Population Registry* 49(5) PD 693 (1996).

[84]Talia Einhorn, *Same-Sex Family Unions in Israeli Law*, 4 Utrecht L. Rev. (2008), pp. 222, 227.

6.4.2.4 Succession

Section 55 of the Succession Law grants reputed spouses rights of inheritance similar to spouses in cases of intestate death.[85] It should also be noted that the right of reputed spouses to inherit is the only right that is conditioned on both parties not being formally married to others. Other rights of reputed spouses are given to them even if one of them, or both, is formally married to another. This legal situation was explained by the difficulties in obtaining divorce in Israel.[86]

A question may arise as to whether same-sex couples who married abroad – can inherit under section 11 as "spouses" or under section 55 as "reputed spouses." Although, the inheritance rights provided under each of these sections are similar, in *Ploni v. Plonit* Justice Barak held that for purposes of the Inheritance Law, couples who were married abroad shall inherit under section 11 as spouses, even if their status as "married" is not considered valid for all purposes under Israeli law.[87] It is an open question whether this ruling applies to same-sex couples, since in their case it is supposedly not only the *validity* of the marriage that was left open, but the very definition of "marriage" under Israeli law, and whether a legal framework of same-sex marriage is recognized in Israel.

In a 2004 groundbreaking case, the District Court in Nazareth applied section 55 to same-sex couples, despite the wording of the section that refers to "*a man and a woman* who lived in a joint household but were not married to each other."[88] Judge Maman used purposive interpretation, holding that section 55's purpose was to guarantee the inheritance rights of couples who could not marry and that the law should take contemporary norms into consideration. Judge De-Leo Levi added that any other interpretation of section 55 would be discriminatory and contradict Israel's Basic Laws and fundamental principles.

While this case is not Supreme Court precedent,[89] the State decided not to ask for leave to appeal the district court's decision. Furthermore, following this decision, the Attorney General stated: "The Attorney General's principled position is that one has to distinguish, for the purpose of the recognition of same-sex couples, between monetary issues and other practical arrangements, where the attitude should be pragmatic and flexible, in the spirit of the times and the changing reality, and

---

[85]The Succession Law, 1965, 19 L.S.I. 58.

[86]See *e.g.* Blecher-Prigat & Shmueli, *supra* note 25, pp. 298–299. In case of inheritance, once there is a formal spouse, that spouse inherits, even if the spouses are separated and have other partners. Nevertheless, on August 2012, Judge Shifra Glick from the Tel-Aviv family court denied a wife's claim to inherit after the spouses were separated for over 40 years. Estate File 108091/08 *Estate of Y.A. v. R.A* (Aug. 11, 2012) (unpublished officially).

[87]F.A. 9607/03, *Ploni v. Plonit*, 61(3) P.D.726 (2006).

[88]CA (Nazareth) 3245/03 *Anonymous v. The Custodian Gen.* (2004) [emphasis added – A.B.P].

[89]According to Israeli law, a precedent by the Supreme court binds all the lower courts, although it does not bind the Supreme Court itself. A precedent set by the District Court instructs and directs the lower jurisdictions family courts, in this case, but they can deviate from it if they present good reasoning for doing so.

between issues of the creation of new statutory personal status, which requires a more careful approach, and which is usually in the domain of the legislature."[90] Nevertheless, given that a District Court's decision does not bind lower courts, in October 2010 a family court judge in Be'er Sheva, rejected the Nazareth court decision and refused to apply the Inheritance Law rules regarding reputed spouses to same-sex couples.[91] The deceased's sister and alleged partner submitted an appeal to the Be-er Sheva district court, however, the parties eventually settled outside the court.[92]

6.4.2.5 Social Rights

Courts recognized same-sex couples as reputed spouses for a wide range of social rights under Israeli law: pension rights under the National Insurance Law,[93] pension rights under the Permanent Service in the Israel Defense Forces Pension Law,[94] bereavement pension from Mivtachim Fund,[95] and more. The accumulated case law suggests that for social rights purposes, same-sex couples are considered reputed spouses. In this regard, Israeli law extends social rights to reputed spouses, as it does to spouses.

6.5 Consequences of Relationships: Marriage and Cohabitation

6.5.1 Property Relations

Secular law governs property relations between spouses or cohabitants. The Spouse (Property Relations) Law, applies to spouses married after January 1st 1974, and adopts a regime of deferred community of property, according to which a separation of property exists during marriage, and following separation or death, a resource-balancing arrangement applies. Property relations among spouses married prior to

---

[90]Translation is taken from International Gay and Lesbian Human Rights Commission asylum Documentation Program – Status of Sexual Minorities: Israel: http://209.85.229.132/search?q=cache:QVI-_4RS3JoJ:www.asylumlaw.org/docs/sexualminorities/Israel%2520CU%2520SO.pdf+3245/03+%22attorney+general%22+%22not+to+appeal%22&cd=1&hl=iw&ct=clnk&gl=il

[91]Estate File (Be'er Sheva) 1320/08 *Ploni v. Plonit* (Aug. 23, 2010) (unpublished officially).

[92]Information provided by Adv. Dan Yakir, Chief Legal Counsel Attorney for the Association for Legal Rights in Israel (ACRI). ACRI asked to file amicus brief to the appeal proceedings in the Be-er Sheva District Court.

[93]NI (TA) 3536/04 *Raz v. National Insurance Institute*, (Feb. 28, 2005) (unpublished officially).

[94]MA (TA) 369/94 *Steiner v. IDF* (1996).

[95]LabC (TA) 3816/01 Levy v. Mivtahim.

1974 and among reputed spouses are governed in Israel by the presumption of co-ownership, an immediate community of property regime created by case law. According to this presumption, the court considers property accumulated during the time of marriage as joint property regardless of formal registration of this property.[96]

The Presumption of Community Property will probably apply to unmarried same-sex couples. A question may arise as to whether the Presumption of Community Property applies to same sex couple married in a civil ceremony abroad, or the Spouse (Property Relations) Law, which applies to spouses who married after January 1st 1974.[97]

6.5.2 *Maintenance Obligations*

According to the Family Law Amendment (Maintenance) Law,[98] the parties' religious laws govern spousal maintenance issues. Nonetheless, in *A v. B*,[99] the Supreme Court held that the Maintenance Law does not apply to couples married in a civil ceremony abroad, and to reputed spouses. Civil-contractual principles and the principle of good faith govern maintenance obligations among the latter couples. The Court emphasized that this contractual obligation does not follow from the marital bond but rather from the actual relationship between the parties, and therefore applies to reputed spouses as well. Nonetheless, having a civil marriage ceremony relieves a couple from having to prove their commitment for purposes of financial support obligations, whereas unmarried cohabitants should prove that they have passed the trial phase in their relationship and can be considered reputed spouses for this purpose.[100]

---

[96]As noted above, since religious law is often patriarchal in a way incompatible with modern liberal values, Israeli civil court judges have sought jurisdiction over matters relating to family life and have attempted to subject these matters to civil secular laws. One method of doing so is by characterizing various matters as civil, and giving a narrow interpretation to personal status matters. For example in developing the presumption of community property the Supreme Court characterized property relations as exogenous to "matters of marriage" over which religious laws would hold sway, and instead as questions of civil property, the provenance of secular laws. The presumption of community property was originally developed based on contractual principles according to which spouses implicitly consented to jointly own property accumulated during their marriage. Framing the issue in terms of an implied contract assisted the court in portraying the issue as a civil, rather than a personal status matter. Also, since the community property presumption was characterized as exogenous to "matters of marriage" and based on "implied contract" it was easy to apply it to unmarried cohabitants as well. See C.A. 52/80 *Shachar v. Friedman* P.D. 38(1) 443 (1984).

[97]The Spouses (Property Relations) Law, 5733–1973, 27 LSI 313 (1972–1973) (hereinafter: "The Spouses Property Relations Law").

[98]The Family Law Amendment (Maintenance) Law, 1959, 13 L.S.I. 73 (hereinafter: "the Maintenance Law").

[99]LCA 8256/99 *Plonit v. Ploni*,. 58(2) P.D 213 (2004).

[100]*Ibid.*, p. 238.

Following *A v. B*, several family courts awarded temporary rehabilitative maintenance to reputed spouses following separation. To date, there has been no reported case where civil-contractual maintenance was awarded to same-sex partners. Nonetheless, the concept of civil-contractual maintenance obligation is a novel concept within Israeli law, and in general it has been applied to few cases. There is good reason to believe that civil-contractual maintenance shall apply to same-sex couples as well, as in the context of economic rights, the rights of same-sex couples equate those of heterosexual couples.[101]

6.6 Parenthood in Same-Sex Families

6.6.1 Becoming Parents by Adoption

The Israeli Adoption Law addressing the capacity to adopt states in section 3 that "Adoption may only be done by a man and his wife together."[102] Nonetheless, in 2008 following the Supreme Court's *Yaros-Hakak* case[103] allowing second-parent adoption, the Attorney General issued guidelines interpreting the Adoption Law to allow reputed spouses, including same-sex couples, to adopt children.[104] The Attorney General clarified in his guidelines that he refers merely to the capacity to adopt, and that a decision regarding the placement of a particular child should consider the child's best interest. Therefore, in practice, and given the scarcity of children placed for adoption, same-sex couples cannot adopt children unrelated to either of them, as the Welfare Services give preference to heterosexual married couples as the best familial framework for children. The Attorney General's guidelines recognizing the capacity of same-sex couples to adopt will likely apply mainly to cases such as that of Amit Kama and Uzi Even, a couple that took into their home, a child who was driven out of his own home after coming out of the closet.[105]

In principle, same-sex Israeli couples can adopt children from abroad.[106] Unlike internal adoption, inter-country adoptions are organized by private adoption agencies licensed by the State. However, adoptions from abroad have to satisfy the conditions for adoption under the law of the child's country of origin. Thus, it

[101] HCJ 3045/05 *Ben-Ari v. Ministry of the Interior*, 61(3) P.D 537 (2006).

[102] Adoption of Children Law, 1981, S.H. 293 [hereinafter: Adoption Law].

[103] CA 10280/01, Yaros-Hakak v. Atty. Gen., P.D. 59(5) 64 (2005). See discussion of this case in Section 6.B.

[104] *Guidelines of the Attorney General regarding Adoption by Same-Sex Couples* [Hebrew]: http://www.justice.gov.il/MOJHeb/News/imuz.htm

[105] *Court Grants Gay Couple Right to Adopt 30-Year-Old Foster Son*: http://www.haaretz.com/hasen/spages/1070060.html

[106] Adoption of Children Law, 1981, 35 L.S.I.360.

will only be possible for same-sex couples to adopt children from countries that allow same-sex adoptions. An adoption order given abroad to a same-sex couple will enable registration of both parties as parents in the population registry in Israel.[107]

6.6.2 Becoming Parents Through Reproductive Technologies

Israeli national health insurance fully subsidizes fertility treatments in Israel. In Vitz v. Minister of Health the Supreme Court, with the state's consent, abolished provisions of subordinate legislation, which required unmarried women and lesbians to undergo a psychiatric test, a requirement not imposed on married women, as a condition for receiving artificial insemination and in-vitro fertilization services.[108] Today, lesbian couples have access to sperm donation, egg donation, IUI and IVF treatments similar to married and single women.

Surrogacy, however, is limited to heterosexual couples married or reputed spouses, according to the Surrogate Motherhood Agreements (Approval of Agreement and Status of Newborn) Law, hereinafter "the Surrogacy Law."[109] In 2001, the first attempt to challenge this limitation in the Supreme Court failed.[110] In 2010, a same-sex couple brought an additional challenge to this limitation. A gay couple, Yoav Arad Pinkas and Itay Pinkas, petitioned the Supreme Court sitting as a High Court for Justice, and challenged the constitutionality of the Surrogacy Law. Following the petition, the Health Ministry appointed a public committee tasked with examining the surrogacy law and its limitations, as well as other issues regarding fertility treatments in Israel. In May 2012, the committee published its recommendations and advised that single men and single women, with a medical problem, be allowed to have children using surrogate mothers. The committee's recommendation, however, applies only to altruistic surrogacy and not to paid surrogacy services when it concerns single men.

In 2006, the Health Ministry permitted a woman to be impregnated with an egg of her female partner fertilized in vitro by sperm from an anonymous donor.[111] The couple underwent this procedure following a medical reason that necessitated fertility treatments. Following this case, several lesbian couples became joint parents using this procedure. Although in all cases the Health Ministry required a showing of a medical reason for fertility treatments, in practice, there was no in-depth inquiry

---

[107] See discussion in part 6.B. *infra*.

[108] HCJ 2078/96 *Vitz v. Minister of Health* (unpublished officially).

[109] 1996, S.H. 1577, 176.

[110] HCJ 2458/01, *New Family v. Approvals Comm. for Surrogate Motherhood Agreements, Ministry of Health*, 57(1) P.D. 419 (2002).

[111] Ruth Zafran, *More Than One Mother: Determining Maternity for the Biological Child of a Female Same-Sex Couple–The Israeli View*, 9 Geo. J. Gender & L. 115 (2008).

as to whether there was truly a fertility problem.[112] In 2009, the Attorney General instructed the Health Ministry to allow lesbian couples to use this procedure.[113] However, since the enactment of the Egg Donation Law on June 2010, the Health Ministry perceives this procedure as impermissible, since the Egg Donation Law generally requires, anonymous donations.[114] Although a special committee may permit exceptions to the anonymity requirement, the committee has yet to grant approval to a lesbian couple who wish to have a child together in a manner that was possible prior to the enactment of the Egg Donation Law.[115]

In September 2013 an extended panel of the Supreme Court, sitting as a High Court of Justice, denied an appeal submitted by a lesbian couple asking to enable one of them to be impregnated with the egg of her partner without a medical reason justifying fertility treatments. The Court held that under existing laws regarding egg donation and surrogacy such a procedure is illegal in Israel.[116]

6.6.3 Being Legally Recognized as Co-parents

The 2000 case of *Brenner-Kaddish* concerned two Israeli citizens who resided in Los Angeles for 2 years. While in Los Angeles, one of the women gave birth to a child through artificial insemination of a donated sperm. Through adoption by a California court, the Court recognized her partner as the child's mother. Upon their return to Israel, the women asked the State to list them both as mothers in the population registry. The Ministry of Interior denied the request arguing that the listing would be "erroneous on its face" invoking the *Funk-Schlezinger* exception, and technically impossible. The women appealed to the Supreme Court, and the Court by a majority decision granted the petition and ordered the registration of both women as the child's mothers based on the Californian adoption decree. The Court, however, explicitly avoided any substantive evaluation of dual motherhood or co-parent adoption. The State submitted a motion for further hearing of this case,[117]

---

[112]Information provided by Adv. Na'ama Zoref, who represented the couple, as well as other couples who underwent this procedure. Since, there was a medical justification for fertility treatments, the National Health Insurance also covered theses treatments, although, according to Adv. Zoref, it required the intervention of the legal advisor of the Health Ministry to get the funding.

[113]http://www.ynet.co.il/articles/0,7340,L-3812367,00.html [Hebrew].

[114]*Ibid.* Egg Donation Law, 2010, section 39.

[115]Even in a case where there was a clear need for fertility treatments, the Health Ministry did not approve a procedure in which one partner provides the egg and the other carries the pregnancy.

[116]HCJ 5771/12 *Moshe v. Approvals Comm. for Surrogate Motherhood Agreements* (Sept 11, 2013).

[117]A further hearing is a rather unique Israeli invention. Under British Mandatory rule, rulings of the local Supreme Court could be appealed to the Privy Council in London, England. This option was obviously eliminated upon the establishment of the State of Israel and its independent

but eventually withdrew its request. In its assent to withdraw the application for further hearing, the State clarified that the judgment of the Court applies only to cases similar to the *Brenner-Kaddish* case. Furthermore, it understood the original judgment as applying only to the question of registration in the population registry, which is understood as merely collecting statistical information and has no bearing on questions of validity of status.[118]

In 2005, the Supreme Court handed down a far more significant decision in the *Yaros-Hakak* case, where the Israeli Supreme Court interpreted the Israeli Adoption Law as enabling second parent adoption. The case concerned two women, Tal and Avital Yaros-Hakak, who shared a long-term relationship. The women together raised three children, born through anonymous sperm donations two of them carried by one woman, and the third by the other woman. The women sought official adoption to anchor the relationship of each of them to the children conceived by her partner. The family court initially denied their petition, and the District Court denied an appeal by a majority. The Supreme Court recognized the possibility of a co-parent adoption in a same-sex family and thus the possibility of dual motherhood or fatherhood following such an adoption. The Court remanded the case to the court of first instance to examine whether adoption would serve the children's best interest. The family court, to which the Court remanded the case, issued an adoption decree.

Despite the significance of the *Yaros-Hakak* decision, the law still requires the adoption process to establish dual motherhood to be recognized. Furthermore, the law requires non-biological co-mothers to adopt their own children in order to be legally recognized as their parents. A lesbian couple that split the gestational and genetic motherhood between them brought the first challenge to this state of affairs.[119] Following the birth of their son, both women asked to be registered as the child's mothers, but were refused. The State only recognized the birth mother as the child's legal mother. The women turned to the family court to have their dual motherhood recognized without the adoption procedure. The Attorney General objected to the petition, arguing that adoption was the only way both women could achieve legal recognition as mothers. In March 2012, Judge Alysa Miller from the Ramat Gan family court held that adoption was an inappropriate procedure to recognize the dual motherhood in this case, and stated that there was no reason

judicature. In a further hearing, a panel of five or more Supreme Court judges hears a matter on which the Supreme Court has already ruled in a panel of three or more judges. In a way, the further hearing was established as a substitute for the additional option of appeal to the Privy Council. Chanan Goldschmidt, Further Hearing: Theoretical and Empirical Aspects, 35 Isr. L. Rev. 320, 328–329 (2001). A petition to have a further hearing is made by a litigant, and the Chief Justice or a judge empowered by a Chief Justice decides whether to accept the petition. There is no vested right to a further hearing, and it should only be granted when "the Supreme Court makes a ruling inconsistent with a previous ruling of the Supreme Court or where the importance, difficulty, or novelty of a ruling made by the Supreme Court justifies, in their view, such a further hearing." See Sec. 30 of the Courts Law [Consolidated Version] 1984, 38 L.S.I. 271.

[118]FH 4252/00 *Interior Minister v. Brenner Kaddish* (2008).

[119]FamC (Tel Aviv) 60320–07 *T.Z. v. Attorney General* (March 4, 2012) (unpublished officially).

for a genetic mother to adopt her son.[120] Nonetheless, Judge Miller held that determination of legal motherhood in such cases cannot be automatic but requires a legal procedure. She turned to the procedure determined in the Surrogacy Law for establishing the legal parental status of the intended parents, who are usually the genetic parents. Though this procedure still necessitates a welfare officer's report, it is a relatively quick and effective mechanism to establish legal parenthood, which can be done immediately following birth.[121]

6.7 Conclusions

Israeli law has come a long way since abolishing the criminal prohibition against male homosexual intercourse in 1988. Same-sex couples are recognized as reputed spouses for a wide range of purposes under Israeli law, and they enjoy the vast majority of rights and benefits that heterosexual married couples enjoy; their marriages celebrated abroad are registered in the population registry, and mainly through adoption their joint parenthood is also recognized. The Israeli Supreme Court played a significant role in advancing the recognition of same-sex familial relationships. In some respects, same-sex couples in Israel benefitted from the traditional legal background of family law in Israel, against which their plight for recognition of their familial relationship is shared by numerous heterosexual couples who are denied recognition by religious family laws.

This is not to suggest that nothing else can be done to advance the legal status of same-sex couples under Israeli law. The Supreme Court, having adopted a pragmatic approach and advance through a case-by-case solution, has not guaranteed same-sex families certainty and stability. The absence of precedence on many significant issues also leaves same-sex couples vulnerable to the discretion of individual family law judges and their world view.

[120]The Surrogate Motherhood Agreements (Approval of Agreement and Status of Newborn) Law, 1996, S.H. 176 [hereinafter Surrogacy Law] statute legalizes only gestational (full) surrogacy meaning that the egg to be used cannot be that of the surrogate mother. The egg can be either the egg of the intended mother or the egg of a donor. The sperm to be used must, however, be the sperm of the intended father. The basic premise of the Surrogacy Law is that the intended parents are the legal parents of the ensuing child. To formalize this principle, the intended parents must apply for a "parenthood order" within a week of the child's birth. The Surrogacy Law instructs the court to grant the order unless it is persuaded that such an order would be contrary to the best interests of the child. The parenthood order recognizes the intended parents as the child's parents in all respects.

[121]Ruth Zafran, *More Than One Mother: Determining Maternity for the Biological Child of a Female Same-sex Couple - the Israeli View*, 9 Geo. J. Gender & L., (2008), 115, 159.

Bibliography

Books

1. Elon, Menachem. 1975. *The principles of Jewish Law*. Jerusalem: Keter Publishing House.
2. Halperin-Kaddari, Ruth. 2004. *Women in Israel: A state of their own*. Philadelphia: University of Pennsylvania Press.
3. Rubinstein, Amnon, and Barak Medina. 1997. *The constitutional law of the State of Israel*, vol. I, 5th ed. (Hebrew).[100]

Articles

4. Barak-Erez, Daphna. 1995. From an unwritten to a written constitution: The Israeli challenge in American perspective. *Columbia Human Rights Law Review* 26: 309.
5. Blecher-Prigat, Ayelet, and Benjamin Shmueli. 2009. The interplay between tort law and religious family law: The Israeli case. *Arizona Journal of International and Comparative Law* 26: 279.
6. Blecher-Prigat, Ayelet. 2014. A basic right to marry: Israeli style. *47 Israel Law Review* 433.
7. Dorner, Dalia. 2003. *Between equality and human dignity*, Shamgar Book 9 (Articles, vol. 1).
8. Dotan, Yoav. 2005. The spillover effect of bills of rights: A comparative assessment of the impact of bills of rights in Canada and Israel. *American Journal of Comparative Law* 53: 293.
9. Einhorn, Talia. 2008. Same-sex family unions in Israeli law. *Utrecht Law Review* 4: 222.
10. Goldschmidt, Chanan. 2001. Further hearing: Theoretical and empirical aspects. *Israel Law Review* 35: 320.
11. Halperin-Kaddari, Ruth. 2001. Towards concluding civil family law – Israel style. *Mehkarei Mishpat* 17: 105.
12. Karp, Yehudit. 1992. Basic law: Human dignity and freedom — A biography of power struggles. *Mishpat Umimshal (Law and Government)* 1: 323 (Hebrew).
13. Karp, Yehudit. 1995. Several questions on human dignity under the basic law: Human dignity and liberty. *Hebrew University Law Review (Mishpatim)* 25: 129 (Hebrew).
14. Levontin, Eitan. 2008. Figment of the imagination: Funk-Schlezinger and civil registry law. *Mishpat Umimshal (Law and Government)* 11: 125.
15. Lifshitz, Shahar. 2003–2004. The external rights of cohabiting couples in Israel. *Israel Law Review* 37: 346.
16. Rabin, Yoram, and Yuval Shany. 2003. The Israeli unfinished constitutional revolution: Has the time come for protecting economic and social rights. *Israel Law Review* 37: 299.
17. Rosen-Zvi, Ariel. 1989. Forum shopping between religious and secular courts (and its impact on the legal system). *Tel Aviv University Studies in Law* 9: 347.
18. Rosen-Zvi, Ariel. 1995. Family and inheritance law. In *Introduction to the law of Israel* 75, eds. Amos Shapira, and Keren C. DeWitt-Arar. Hague: Kluwer Law International.
19. Sapir, Gidon. 1999. Religion and state in Israel: The case for reevaluation and constitutional entrenchment. *Hastings International and Comparative Law Review* 22: 617.
20. Shava, Menashe. 1981. Matters of personal status of Israeli citizens not belonging to a recognized religious community. *Israel Yearbook on Human Rights* 11: 238.
21. Shava, Menashe. 1983. The property rights of spouses cohabiting without marriage in Israel – A comparative commentary. *Georgia Journal of International and Comparative Law* 13: 465.
22. Shava, Menashe. 1989. Civil marriage celebrated abroad: Validity in Israel. *Tel-Aviv University Studies in Law* 9: 65.

23. Shifman, Pinhas. 1980. Religious affiliation in Israel interreligious law. *Israel Law Review* 15(31).
24. Sommer, Hillel. 1997. The non-enumerated rights: On the scope of the constitutional revolution. *Hebrew University Law Review* 28: 257 (Hebrew).
25. Zafran, Ruth. 2008. More than one mother: Determining maternity for the biological child of a female same-sex couple–the Israeli view. *Georgetown Journal of Gender and the Law* 9: 115.

Cases

26. *Baehr v. Lewin*, 852 P.2d 44 (Haw. 1993).
27. C.A. 191/51 *Skornik v. Skornik*, P.D. 8 141 (1954).
28. C.A. 52/80 *Shachar v. Friedman*, P.D. 38(1) 443 (1984).
29. C.A. 2000/97 *Lindorn v. Karnit*, 55(1) P.D. 12 (1999).
30. CA 6821/93 *Bank Hamizrachi Ltd. v. Migdal et al.* P.D. 49(4) 221 (1995).
31. CA 2316/95 *Ganimat v. the State of Israel*, P.D. 49(4) 589 (1995).
32. CA 3077/90 *Plonit v. Plonit*, P.D. 49(2) 578 (1995).
33. CA 2622/01 *Manager of Land Betterment Tax v. Levanon*, P.D. 57(5) 309 (2003).
34. CA (Nazareth) 3245/03 Anonymous v. The Custodian Gen. (2004).
35. CA 10280/01 Yaros-Hakak v. Atty. Gen., P.D. 59(5) 64 (2005).
36. C.C. (Jerusalem) 2/85 *Kleidman v. Kleidman*, P.M. 1979(b) 377 (1985).
37. CCT 60/04 Minister of Home Affairs v. Fourie 2006 (3) BCLR (CC) at 27 (S. Afr.).
38. EF (Estate File) (Be'er Sheva) 1320/08 Jhon Dow v. Jane Dow, [Aug. 23, 2010] (unpublished officially).
39. EF (Estate File) (Tel-Aviv) 108091/08 *Estate of Y.A. v. R.A.*, [Aug. 11, 2012] (unpublished officially).
40. Egale Canada Inc. v. Canada (Attorney General) (2003), 225 D.L.R. (4th) 472 (C.A.).
41. F.A. 9607/03 Ploni v. Plonit., P.D. 61(3) 726 (2006).
42. FamC (Haifa) 32520/97 Roe v. Doe (1997).
43. FamC (Beer-Sheva) 8510/01 *In the matter of A & G* (2002).
44. FamC (Tel-Aviv) 6960/03 *K.Z. v. State of Israel* (2004).
45. FamC (Tel-Aviv) 3140/03 *In the matter of R.A. & L.M.F* (2004).
46. FamC (Tel-Aviv) 16610/04 *A v. Attorney-General* (2005).
47. FamC (Ramat-Gan) 1630/08 Roe v. Doe (2008).
48. FamC (Tel-Aviv) 23849-08-10 *Y.K. v. B. Sh. K.* [Oct. 9, 2011] (unpublished officially).
49. FamC (Tel-Aviv) 35371-02-10 *A.A L. B. v. Ch. B.* [Oct. 11, 2011] (unpublished officially).
50. FamC (Rishon Lezion) 9877/02*P.E. v. P. Y.* (Aug. 17, 2011) (unpublished officially).
51. FH 4252/00 Interior Minister v. Brenner Kaddish (2008).
52. *Goodridge v. Dep't of Pub. Health*, 798 N.E. 2d 941 (Mass. 2003).
53. Halpern v. Attorney General of Canada (2002), 60 O.R. (3d) 321 (Div. Gen) (Ontario).
54. HCJ 143/62 *Funk Shlezinger v. Minister of the Interior*, P.D. 17 225 (1963).
55. HCJ 3/73 *Cahanoff v. the Rabbinical Court*, P.D. 29(1) 449 (1974).
56. HCJ 51/80 *Cohen v. Rabbinical High Court of Appeals*, P.D. 35(2) 8 (1980).
57. HCJ 693/91 *Efrat v. Commissioner of the Population Registry*, P.D. 47(1) 749 (1993).
58. HCJ 721/94 *El-Al Israel Airlines Ltd v. Danielowitz*, P.D. 48(5) 749 (1994).
59. HCJ 6086/94 Nizri v. Commissioner of the Population Registry, P.D. 49(5) 693 (1996).
60. HCJ 1779/99 *Brener-Kadish v. Minister of the Interior*, P.D. 54(2) 368 (2000).
61. HCJ 2458/01, *New Family v. Approvals Comm. for Surrogate Motherhood Agreements, Ministry of Health*, P.D. 57(1) 419 (2002).
62. HCJ 7052/03 *Adalah v. Minister of Interior*, P.D. 61(2) 202 (2006).
63. HCJ 3045/05 *Ben-Ari v. Ministry of the Interior*, P.D. 61(3) 537 (2006).
64. HCJ 2232/03 *Plonit v. The Regional Rabbinical Court Tel Aviv*, P.D. 61(3) 496 (2006).

65. HCJ 6427/02 *Movement for Quality Government in Israel v. Knesset*, P.D. 61(3) 619 (2006).
66. HCJ 2078/96 *Vitz v. Minister of Health*, (unpublished officially).
67. Hendricks and Leboeuf v. Quebec (Attorney General), [2002] R.J.Q. 2506 (C.S.) (Quebec).
68. LabC (TA) 3816/01 Levy v. Mivtahim.
69. LCA 8256/99 *A v. B*, P.D. 58(2) 213 (2004).
70. LCA 3497/09 *John Dow v. Jane Dow*, [May 4, 2011] (unpublished officially).
71. MA (TA) 369/94 Steiner v. IDF (1996).
72. NI (TA) 3536/04 Raz v. National Insurance Institute, [Feb. 28, 2005] (unpublished officially).

Legislation

73. Adoption of Children Law, 1981, 35 L.S.I. 360.
74. Basic Law: Human Dignity and Liberty, 1992, S.H. 150.
75. Basic Law: Freedom of Occupation, 1992, S.H. 114.
76. Basic Law: Freedom of Occupation, 1994, S.H. 90.
77. Egg Donation Law, 2010.
78. Jurisdiction in the Matter of Dissolution of Marriage (Special Cases & International Jurisdiction) Act of 1969.
79. Matters of Dissolution of Marriage (Jurisdiction in Special Cases) Law, 1969, 23 L.S.I..
80. Palestinian Order in Council, Articles 46, 47, 64(2).
81. Partnership Covenant for the Religionless Law, 2010.
82. Population Registry Law, 5725–1965, 19 LSI 288 (1964–65) (Isr.).
83. Rabbinical Courts Jurisdiction (Marriage and Divorce) Law-1953, 7 L.S.I 139.
84. The Courts Law (Consolidated Version), 1984, 38 L.S.I. 271.
85. The Family Courts Law, 1995, S.H. 393.
86. The Family Law Amendment (Maintenance) Law, 1959, 13 L.S.I. 73.
87. The Prevention of Family Violence Law, 1991, S.H. 138.
88. The Spouses (Property Relations) Law, 5733–1973, 27 LSI 313 (1972–1973).
89. The Succession Law, 1965, 19 L.S.I. 58.
90. The Surrogate Motherhood Agreements (Approval of Agreement and Status of Newborn) Law, 1996, S.H. 1577, 176.

Others

91. Edelman, Ofra. 2009. *Court Grants Gay Couple Right to Adopt 30-Year-Old Foster Son*, Haaretz, Mar. 11, www.haaretz.com/hasen/spages/1070060.html.
92. Gross, Aeyal. 2006. *Israel's supreme court orders registration of same-sex marriage conducted in Canada*, Lesbian/Gay law notes 226.
93. International Gay and Lesbian Human Rights Commission, asylum Documentation Program – Status of Sexual Minorities: Israel, *available at* www.asylumlaw.org/docs/sexualminorities/Israel%20CU%20SO.pdf.
94. www.ynet.co.il/articles/0,7340,L-3812367,00.html [Hebrew].
95. Yoram Yarkoni, *Gay couple turns to rabbis for divorce*, Ynet News, July 9, 2012, www.ynetnews.com/articles/0,7340,L-4276046,00.html.

Chapter 7
Same-Sex Marriage in the Commonwealth Caribbean: Is It Possible?

Toni Holness

Abstract Respect for LGBTI rights in the Commonwealth Caribbean is a fast-moving target. However, human rights advocates are working tirelessly to generate both legal reform and social tolerance for sexual minorities. LGBTI rights, or lack thereof, is evident in several bodies of law, including but not limited to sodomy law and marriage law. Additionally, a dialogue on LGBTI rights would be incomplete without an honest account of ongoing violence and other manifestations of homophobia and transphobia in the region. This chapter seeks to give as comprehensive a perspective as possible on the current state of LGBTI rights in the Caribbean regarding marriage. It looks at specific regulations in each country of the region and it shows that heteronormativity in family law is a vestige of British colonialism. Today Great Britain as other European countries, are moving away of the heterosexual paradigm in family law. Post colonialist Caribbean is not following this trend, at least not yet.

This chapter explores the development of same sex marriage rights in the Commonwealth Caribbean. Importantly, this chapter examines only the Commonwealth Caribbean countries, not the entire Caribbean region.[1] However, because same sex marriages may not be performed legally in the Caribbean, the bulk of this discussion will examine factual and legal contexts within which same sex marriage may eventually gain recognition.

[1]The Commonwealth is a voluntary association of sovereign nations who either share the common former colonial power, the United Kingdom, or have voluntarily joined the association. The Commonwealth Caribbean refers to those Commonwealth nations in the Caribbean. These include Antigua and Barbuda, The Bahamas, Barbados, Belize, Dominica, Guyana, Jamaica, St Kitts and Nevis, St. Lucia, St. Vincent and the Grenadines, and Trinidad and Tobago. *See* The website of The Commonwealth of Nations (available at www.commonwealthofnations.org) (last visited Dec. 1, 2013).

T. Holness (✉)
American Civil Liberties Union (ACLU), 3600 Clipper Mill Rd, Suite 350,
Baltimore, MD 21211, USA
e-mail: toni.holness@gmail.com

M. Sáez (ed.), *Same Sex Couples - Comparative Insights on Marriage and Cohabitation*, Ius Gentium: Comparative Perspectives on Law and Justice 42,
DOI 10.1007/978-94-017-9774-0_7

The chapter opens with a description of the existing hostile atmosphere toward Lesbian, Gay, Bisexual, Trans, and Intersex (LGBTI) communities in the Caribbean, paying specific attention to incidents of violence, sociocultural trends, and state complicity. An overview of the heteronormative character of marriage laws in the Commonwealth Caribbean will then be discussed, followed by a more in-depth look at the marriage laws of The Bahamas, Jamaica, and Trinidad and Tobago. For many Commonwealth Caribbean countries, sexual activity between consenting adults of the same sex is proscribed by anti-sodomy or anti-buggery laws; these laws will also be discussed. After examining the landscape of local marriage and sexuality laws, the chapter looks at regional jurisprudence around LGBTI rights, specifically the jurisprudence of the Inter-American Court of Human Rights, the Inter-American Commission on Human Rights, the Caribbean Court of Justice, and the United Kingdom's Judicial Committee of the Privy Council (hereafter "United Kingdom Privy Council" or "Privy Council").

7.1 Current Atmosphere of Hostility Toward LGBTI Communities in the Commonwealth Caribbean

A discussion of same sex marriage in the Caribbean must necessarily account for the hostile and often dangerous environment in which sexual minorities exist and with which LGBTI rights advocates must contend. The charged social and political atmosphere is indicative of the challenges ahead for same sex marriage advocates and the seemingly insurmountable obstacles to legislative recognition of same sex relationships. In the region, hostility toward sexual minorities manifests itself most vociferously through violence, sociocultural resistance, and state complicity. To be clear, the three categories are not discrete. Violence and sociocultural resistance are perpetrated largely by private actors, but state complicity implicates the government's responsibility, capacity, and (un)willingness to protect LGBTI persons from these private actions.

7.1.1 Violence Against LGBTI Persons

Although widely acclaimed for its scenic beaches and carefree attitude, the Caribbean has earned equal infamy for its violence toward LGBTI persons. This section discusses homophobic and transphobic violence in the Commonwealth, with special attention to Jamaica, whose notoriety for violence far surpasses other Commonwealth nations.

Across the Caribbean, sexual minorities experience actual and persistent threats of physical harm and even death. This violence may take the form of mob attacks, corrective rapes, murder, or destruction of real property thought to be occupied by

LGBTI persons. Tourists to the region are not immune to these attacks. As recently as 2012, two gay male tourists were arrested in Dominica on suspicion of having committed sexual conduct with each other. The two were purportedly seen engaged in intercourse by someone on the dock.[2] Similarly, in 2008, St. Lucian tourism authorities scrambled to do damage control after three gay tourists were robbed and assaulted while vacationing on the island. The attackers yelled profanities and demanded that the men leave the island because they were not welcome.[3] In 2004, a gay cruise hosting about 1,150 passengers confronted about 100 angry protestors on the island of Nassau in The Bahamas. The protestors hurled anti-gay slurs at the visitors.[4] Again, in 2010, a gay cruise was turned away from the Cayman Islands, in response to local protests by religious groups.[5]

Although the entire Caribbean region has gained notoriety, Jamaica stands head and shoulders above its neighbors with an astonishing record of homophobic and transphobic violence. In 2006, Time Magazine boldly declared the island paradise, "the most homophobic place on earth."[6] In 2004, Brian Williamson, a vocal Jamaican gay rights activist was murdered in his home. Upon discovering his body, his neighbors gathered to celebrate around the mutilated corpse, hailing the murder as a step in the right direction and an elimination of sinful behavior.[7] More recently, in June 2012, the bodies of two men believed to be gay were found chopped and mutilated, with blood stained rocks nearby. According to the Inter-American Commission on Human Rights, the double murder came on the heels of a frenzy of homophobic violence—eight gay men had been murdered within the prior 3 months, in addition to other non-fatal attacks.[8] In what was perhaps the most egregious act of defilement, the 2007 funeral of a gay businessman was brashly interrupted by an angry mob outside the church.[9] The mob of protestors barged into the church and demanded that the service be called to an end. No prosecutions were made against members of the mob.[10] These and countless other incidents of violence against LGBTI persons demonstrate the caustic atmosphere within which same sex marriage rights must not only emerge, but also survive.

---

[2]Carlisle Jno Baptiste, *2 US men arrested on gay cruise in Caribbean*, MSNBC, Mar. 22, 2012.

[3]Guy Ellis, *St. Lucia Responds To Attack On 3 Gay American Tourists*, Huffington Post, Mar. 14, 2012.

[4]Associated Press, *Rosie O'Donnell Cruise for Gay Families Cuts Bermuda Stop, Fearing Protests*, FoxNews.com, Apr. 18, 2007.

[5]Carlisle Jno Baptiste, *2 US men arrested on gay cruise in Caribbean*, MSNBC, Mar. 22, 2012.

[6]Tim Padgett, *The Most Homophobic Place on Earth?*, Time World, Apr. 12, 2006.

[7]Human Rights Watch, Hated to Death: Homophobia, Violence and Jamaica's HIV/AIDS Epidemic 2 (November 2004).

[8]*IACHR Condemns Murder of Two Gay Men in Jamaica*, Organization of American States, Jul. 9, 2012.

[9]Mark Lacey, *Anti-gay violence defies laid-back image of Jamaica*, New York Times, Feb. 24, 2008.

[10]*Ibid.*

7.1.2 Sociocultural Resistance to Sexual Minorities

Beyond incidents of violence, there also exists a culture of hate toward LGBTI persons in the Caribbean. In 2011, the University of the West Indies – Mona, Department of Sociology, Psychology, and Social Work issued a report on the attitudes of Jamaicans toward same sex relationships. The report's findings illustrate the deep-rooted and pervasive cultural aversion of Jamaican citizens to sexual minorities. The authors designate as their most important finding the fact that strong negative perceptions of homosexuality transcend social classes, gender, and social groups in Jamaica. In other words, homophobia is not culturally isolated; it runs the gamut of society.[11] Additionally, the study found that the overwhelming majority of respondents (85.2 %) did not think that homosexuality between consenting adults should be legalized.[12] This cultural resistance tends to manifest itself through fundamentalist religious discourse as well as homophobic and transphobic music.

As with most regions and countries across the globe, resistance to LGBTI rights, and especially same sex marriage rights, often stems from the religious community. For example, when the United Kingdom Privy Council demanded that the Caribbean repeal its various anti-gay laws, the region rejected the plea in a unified voice, claiming that homosexuality was against their religion.[13] As another example, in Belize, the religious right has held steadfast in its opposition to LGBTI rights advocacy, refusing to "surrender [their] moral foundations [. . .] to predatory foreign interests."[14]

The region's faith-based resistance to LGBTI rights can be traced to colonialism, during which a tradition of Christianity was imposed upon the Caribbean by the British Empire. Much of British common law finds its roots in the Christian Bible and as a result, the laws of the British territories were similarly ruled by a de facto theocracy.[15] The colonial rulers invoked their Christian belief systems in ruling the territories, using Biblical references to instill discipline and subordination in the region.[16]

---

[11] Department of Sociology, Psychology, and Social Work – University of the West Indies, Mona, National Survey of Attitudes and Perceptions of Jamaicans Towards Same Sex Relationships 3 (September 2011).

[12] *Ibid.*

[13] *Caribbean Rejects UK Justice*, British Broadcasting Corporation, Feb. 15, 2001.

[14] *Global campaign to decriminalise homosexuality to kick off in Belize court*, The Guardian, Nov. 16, 2011.

[15] James Wilets, *Conceptualizing Private Violence against Sexual Minorities as Gendered Violence: An International and Comparative Law Perspective*, 60 Alb. L. Rev. 989, 1,028 (1997) ("In Asia and Africa the extensive list of countries with anti-sodomy laws can be traced back to the lingering effects of colonialism and Christianity, Islam, and Marxist-Leninism.").

[16] *Ibid.*

With regard to the region's music, the Caribbean's iconic dancehall[17] music has grown notorious for its homophobic and transphobic lyrical content. Ironically, the genre otherwise embraces sexual freedom, with little censorship for sexually provocative content. Perhaps most notorious, is Jamaican artist Buju Banton. Early in his career, Banton penned the song, Boom Bye Bye, advocating fatal violence against gay men.[18] Similarly, the artist Capleton also released a song, chanting "All boogaman and sodomites fi get kill," which means all gays and lesbians should be killed.[19] Banton and Capleton stand among numerous other musicians who advocate violence against LGBTI persons in their lyrics, including Elephant Man, Bounty Killa, and Capleton.[20] As a result of the blatant and violent lyrical content of their music, many dancehall artists have been banned or boycotted by international LGBTI groups.[21]

However, the dynamic between gay rights groups and dancehall artists seems to have grown more amicable in recent years. In 2007, three artists, Beenie Man, Capleton, and Sizzla, signed the Reggae Compassionate Act, which rejects homophobic and transphobic musical lyrics.[22] The Act reportedly came in response to an estimated £2.5 million loss suffered by the artists as a result of boycotts across Europe.[23] Also in 2012, gay and transgender rights groups in Belgium agreed to let up on their protest activities, after dancehall artist Beenie Man released a video apologizing for his homophobic lyrics and committed to respecting all persons, regardless of sexual orientation.[24]

The impact of homophobic and transphobic music is unclear. Many dancehall artists will profess to be simply voicing the views of the public, absolving themselves of culpability for homophobic violence; in their view, the violence came before the music, not vice versa.[25] Although the causative direction is unclear, the correlation is likely. The earlier noted study by the University of the West Indies

[17]Note that homophobic lyrics plague dancehall music, which is a subgenre of reggae music. The distinction is important because several reggae artists have decried getting lumped together with the homophobic lyrics of dancehall artists, when they themselves have not espoused a homophobic view. *See for example*, Teino Evans, *Artistes not 'compassionate' to the act – Reggae artistes want clauses changed*, Jamaica Star, Jun. 29, 2007.

[18]Eric Kreindler and Frank Heinz, *Homophobic Lyrics Lead to Concert Cancellations*, NBC Chicago, Aug. 31, 2009.

[19]Christopher Thompson, *Curbing Homophobia in Reggae*, Time Entertainment, Aug. 7, 2007.

[20]*Ibid.*

[21]*See for example* Stephen Jackson, *Reggae Artists Blacklisted*, Jamaica Observer, Feb. 28, 2010. (Germany blacklisted at least 11 dancehall albums between 2008 and 2010 because of their homophobic and violent content).

[22]Teino Evans, *Artistes not 'compassionate' to the act – Reggae artistes want clauses changed*, Jamaica Star, Jun. 29, 2007.

[23]Rosie Swash, *Beenie Man, Sizzla and Capleton renounce homophobia*, The Guardian, Jun. 14, 2007.

[24]*Belgian gays grant reprieve to Beenie, Sizzla and Shabba*, Jamaica Observer, May 18, 2012.

[25]Christopher Thompson, *Curbing Homophobia in Reggae*, Time Entertainment, Aug. 7, 2007.

revealed that homophobic views were most prominent among male respondents in lower socioeconomic groups who were not university educated and listened mostly to dancehall and reggae music.[26]

7.1.3 State Complicity in Violence and Discrimination Against LGBTI Persons

The violence and sociocultural expressions of homophobia and transphobia discussed in the two previous sections are activities carried out by private actors and members of the general public. This section addresses state action (or inaction), which creates, perpetuates, or tolerates homophobia and transphobia.

The most frequent complaint of state activity centers on the unresponsiveness of local police forces to pleas from the LGBTI community. For example, in Trinidad, LGBTI groups expressed a reluctance to report violence and harassment to the local authorities for fear of re-traumatization by members of the police force, who frequently harass LGBTI persons.[27] In Jamaica, police officers have turned the issue of violence against LGBTI persons on its head by blaming gay men for the murder rate against gays. In 2012, the Jamaican Assistant Police Commissioner, Les Green, stated that the majority of murders of gay men were committed by intimate partners and these murders are therefore not indicative of homophobic violence.[28] Green also suggested that Jamaica's LGBTI community invites harassment by "cross-dressing," and asks "do they do that to create a media blitz?"[29] Prominent LGBTI and AIDS activist, Maurice Tomlinson, can attest to the police apathy toward sexual minorities. On one instance, Tomlinson sought protection from the local police force, but was greeted with a sharp refusal. The officer in charge turned him away, saying, "I hate gays, they make me sick."[30] Tomlinson was later contacted for an investigation, but the police force has not followed up.[31]

In other instances, members of the police force themselves engage in homophobic or transphobic violence. As recently as November 2012, two security guards stationed at Jamaica's University of Technology were involved in an assault of a student thought to be gay. The male student was allegedly found in a compromising position with another male and after fleeing an angry mob, the young man wound up

---

[26]Department of Sociology, Psychology, and Social Work – University of the West Indies, Mona, National Survey of Attitudes and Perceptions of Jamaicans Towards Same Sex Relationships 3 (September 2011).

[27]U.S. Department of State, 2010 Human Rights Report: Trinidad (Apr. 2011).

[28]Julie Bolcer, *Jamaica Police Commissioner Blames Gays for Violence*, Advocate.com, Jul. 13, 2012.

[29]*Ibid.*

[30]Human Rights Watch, *Jamaica: Combat Homophobia*, July 18, 2012.

[31]*Ibid.*

in a room with the security guards. A YouTube video shows that, instead of offering protection, one guard punched, kicked, and slapped the student, while another held the student in place.[32] The two guards had reportedly been fired since the incident.[33]

Officials higher on the governmental totem pole can sometimes be equally damaging; Caribbean state leaders have often been complicit in discrimination against LGBTI communities. For example, the Antiguan Attorney General once told the press, "Being gay is morally wrong, and to be honest personally, I am still homophobic."[34]

However, some state leaders have taken notable steps to ameliorate their state's homophobic reputation. In Jamaica and Trinidad, featured above in the examples of police apathy or violence, state leaders have actually voiced pro-LGBTI rhetoric. During her run for office, Jamaica's Prime Minister, Portia Simpson Miller stated, "no one should be discriminated against because of their sexual orientation."[35] Simpson Miller further stated that her cabinet was open to be filled by LGBTI persons, so long as they were qualified.[36] Not only did Simpson Miller accomplish a landslide victory in the upcoming election, she was recently named one of Time Magazine's 100 Most Influential People for 2012. Among other attributes and accomplishments, the magazine took notice of her courageous battle against homophobia.[37]

Trinidadian Prime Minister, the Hon. Kamla Persad-Bissessar, was similarly supportive of LGBTI rights in a recent statement. Persaud-Bissessar vowed to end discrimination based on sexual orientation, stating, "The stigmatization of homosexuality in Trinidad and Tobago is a matter which must be addressed on the grounds of human rights and dignity to which every individual is entitled under international law."[38] Therefore, although some state actors may demonstrate homophobic tendencies, this perspective is not necessarily indicative of a statewide policy of homophobia.

To briefly conclude, the factual context of LGBTI rights in the region demonstrates the hostility and resolute resistance of local interest groups and the broader public. Although some state leaders demonstrate support for LGBTI rights, the

---

[32] *UTech, Marksman Condemn Beating Of Alleged Gay Student*, Jamaica Gleaner, Nov. 2, 2012. *See also* Associated Press, *2 guards in Jamaica accused of beating gay student*, Fox News, Nov. 3, 2012.

[33] *Ibid.*

[34] U.S. Department of State, 2010 Human Rights Report: Antigua and Barbuda (May 2012).

[35] Sarah Boseley, *Jamaican gay rights activists hopeful of repealing anti-homosexuality law*, The Guardian, Feb. 10, 2012.

[36] Toni Holness, *Jamaica's Portia Simpson Miller: Out with the Old and in with the New*, Intlawgrrls.com, Jan. 18, 2012.

[37] Yvette D. Clarke, *2012 Time 100: The Most Influential People in the World – Portia Simpson Miller*, Time Magazine, Apr. 18, 2012.

[38] *IACHR Welcomes Anti-Discrimination Statement by the Prime Minister of Trinidad and Tobago*, Organization of American States, Dec. 20, 2012.

frequency of homophobic and transphobic acts of violence and discrimination evidence a widely held sentiment of hostility toward LGBTI persons. This hostility must be accounted for in any legislative or other advocacy efforts to recognize same sex marriages in the region.

7.2 Overview of Marriage Laws in the Commonwealth Caribbean

Currently, same sex unions are not recognized in the domestic legal system of any Commonwealth Caribbean country. In fact, recognition and respect for broader sexual minority rights has been a long, slow, and often painful process for LGBTI rights activists. This section will first discuss the heteronormative trends in Commonwealth Caribbean marriage laws, followed by a closer examination of the domestic laws of The Bahamas, Jamaica, and Trinidad and Tobago.

7.2.1 Heteronormative Trends in the Domestic Marriage Laws of Commonwealth Caribbean Countries

As an initial matter, same sex marriage is not recognized in the domestic jurisprudence of any Commonwealth Caribbean country. This trend against recognizing same sex relationships stems largely from residual colonial influences. The legacy of the former British colonial power endures and is evident in the marriage laws of many Caribbean countries. In fact, many of the Caribbean's early legislatures enacted marriage laws with an eye toward achieving likeness with the British laws.[39] For example, the Barbadian legislature is said to have enacted its first Marriage Act of 1734, "An Act to Prevent Clandestine Marriage," with the hope of bringing the domestic jurisprudence "on the same footing as the law in England."[40] Despite gaining independence, many Commonwealth Caribbean countries retain heteronormative norms in their marriage laws.

The marriage laws of many Commonwealth states employ deceptively gender-neutral language. For example, the Marriage Act of Antigua and Barbuda uses language such as "the consent of each party to accept the other as his or her wife or husband."[41] However, the official Form of Notice of Marriage reveals that marriage is in fact reserved for heterosexual couples. The form consists of two slots for the marrying parties, with directions, "The names and particulars relating to the

---

[39] Andrew Bainham Ed., The International Survey of Family Law, (1995), p. 52.

[40] *Ibid.*

[41] Marriage Act, Part V: Solemnization or Celebration of Marriage, 1925, Cap. 261, Sec. 47(b) (Antigua and Barbuda) (available at http://www.laws.gov.ag/acts/chapters/cap-261.pdf)

man should be first entered in the several columns, and then the names, etc. of the woman placed below."[42] The Barbadian Marriage Act also appears gender-neutral on its face.[43] Again, however, the Application for Marriage Certificate offers slots for the names of the "husband" and "wife."[44] Similarly, the Guyanese Marriage Act requires that at some point during the marriage ceremony, "the consent of each party to accept the other as *his or her wife or husband* is clearly expressed in the presence of the marriage officer and the witnesses."[45] (emphasis added). The Guyanese Form of Notice of Marriage, however, requires that "the names and particulars relating to the man should be first entered in the several columns, and then the names and particulars of the woman placed below."[46]

Although same sex marriage has not yet gained legal recognition, the LGBTI advocates in many Commonwealth Caribbean countries have pressured their citizenry and legislatures to adopt more LGBTI friendly norms and laws. For example, in 2011, Sir Errol Walrond, a Knight, called on this fellow Barbadians to end discrimination on the basis of sexual orientation. Anticipating sharp criticism, Walrond stated, "I know I have been abused for saying so, but there is absolutely no reason why we as a free community should be discriminating against any minority in our community."[47]

LGBTI activists in other countries proceed more cautiously. For example, with a heightened awareness of the domestic hostility toward sexual minorities, LGBTI activists in Antigua and Barbuda strategically omit same sex marriage from their current advocacy agenda. One local advocate explained that it would be reckless to promote same sex marriages given the tense atmosphere, "For you to just jump on same sex marriage without educating people and getting people to understand who they are, why they exist and how they infringe on people's rights would be senseless."[48]

7.2.2 *Same-Sex Marriage in Non-Commonwealth Caribbean Nations*

Although this chapter's focus is the Commonwealth Caribbean, it is also relevant to review the state of affairs in the Commonwealth's neighboring states. Although

[42]Marriage Act, 1925, Cap. 261 (Antigua and Barbuda) (available at http://www.laws.gov.ag/acts/chapters/cap-261.pdf)

[43]Marriage Act, 1995, Cap. 218A (Barbados).

[44]Application for Marriage Certificate, Barbados (available at http://www.lawcourts.gov.bb/Documents/Application%20for%20Marriage%20Certificate.pdf)

[45]Marriage Act, 1998, Cap. 45:01 (Guyana) (available at http://www.jafbase.fr/DocAmeriques/Guyana/LoiMariage.pdf)

[46]*Ibid.*

[47]*Gay laws an obstacle*, Nation News, Dec. 2, 2011.

[48]Martina Johnson, *Same sex marriages off the radar*, Antigua Observer, Dec. 21, 2012.

same sex unions have not been recognized in the Commonwealth Caribbean, some non-Commonwealth Caribbean states have taken steps toward protecting the rights of sexual minorities. Consider for example, the French Overseas Departments of Guadeloupe and Martinique. The 1999 French Pacte civil de solidarité (PACS) permits civil unions between same sex couples, offering many of the legal protections and tax benefits of marriage.[49] As French overseas departments, Guadeloupe and Martinique also recognize civil unions under the French law.[50]

The Dutch Caribbean has a similar story. In 2001, the Netherlands became the first country to recognize same sex marriages.[51] Nonetheless, LGBTI rights were greeted with a less-than-warm welcome in the Dutch Caribbean territories. For example, Aruba is an autonomous country within the Dutch Kingdom and therefore has substantial autonomy from the Netherlands. As a result, Aruba does not have to legalize same sex marriages, but must recognize those same sex marriages performed in the Netherlands.[52] Despite this advancement, local resistance to LGBTI rights remains vociferous. In 2005, the Aruban Justice Minister refused to recognize same sex marriages formed in the Netherlands, invoking the Christian argument that such unions were unnatural and deviant.[53]

7.3 Same-Sex Marriage in the Bahamas

Bahamian marriage law consists of a host of different pieces of legislation, including the Marriage Act,[54] the Marriage of British Subjects Act,[55] the Marriage of Deceased Wife's Sister Act,[56] and the Matrimonial Causes Act.[57] For the purpose of our discussion, the Marriage Act and Matrimonial Causes Act are most relevant. The Bahamian Marriage Act does not expressly state that marriage must be between a man and a woman.[58] In fact, the law, titled "An Act Relating to Marriage" uses

[49]Loi n° 99–944 du 15 novembre 1999 relative au pacte civil de solidarité. *See also* Scott Sayare and Maia De Law Baume, *In France, Civil Unions Gain Favor Over Marriage*, New York Times, Dec. 15, 2010.

[50]Vanessa Agard-Jones, *Le Jeu de Qui? Sexual Politics at Play in the French Caribbean*, Caribbean Review of Gender Studies (Issue 3 – 2009).

[51]*Popularity of Caribbean island soars after gay wedding*, Jamaica Observer, Dec. 15, 2012.

[52]*Ibid.*

[53]Boris O. Dittrich, *Gay marriage's diamond anniversary*, Los Angeles Times, Apr. 17, 2011.

[54]Marriage Act, 1907, Cap. 106 (The Bahamas) (available at http://laws.bahamas.gov.bs/cms/images/LEGISLATION/PRINCIPAL/1908/1908-0004/MarriageAct_1.pdf)

[55]*Ibid.*

[56]Marriage with Deceased Wife's Sister Act, 1907, Cap. 122 (The Bahamas).

[57]Matrimonial Causes Act, 1879, Cap. 125 (The Bahamas).

[58]Marriage Act, *Supra* note 55.

alternative gender phrases, such as "his or her," and "he or she," quite frequently.[59] The Act calls upon the officiating officer to declare, "I call upon these persons here present to witness that I, A.B., do take (or have now taken) C.D. to be my lawful wife (or husband)."[60] However, the heteronormative norm is evident in the Bahamian 1879 Matrimonial Causes Act.[61] Subsection (c) of paragraph 21 contains the relevant language:

> 21. (1) A marriage shall be void on any of the following grounds:
>
> (a) that it is not a valid marriage in accordance with the provisions of the Marriage Act;
> (b) that at the time of the marriage, either party was already lawfully married;
> (c) *that the parties are not respectively male and female* (emphasis added); or
> (d) that in the case of a polygamous marriage entered into outside The Bahamas, either party was domiciled in The Bahamas.[62]

The application for a Bahamian Marriage Certificate also reveals the heteronormity of the local marriage law. The form requests the "name of husband" and the "maiden name of wife."[63]

One would expect that the Bahamian marriage law would find its grounding in Christianity, in light of its heteronormative character. To the contrary, the marriage law offers broad latitude to the marrying parties to conduct religious marital ceremonies of their choosing. The Act states, "If the parties to a marriage contracted before the registrar or a marriage officer desire that there shall be separately performed any religious service of marriage between them, they may present themselves to any acknowledged minister of religion, and such minister upon the production of the certificate of marriage of the parties before the registrar or a marriage officer may, if he thinks fit, perform such religious service."[64] According to the Act, a religious ceremony may or may not coincide with the marriage.

The future of Bahamian policy regarding marriage equality is difficult to decipher. In 2011, the Bahamian legislature passed a Maritime Marriage Bill to legalize marriages performed in Bahamian waters.[65] During the bill's amendment phase, an unsuccessful attempt was made to remove from the bill the clause which defines marriage as being between a man and a woman. The result of this amendment would

---

59 Marriage Act, *Supra* note 55.

60 Marriage Act, *Supra* note 55, Cap. 106, ¶23.

61 Matrimonial Causes Act, 1879, Cap. 125 (The Bahamas).

62 *Ibid.*

63 Bahamian Application for Marriage Certificate (available at http://www.bahamas.com/sites/bahamas.com/files/pdf/APPLICATION_FOR_MARRIAGE_CERTIFICATE.pdf) (last visited Feb 1, 2013).

64 Marriage Act, Supra note 55, Cap. 106, ¶25.

65 Glen Ferguson, *Bahamas Cruise Weddings to Get Boost from Maritime Marriage Legislations*, The Bahamas Weekly, Jul. 14, 2011.

have been to permit same sex marriages in Bahamian waters.[66] Speaking in relation to the bill, Bahamian Minister of State for Finance, Zhivargo Laing expressed, "As a community in The Bahamas we believe that a marriage must and should be and is between a man and a woman."[67] However, Laing's position stood in stark contrast to the sentiment offered by Deputy Prime Minister and Minister of Foreign Affairs, Brent Symonette, only a month before Laing's statement. Symonette expressed the Bahamian support for the recently passed United Nations Resolution on LGBTI rights.[68] Symonette stated, "[We] continue to support freedom of expression and the right for people to express their opinions."[69] To briefly conclude, Bahamian marriage laws remain heteronormative and while there are glimmers of hope for more LGBTI friendly policies, substantial roadblocks remain.

7.4 Same-Sex Marriage in Jamaica

Like The Bahamas, Jamaica's marriage law is a patchwork of several pieces of legislation.[70] This discussion will consider the two most relevant, being the Marriage Act and the Matrimonial Causes Act.[71] Like the Marriage Acts of neighboring Caribbean countries, Jamaica's Marriage Act is largely gender-neutral.[72] However, the Matrimonial Causes Act enumerates the homosexuality of a couple as a ground for nullifying the marriage:

4(1) Decrees of nullity of marriage may be pronounced by the Court on the ground that the marriage is void on any of the following grounds, that is to say-

...

---

[66] *The FNM Attempted to Make Same Sex Marriage Legal Last Night in the House*, Bahamas Press, Jul. 8, 2011.

[67] Chester Robarbs, *Government against gay marriages*, The Nassau Guardian, Jul. 8, 2011.

[68] *UN rights body hits out against violence based on sexual orientation*, UN News Center, Jun. 17, 2011.

[69] Juan MCartney, *Bahamas backs gay rights*, The Nassau Guardian, Jun. 18, 2011.

[70] Marriage Act, 1897, Cap237 (Jamaica) (available at http://www.moj.gov.jm/sites/default/files/laws/Marriage%20Act.pdf); Maintenance Act, 2005 (Jamaica) (available at http://www.moj.gov.jm/sites/default/files/laws/Maintenance%20Act.pdf); Muslim Marriage Act, 1957 (Jamaica) (available at http://www.moj.gov.jm/sites/default/files/laws/Muslin%20Marriage%20Act.pdf); Property (Rights of Spouse) Act, 2006 (Jamaica) (available at http://www.moj.gov.jm/sites/default/files/laws/Property%20%28Rights%20of%20Spouse%29%20Act.pdf); Deceased Wife's Sister or Brother's Widow Act, 1914 (Jamaica).

[71] Marriage Act, 1897, Cap 237 (Jamaica) (available at http://www.moj.gov.jm/sites/default/files/laws/Marriage%20Act.pdf); Matrimonial Causes Act, 1989 (Jamaica) (available at http://www.moj.gov.jm/sites/default/files/laws/Matrimonial%20Causes%20Act.pdf)

[72] Maintenance Act, 2005 (Jamaica) (available at http://www.moj.gov.jm/sites/default/files/laws/Maintenance%20Act.pdf)

(d) the parties to the marriage were, at the time of the marriage, of the same sex.[73]

In 2011, Jamaica dug its heels further in with the passage of the Charter of Fundamental Rights and Freedoms (Constitutional Amendment) Act. According to Section 18 of the Charter, marriage is limited to heterosexual couples. Section 18 states:

18(1) Nothing contained in or done under any law in so far as it restricts

(a) marriage; or
(b) any other relationship in respect of which any rights and obligations similar to those pertaining to marriage are conferred upon persons as if they were husband and wife,

to one man and one woman shall be regarded as being inconsistent with or in contravention of the provisions of this Chapter.

(2) No form of marriage or other relationship referred to in subsection (1), other than the voluntary union of *one man and one woman* may be contracted or legally recognized in Jamaica.[74]

In light of the hostile sociocultural and legislative atmosphere surrounding LGBTI rights in Jamaica, it is unsurprising that same sex marriage fails to make the advocacy agenda. With astonishing levels of homophobic and transphobic violence as well as firmly grounded and reiterated anti-sodomy laws, Jamaican LGBTI rights advocates have their proverbial hands full, and same sex marriage is likely a long way down the road.

7.5 Same Sex Marriage in Trinidad and Tobago

Trinidad and Tobago's marriage regulations also consist of a host of marriage laws.[75] Most relevant for our discussion of same sex marriage are Trinidad's Marriage Act and Matrimonial Proceedings and Property Act. Trinidad's Marriage Act is also drafted in deceptively gender-neutral terms, using alternative phrases such as "he or she" throughout the legislation.[76] However, Trinidad's Matrimonial Proceedings and Property Act state, under paragraph 13, titled "Nullity, Judicial Separation and Presumption of Death":

[73]Matrimonial Causes Act, 1989 (Jamaica) (available at http://www.moj.gov.jm/sites/default/files/laws/Matrimonial%20Causes%20Act.pdf). Emphasis added.

[74]The Charter of Fundamental Rights and Freedoms (Constitutional Amendment) Act, 2011 (Jamaica). Emphasis added.

[75]*Including* Muslim Marriage and Divorce Act, 1961, Cap 45:02 (Trinidad and Tobago) (available at http://rgd.legalaffairs.gov.tt/laws2/alphabetical_list/lawspdfs/45.02.pdf; Hindu Marriage Act, 1945, Cap 45:03 (Trinidad and Tobago) (available at http://rgd.legalaffairs.gov.tt/laws2/alphabetical_list/lawspdfs/45.03.pdf)

[76]Marriage Act, 1923, Cap 45:01 (Trinidad and Tobago) (available at http://rgd.legalaffairs.gov.tt/laws2/alphabetical_list/lawspdfs/45.01.pdf)

13. (1) A marriage which takes place after the commencement of this Act shall be void on the following grounds only:

...

(c) *that the parties are not respectively male and female.*[77]

Also, in its 1998 Cohabitational Relationships Act, Trinidad expressly reserves cohabitational benefits for heterosexual couples. Under the Act, "A man and a woman who are not married to each other may enter into a cohabitation agreement or a separation agreement for the purpose of facilitating their affairs under this Act."[78] According to the legislative history, the Act's purported purpose was to "redress some of the injustices and hardships caused when parties to common-law unions do not recognize their obligations to each other."[79] Nowhere in the legislative discussion, does the legislature consider extending these benefits to same sex couples.[80]

Although Trinidadian LGBTI activists have not yet lobbied aggressively for same sex marriage, they will likely find a key ally in the current administration.[81] Prime Minister, Kamla Persad-Bissessar has vowed to end discrimination against LGBTI persons.[82] Speaking in regard to the country's immigration law, which currently bars the entry of homosexuals, Persad-Bissessar addressed the issue as a human rights concern and emphasized the importance of equality under law.[83]

7.6 Anti-Sodomy Laws of the Caribbean: The Colonial Legacy

The Caribbean's amenability or resistance to same sex marriage must be considered in light of other legal spheres in which the rights of LGBTI communities are implicated, particularly the region's anti-sodomy statutes.

The uphill legal battle for LGBTI rights in the Commonwealth Caribbean stems largely from the region's colonial history, which left behind egregious anti-sodomy

[77] Matrimonial Proceedings and Property Act, 1972, Cap 45:51 (Trinidad and Tobago) (available at http://rgd.legalaffairs.gov.tt/laws2/alphabetical_list/lawspdfs/45.51.pdf). Emphasis added.

[78] Cohabitational Relationships Act, 1998, Cap 45:55 (Trinidad and Tobago) (available at http://www.ttparliament.org/legislations/a1998-30.pdf)

[79] Parliamentary Legislative Session, Jun. 12, 2008 (Trinidad and Tobago) (available at http://www.ttparliament.org/hansards/hh19980612.pdf)

[80] *Ibid.*

[81] Gyasi Gonzales and Julien Neaves, *Govt to make decision on gay and lesbian marriages*, Trinidad Express, May 11, 2012.

[82] Yvonne Baboolal, *PM promises rights for gays in gender policy*, Trinidad and Tobago Guardian Online, Dec. 18, 2012.

[83] *Ibid.*

laws.[84] These British imperial laws are therefore a key point of reference when discussing sexual rights in the region.

During its colonial rule, the British imperial power imposed a range of laws to govern its territories, including anti-sodomy laws. Section 377 of the British Penal Code proscribes "unnatural offences."[85] Under this section, "Whoever voluntarily has carnal intercourse against the order of nature with any man, woman or animal, shall be punished with imprisonment for life, or with imprisonment of either description for term which may extend to 10 years, and shall also be liable to fine."[86]

Section 377 served as a model for British territories beyond the Caribbean, including Africa, Asia, and the Pacific Islands.[87] Although the domestic iterations of Section 377 varied textually and substantively, many mandated capital punishment for consensual same sex relations.[88]

Despite gaining independence from the British rule, many Commonwealth nations retain vestiges of Section 377 in their domestic jurisprudence. The next few paragraphs describe what remains of the colonial law in the Commonwealth Caribbean, first looking at the three featured nations, The Bahamas, Jamaica, and Trinidad and Tobago, then turning attention to the Independent Commonwealth Caribbean, and finally the British Overseas Territories.

7.6.1 Anti-Sodomy Laws in the Bahamas, Jamaica, and Trinidad and Tobago

In 1991, The Bahamas repealed its anti-sodomy laws substantially. Prior to 1991, all same sex activity was criminal *per se*. Since the repeal, only public same sex conduct and same sex conduct between an adult and a minor are criminalized under Section 16 of the Bahamian Sexual Offences and Domestic Violence Act.[89]

---

[84] In fact, worldwide, colonial influences are largely to blame for homophobic legislation that persists today. As of 2008, more than 80 nations criminalized consensual homosexual conduct and more than half of these countries inherited their anti-sodomy laws from former colonial powers Human Rights Watch, This Alien Legacy: The Origins of "Sodomy" Laws in British Colonialism 5 (December 2008).

[85] Human Rights Watch, This Alien Legacy: The Origins of "Sodomy" Laws in British Colonialism 18 (December 2008).

[86] Bart Rwezaura, *To Be or Not To Be: Recognition of Same-Sex Partnerships in Hong Kong*, 34 Hong Kong L. J. 557, 564 n. 38 (2004).

[87] Bart Rwezaura, *To Be or Not To Be: Recognition of Same-Sex Partnerships in Hong Kong*, 34 Hong Kong L. J. 557, 564 n. 38 (2004).

[88] *Ibid.*

[89] Sexual Offences and Domestic Violence Act, 2006, Cap 99 (The Bahamas).

Section 13 of Trinidad and Tobago's Sexual Offences Act defines the offence of buggery as, "sexual intercourse per anum by a male person with a male person or by a male person with a female person." Buggery is punishable by life imprisonment if committed by an adult upon a minor; by 25 years if committed between two adults; and 5 years if committed by a minor.[90]

Sections 76, 77, and 79 of the Jamaican Offences Against the Person Act criminalize buggery, defined as consensual sex between adult men.[91] The offense is punishable by imprisonment with hard labor for up to 10 years. Attempts to commit buggery are also punishable by up to 7 years, with or without hard labor. These homophobic laws were further entrenched in 2011, when Jamaica passed the Charter of Fundamental Rights and Freedoms to replace the Jamaican Bill of Rights. Section 13(12) of the Charter shelters the anti-sodomy laws from constitutional challenges. The Section states:

> (12) Nothing contained in or done under the authority of any law in force immediately before the commencement of the Charter of Fundamental Rights and Freedoms (Constitutional Amendment) Act, 2011, relating to
>
> (a) *sexual offences;* (emphasis added)
> (b) obscene publications; or
> (c) offences regarding the life of the unborn,
>
> shall be held to be inconsistent with or in contravention of the provisions of this Chapter.[92]

Therefore, as was the case with same sex marriage in Jamaica, opposition to same sex sexual conduct between consenting adults is steadfast and vociferous.

7.6.2 Anti-Sodomy Laws in the Broader Independent Commonwealth Caribbean

Consensual sexual activity between same sex adults continues to be criminalized in many Commonwealth Caribbean countries. However, the language and exact nature of criminal offenses does vary from state to state. For example, Antigua and Barbuda, Dominica, Guyana, Jamaica, St. Kitts and Nevis, St. Lucia, and St. Vincent and the Grenadines criminalize consensual same sex sexual activity between men,

---

[90] Sexual Offences Act, 1986, Cap 11:28 (Trinidad and Tobago) (available at http://rgd.legalaffairs.gov.tt/laws2/alphabetical_list/lawspdfs/11.28.pdf)

[91] Sexual Offences Act, 2009 (Jamaica) (available at http://www.japarliament.gov.jm/attachments/341_The%20Sexual%20Offences%20Act,%202009.pdf)

[92] The Charter of Fundamental Rights and Freedoms (Constitutional Amendment) Act, 2011 (Jamaica).

with no mention of women. Belize, Grenada, and Trinidad and Tobago criminalize all same sex sexual activity, between men and women.[93]

Another distinction exists insofar as the laws of some countries proscribe anal sex between men, while others proscribe anal sex between any two persons, of the same or opposite sex. For example, St. Lucia criminalizes anal sex between men. Section 133 of the St. Lucian Criminal Code defines buggery as, "sexual intercourse per anus by a male person with another male person." The offence is punishable by imprisonment for life if committed with force and without consent and by 10 years in all other cases. Attempt to commit buggery is punishable by imprisonment for 5 years.[94]

By comparison, Antigua and Dominica criminalize anal sex between both same sex and opposite sex couples. Under Section 12(1) of Antigua and Barbuda's Sexual Offenses Act, "A person who commits buggery is guilty of an offence and is liable on conviction to imprisonment."[95] The offense is punishable by life imprisonment if committed by an adult with a minor; 15 years if committed between two adults; and 5 years if committed by a minor. The Act defines buggery as "sexual intercourse per anum by a male person with a male person or by a male person with a female person."[96]

Under Article 16 of Dominica's Sexual Offences Act, buggery is defined as "sexual intercourse per anum" between two males or between a male and a female. Buggery is criminalized and punishable by 25 years if committed by an adult on a minor; 10 years if committed between two adults; and 5 years if committed by a minor. Dominican judges are also permitted to order psychiatric treatment for those convicted under this law. Attempts to commit buggery are also criminalized under the Dominican law.[97]

Other anti-sodomy laws include Section 435 of Grenada's Criminal Code, which defines an unnatural crime as "sexual intercourse per anum."[98] The unnatural crime is punishable by imprisonment for 10 years. In St. Christopher and Nevis (St. Kitts and Nevis), under Section 56 of the Offences Against the Person Act, buggery is punishable by up to 10 years imprisonment, with or without hard labor. Attempts are also punishable by up to 4 years imprisonment, with or without hard labor.[99] Same

[93]AIDS Free World, Unnatural Connexion: Creating Societal Conflict Through Legal Tools, 17 (2004).

[94]Criminal Code, 2004, Cap 273 (St. Lucia) (available at http://www.rslpf.com/site/criminal%20code%202004.pdf)

[95]Sexual Offences Act, 1995 (Antigua and Barbuda) (available at http://laws.gov.ag/acts/1995/a1995-9.pdf)

[96]*Ibid.*

[97]Sexual Offences Act, 1998 (Dominica) (available at http://www.dominica.gov.dm/laws/1998/act1-1998.pdf)

[98]Criminal Code, 1958, Cap 76 (Grenada).

[99]AIDS Free World, Unnatural Connexion: Creating Societal Conflict Through Legal Tools, 62 (2004).

sex conduct (buggery) is criminalized under Section 146 of the Criminal Code of St. Vincent and the Grenadines and punishable by up to 10 years imprisonment.[100]

7.6.3 *Anti-Sodomy Laws in the British Overseas Territories (Anguilla, British Virgin Islands, Cayman Islands, Montserrat, and Turks and Caicos)*

In 2000, in an effort to comply with its own international human rights treaty obligations, Britain called on its Overseas Territories (Anguilla, British Virgin Islands, Cayman Islands, Montserrat, and Turks and Caicos) to repeal their anti-sodomy laws.[101] British Governor, Roger Cousins, explained, "We simply can't be seen to have territories with laws that violate these agreements,"[102] referring to Britain's human rights obligations under various international agreements. Of the five territories, the British Virgin Islands was the only to comply. Anguilla, the Cayman Islands, Montserrat, and Turks and Caicos snubbed the request and held firm to their colonially implanted anti-sodomy laws. In 2001, after an exhausting diplomatic effort, the United Kingdom Privy Council finally issued a unilateral order decriminalizing private homosexual activities between consenting adults in these territories.[103]

7.7 Regional Jurisprudence Around LGBTI Rights

The regional legal systems of the Commonwealth Caribbean do have some persuasive value in the Caribbean and are therefore worth discussing. This section explores LGBTI rights in the Inter-American Human Rights system, the Caribbean Court of Justice and the United Kingdom Privy Council.

7.7.1 *Inter-American Court and Commission on Human Rights Jurisprudence*

The Inter-American Court of Human Rights (hereafter "Inter-American Court") and the Inter-American Commission on Human Rights (hereafter "Inter-American Commission") constitute the judicial arm of the Organization of American States

[100] *Ibid.*

[101] *Scrap Caribbean Anti-Gay Laws*, CBS News, Feb. 11, 2009.

[102] *Ibid.*

[103] *Sexuality and the law*, Jamaica Gleaner, Jul. 25, 2001.

(OAS). The Inter-American Commission may accept petitions and issue rulings for all the Commonwealth Caribbean nations because they are all member states of the OAS, with the exception of the British Overseas Territories (Anguilla, British Virgin Islands, Cayman Islands, Montserrat, and Turks and Caicos).[104] However, the Inter-American Court's jurisdiction is more limited. The Court can only be referred cases arising from states that have ratified the American Convention on Human Rights (hereafter "American Convention"). In the Commonwealth Caribbean, this includes Barbados and Trinidad and Tobago. Note, however, that Trinidad and Tobago withdrew from the American Convention and the Court is therefore only competent to examine petitions related to events that occurred between 1991 and 1999.[105] Although the Inter-American Commission and Inter-American Court lack binding enforcement mechanisms, the jurisprudence of both bodies are widely considered to be effective shaming mechanisms. The persuasion of these bodies is therefore worth discussing.

The Inter-American Commission is unambiguously opposed to the Caribbean's anti-sodomy laws and general homophobic disposition. In 2011, the Inter-American Commission established the Unit on the Rights of Lesbian, Gay, Bisexual, Trans, and Intersex (LGBTI) Persons.[106] The unit was established in recognition of threats and incidents of murder, rape, and other forms of violence and discrimination against LGBTI persons in the region.[107] Although the Court has not issued any rulings pertaining to LGBTI rights in the Caribbean, it has issued such rulings pertaining to Latin America and the Inter-American Commission has also issued press releases concerning the welfare of LGBTI communities in the Caribbean.

With regard to the Inter-American Court's rulings, the landmark 2012 Atala case is directly relevant. The case arose out of a Chilean court's denial of custody to Karen Atala of her three daughters based on Atala's sexual orientation. The Inter-American Court ruled for the first time that sexual orientation is a protected class and discrimination based on sexual orientation is barred under the American Convention on Human Rights.[108] In 1999, the Inter-American Commission issued an admissibility ruling in the case of Marta Lucia Alvarez Giraldo. Giraldo alleged that her personal integrity, honor, and equality were violated when Colombian prison authorities denied her intimate visits because of her sexual orientation. The Commission found the petition to be admissible.[109] Again, in the 2011 admissibility determination concerning Angel Alberto Duque, the Commission considered the

[104]Petition and Case System: Informational Brochure, Organization of American States (2010).

[105]Petition and Case System: Informational Brochure, Organization of American States (2010).

[106]*IACHR Creates Unit on the Rights of Lesbian, Gay, Bisexual, Trans, and Intersex Persons*, Organization of American States, Nov. 3, 2011.

[107]*IACHR Creates Unit on the Rights of Lesbian, Gay, Bisexual, Trans, and Intersex Persons*, Organization of American States, Nov. 3, 2011.

[108]*Karen Atala and Daughters v. Chile*, (IACHR Sept. 17, 2010).

[109]*Marta Lucía Álvarez Giraldo v. Colombia* (IACHR My 4, 1999) (Admissibility Report).

denial of social security benefits to the same sex partner of a deceased man. Some of the claims brought were deemed admissible, others were not.[110]

At the conclusion of the 140th sessions in 2010, the Inter-American Commission issued a press release expressing deep concern for the "systematic discrimination and violence against lesbian, gay, bisexual, trans, and intersex persons (LGBTI) in the region. Most particularly, the IACHR [was] concerned about the situation in those countries of the English-speaking Caribbean where the conduct of LGBTI persons is criminalized, through laws in effect that impose criminal sanctions ranging from 10 years in prison or forced labor to life imprisonment for consensual sexual conduct between adults of the same sex."[111] The Commission further called for a repeal of these laws.[112]

To briefly summarize, the Inter-American Commission has not issued any reports directly addressing LGBTI rights in the Caribbean and the Inter-American Court lacks jurisdiction over the vast majority of the Commonwealth Caribbean. However, the Court and Commission's pro-LGBTI persuasion may offer some hope.

7.7.2 The United Kingdom Privy Council and the Caribbean Court of Justice

The disposition of the United Kingdom Privy Council and the Caribbean Court of Justice (hereafter "Caribbean Court") are relevant in light of their binding appellate functions in the Caribbean.

As an initial matter, the institutional history and functional similarities between the two bodies are important for understanding the role these courts assume in the Caribbean. The United Kingdom Privy Council sits in London, England, as part of the House of Lords. Prior to the establishment of the Caribbean Court, the Privy Council was the final court of appeal for Commonwealth countries.[113] The Privy Council is governed by domestic legislation in the United Kingdom as well as the laws of the country or territory from which an appeal is brought.[114]

---

[110] *Ibid.*

[111] *IACHR Concludes its 140th Period of Sessions*, Inter-American Commission on Human Rights, Nov. 5, 2010.

[112] *Ibid.*

[113] Website of the Judicial Committee of the Privy Council (available at http://www.jcpc.gov.uk/)(last visited Feb. 3, 2013).

[114] *Ibid.*

In 2001, the Caribbean Court was established through the Agreement Establishing the Caribbean Court of Justice.[115] The agreement took effect upon the signing of twelve Caribbean states.[116] The Caribbean Court grew out of a regional sentiment desiring greater autonomy from the former colonial powers.[117] For many, the United Kingdom Privy Council symbolized a remnant of colonialism and so the Caribbean Court represented a sort of judicial liberation from the British Empire.[118] However, in 2004, the Jamaican legislature passed two pieces of legislation, the Judicature Act and the Caribbean Court of Justice Act, both intended to strip the Privy Council of its appellate functions over the island and give domestic effect to the Caribbean Court. In a 2005 decision, the Privy Council itself deemed the acts to be unconstitutional and therefore void.[119] Even as recently as 2011, Jamaican Prime Minister Portia Simpson Miller vowed to rid Jamaicans of "judicial surveillance from London" by replacing the Privy Council with the Caribbean Court.[120]

Therefore, it is clear that a battle of attrition has ensued between the competing appellate powers of the Privy Council and the Caribbean Court. Although the Caribbean Court was established to supplant the Privy Council, the Privy Council retains some judicial authority over the Commonwealth Caribbean. Accordingly, the jurisprudence of both courts are discussed below.

7.7.2.1 Privy Council Jurisprudence

The Privy Council has taken a clear opposition to the Commonwealth's anti-gay legislations. Take for example the aforementioned orders for the British Overseas Territories to repeal their anti-gay laws, which came from the Privy Council.[121] Also, in a 2009 decision, appealed from Gibraltar, *Rodriguez v Minister of Housing of the Government & Anor*, the Privy Council noted the distinction between heterosexual and homosexual couples to be illegitimate and inconsistent with the

[115] Website of the Caribbean Court of Justice (available at http://www.caribbeancourtofjustice.org/court-instruments)(last visited January 22, 2013).

[116] *Ibid.* (Signatories to the Agreement Establishing the Caribbean Court of Justice include Antigua & Barbuda; Barbados; Belize; Dominica; Grenada; Guyana; Jamaica; St. Kitts & Nevis; St. Lucia; St. Vincent & The Grenadines; Suriname; and Trinidad & Tobago).

[117] Jamaicans for Justice, Brochure on the Privy Council and the Proposed Caribbean Court of Justice, June 5, 2006 (available at http://www.jamaicansforjustice.org) (last visited Feb. 3, 2013).

[118] *See for example* Leonard Birdsong, *Formation of the Caribbean Court of Justice: the Sunset of British Colonial Rule in the English Speaking Caribbean*, 36 U. Miami Inter-Am. L. Rev. 197, 200 (Winter-Spring 2005).

[119] *Independent Jamaica Council for Human Rights (1998) Limited and Others v. Hon. Syringa Marshall- Burnett and Attorney General of Jamaica*, Privy Council Appeal No. 41 of 2004 (Feb. 3, 2005).

[120] Owen Bowcott, *Jamaica's colonial-era ties to UK legal system continue to fray*, The Guardian, Jan. 6, 2012.

[121] *Sexuality and the law*, Jamaica Gleaner, Jul. 25, 2001.

right of homosexual couples to enjoy respect for private life.[122] In issuing its decision, the Council referred to the landmark European Court of Human Rights case, *Dudgeon v. United Kingdom.*[123]

7.7.2.2 Caribbean Court Jurisprudence

As of this publication, there appears to be no litigation regarding sexual minorities in the Caribbean Court. However, Jamaican LGBTI activist, Maurice Tomlinson, has initiated challenges to Belize's and Trinidad's discriminatory immigration laws in the Caribbean Court. The immigration laws of both countries prohibit the entry of homosexuals.[124] This will likely be the first opportunity for the Caribbean Court to weigh in on the issue of LGBTI rights.

Moving forward, LGBTI rights advocates may find limited redress in the Privy Council, in light of its waning influence over the Commonwealth. The Inter-American Commission may offer persuasive, though non-binding influence, and the Inter-American Court is simply a non-starter for all Commonwealth states except Barbados. Therefore, the Caribbean Court of Justice may be the most promising avenue for binding judicial recourse. However, the Caribbean Court is relatively young and therefore somewhat unpredictable.

7.8 Limitations and Conclusion

This discussion of marriage, anti-sodomy, and other relevant laws demonstrates the broad and diverse range of progress for LGBTI rights within the Commonwealth Caribbean. Some states have progressed remarkably, most notably the French and Dutch Caribbean. In other states, the possibility of recognizing same sex marriage appears remote and must certainly be preceded by an overhaul of anti-sodomy laws, which outlaw homosexuality itself.

What is clear, however, is the importance of exhausting all available avenues for change, including legislative reform, litigation in domestic and regional courts, and community education. With rampant discrimination plaguing the region's LGBTI communities, advocates must exploit all windows of opportunity to effectuate progress.

---

[122] *Nadine Rodriguez v. Minister of Housing of the Government and The Housing Allocation Committee*, Privy Council Appeal No 0028 of 2009 (Dec. 14, 2009).

[123] *Dudgeon v United Kingdom* (1981) 4 EHRR 149.

[124] *Gay Activist Vows To Fight Belize's Immigration Law*, Jamaica Gleaner, Dec. 27, 2012.

Bibliography

Books

1. Bainham, Andrew (ed.). 1995. *The international survey of family law*, 52. Hague/Boston: Martinus Nijhoff.

Cases

2. *Dudgeon v United Kingdom.* (1981). 4 EHRR 149.
3. *Independent Jamaica Council for Human Rights. (1998). Limited and Others v. Hon. Syringa Marshall- Burnett and Attorney General of Jamaica*, Privy Council Appeal No. 41 of 2004 (Feb. 3, 2005).
4. *Karen Atala and Daughters v. Chile*, (IACHR Sept. 17, 2010).
5. *Marta Lucía Álvarez Giraldo v. Colombia* (IACHR My 4, 1999) (Admissibility Report).
6. *Nadine Rodriguez v. Minister of Housing of the Government and The Housing Allocation Committee*, Privy Council Appeal No 0028 of 2009 (Dec. 14, 2009).

Journal Articles

7. Agard-Jones, Vanessa. 2009. Le Jeu de Qui? Sexual politics at play in the French Caribbean. *Caribbean Review of Gender Studies* (Issue 3).
8. Birdsong, Leonard. Winter-Spring 2005. Formation of the Caribbean Court of Justice: The sunset of British Colonial Rule in the english speaking Caribbean. *University of Miami Inter-American Law Review* 36: 197.
9. Rwezaura, Bart. 2004. To be or not to be: Recognition of same-sex partnerships in Hong Kong. *Hong Kong Law Journal* 34: 557.
10. Wilets, James. 1997. Conceptualizing private violence against sexual minorities as gendered violence: An international and comparative law perspective. *Albany Law Review* 60: 989.

News Articles

11. *Belgian gays grant reprieve to Beenie, Sizzla and Shabba*, Jamaica Observer, May 18, 2012.
12. *Caribbean Rejects UK Justice*, British Broadcasting Corporation, February 15, 2001.
13. *Gay Activist Vows To Fight Belize's Immigration Law*, Jamaica Gleaner, December 27, 2012.
14. *Gay laws an obstacle*, Nation News, December 2, 2011.
15. *Global campaign to decriminalise homosexuality to kick off in Belize court*, The Guardian November 16, 2011.
16. *IACHR Concludes its 140th Period of Sessions*, Inter-American Commission on Human Rights, November 5, 2010.
17. *IACHR Condemns Murder of Two Gay Men in Jamaica*, Organization of American States, July 9, 2012.

18. *IACHR Creates Unit on the Rights of Lesbian, Gay, Bisexual, Trans, and Intersex Persons*, Organization of American States, November 3, 2011.
19. *IACHR Welcomes Anti-Discrimination Statement by the Prime Minister of Trinidad and Tobago*, Organization of American States, December 20, 2012.
20. *Jamaica: Combat Homophobia*, Human Rights Watch, July 18, 2012.
21. *Popularity of Caribbean island soars after gay wedding*, Jamaica Observer, December 15, 2012.
22. *Scrap Caribbean Anti-Gay Laws*, CBS news, February 11, 2009.
23. *Sexuality and the law*, Jamaica Gleaner, July 25, 2001.
24. *The FNM Attempted to Make Same Sex Marriage Legal Last Night in the House*, Bahamas Press, July 8, 2011.
25. *UN rights body hits out against violence based on sexual orientation*, UN News Center, June 17, 2011.
26. *UTech, Marksman Condemn Beating Of Alleged Gay Student*, Jamaica Gleaner, November 2, 2012.
27. Associated Press, *2 guards in Jamaica accused of beating gay student*, Fox News, November 3, 2012.
28. Associated Press, *Rosie O'Donnell Cruise for Gay Families Cuts Bermuda Stop, Fearing Protests*, FoxNews.com, April 18, 2007.
29. Baboolal, Yvonne. *PM promises rights for gays in gender policy*, Trinidad and Tobago Guardian Online, December 18, 2012.
30. Baptiste, Carlisle Jno. *2 US men arrested on gay cruise in Caribbean*, MSNBC, March 22, 2012.
31. Bolcer, Julie. *Jamaica Police Commissioner Blames Gays for Violence*, Advocate.com, July 13, 2012.
32. Boseley, Sarah. *Jamaican gay rights activists hopeful of repealing anti-homosexuality law*, The Guardian, February 10, 2012.
33. Bowcott, Owen. *Jamaica's colonial-era ties to UK legal system continue to fray*, The Guardian, January 6, 2012.
34. Clarke, Yvette D. *2012 Time 100: The Most Influential People in the World – Portia Simpson Miller*, Time Magazine, April 18, 2012.
35. Dittrich, Boris O. *Gay marriage's diamond anniversary*, Los Angeles Times, April 17, 2011.
36. Ellis, Guy. *St. Lucia Responds To Attack On 3 Gay American Tourists*, Huffington Post, March 14, 2012.
37. Evans, Teino. *Artistes not 'compassionate' to the act - Reggae artistes want clauses changed*, Jamaica Star, June 29, 2007.
38. Ferguson, Glen. *Bahamas Cruise Weddings to Get Boost from Maritime Marriage Legislations*, The Bahamas Weekly, July 14, 2011.
39. Gonzales, Gyasi, and Julien Neaves, *Govt to make decision on gay and lesbian marriages*, Trinidad Express, May 11, 2012.
40. Holness, Toni. *Jamaica's Portia Simpson Miller: Out with the Old and in with the New*, Intlawgrrls.com, January 18, 2012.
41. Jackson, Stephen. *Reggae Artists Blacklisted*, Jamaica Observer, February 28, 2010.
42. Johnson, Martina. *Same sex marriages off the radar*, Antigua Observer, December 21, 2012.
43. Kreindler, Eric, and Frank Heinz, *Homophobic Lyrics Lead to Concert Cancellations*, NBC Chicago, August 31, 2009.
44. Lacey, Mark. *Anti-gay violence defies laid-back image of Jamaica*, New York Times, February 24, 2008.
45. MCartney, Juan. *Bahamas backs gay rights*, The Nassau Guardian, June 18, 2011.
46. Padgett, Tim. *The Most Homophobic Place on Earth?*, Time World, April 12, 2006.
47. Robarbs, Chester. *Government against gay marriages*, The Nassau Guardian, July 8, 2011.
48. Sayare, Scott, and Maia De Law Baume, *In France, Civil Unions Gain Favor Over Marriage*, New York Times, December 15, 2010.

49. Swash, Rosie. *Beenie Man, Sizzla and Capleton renounce homophobia*, The Guardian, June 14, 2007.
50. Thompson, Christopher. *Curbing Homophobia in Reggae*, Time Entertainment, August 7, 2007.

Legislation and Related Documents

51. Application for Marriage Certificate, The Bahamas (available at http://www.bahamas.com/sites/bahamas.com/files/pdf/APPLICATION_FOR_MARRIAGE_CERTIFICATE.pdf).
52. Application for Marriage Certificate, Barbados (available at http://www.lawcourts.gov.bb/Documents/Application%20for%20Marriage%20Certificate.pdf).
53. Charter of Fundamental Rights and Freedoms (Constitutional Amendment) Act, 2011 (Jamaica).
54. Cohabitational Relationships Act, 1998, Cap 45:55 (Trinidad and Tobago)(available at http://www.ttparliament.org/legislations/a1998-30.pdf).
55. Criminal Code, 1958, Cap 76 (Grenada).
56. Criminal Code, 2004, Cap 273 (St. Lucia) (available at http://www.rslpf.com/site/criminal%20code%202004.pdf).
57. Deceased Wife's Sister or Brother's Widow Act, 1914 (Jamaica).
58. Hindu Marriage Act, 1945, Cap 45:03 (Trinidad and Tobago) (available at http://rgd.legalaffairs.gov.tt/laws2/alphabetical_list/lawspdfs/45.03.pdf).
59. Maintenance Act, 2005 (Jamaica) (available at http://www.moj.gov.jm/sites/default/files/laws/Maintenance%20Act.pdf)
60. Marriage Act, 1897, Cap 237 (Jamaica) (available at http://www.moj.gov.jm/sites/default/files/laws/Marriage%20Act.pdf)
61. Marriage Act, 1907, Cap. 106 (The Bahamas) (available at http://laws.bahamas.gov.bs/cms/images/LEGISLATION/PRINCIPAL/1908/1908-0004/MarriageAct_1.pdf).
62. Marriage Act, 1923, Cap 45:01 (Trinidad and Tobago) (available at http://rgd.legalaffairs.gov.tt/laws2/alphabetical_list/lawspdfs/45.01.pdf).
63. Marriage Act, 1925, Cap. 261 (Antigua and Barbuda) (available at http://www.laws.gov.ag/acts/chapters/cap-261.pdf).
64. Marriage Act, 1995, Cap. 218A (Barbados).
65. Marriage Act, 1998, Cap. 45:01 (Guyana) (available at http://www.jafbase.fr/DocAmeriques/Guyana/LoiMariage.pdf).
66. Marriage with Deceased Wife's Sister Act, 1907, Cap. 122 (The Bahamas).
67. Matrimonial Causes Act, 1879, Cap. 125 (The Bahamas).
68. Matrimonial Causes Act, 1989 (Jamaica) (available at http://www.moj.gov.jm/sites/default/files/laws/Matrimonial%20Causes%20Act.pdf).
69. Matrimonial Proceedings and Property Act, 1972, Cap 45:51 (Trinidad and Tobago) (available at http://rgd.legalaffairs.gov.tt/laws2/alphabetical_list/lawspdfs/45.51.pdf).
70. Muslim Marriage Act, 1957 (Jamaica) (available at http://www.moj.gov.jm/sites/default/files/laws/Muslin%20Marriage%20Act.pdf).
71. Muslim Marriage and Divorce Act, 1961, Cap 45:02 (Trinidad and Tobago) (available at http://rgd.legalaffairs.gov.tt/laws2/alphabetical_list/lawspdfs/45.02.pdf).
72. Parliamentary Legislative Session, Jun. 12, 2008 (Trinidad and Tobago) (available at http://www.ttparliament.org/hansards/hh19980612.pdf).
73. Property (Rights of Spouse) Act, 2006 (Jamaica) (available at http://www.moj.gov.jm/sites/default/files/laws/Property%20%28Rights%20of%20Spouse%29%20Act.pdf).
74. Sexual Offences Act, 1986, Cap 11:28 (Trinidad and Tobago) (available at http://rgd.legalaffairs.gov.tt/laws2/alphabetical_list/lawspdfs/11.28.pdf).

75. Sexual Offences Act, 1995 (Antigua and Barbuda) (available at http://laws.gov.ag/acts/1995/a1995-9.pdf).
76. Sexual Offences Act, 1998 (Dominica) (available at http://www.dominica.gov.dm/laws/1998/act1-1998.pdf).
77. Sexual Offences Act, 2009 (Jamaica) (available at http://www.japarliament.gov.jm/attachments/341_The%20Sexual%20Offences%20Act,%202009.pdf).
78. Sexual Offences and Domestic Violence Act, 2006, Cap 99 (The Bahamas).

Published Reports

79. AIDS Free World, Unnatural Connexion: Creating Societal Conflict Through Legal Tools, 17 (2004).
80. Department of Sociology, Psychology, and Social Work – University of the West Indies, Mona, National Survey of Attitudes and Perceptions of Jamaicans Towards Same Sex Relationships (September 2011).
81. Human Rights Watch, Hated to Death: Homophobia, Violence and Jamaica's HIV/AIDS Epidemic (November 2004).
82. Human Rights Watch, This Alien Legacy: The Origins of "Sodomy" Laws in British Colonialism 5 (December 2008).
83. Jamaicans for Justice, Brochure on the Privy Council and the Proposed Caribbean Court of Justice, June 5, 2006 (available at http://www.jamaicansforjustice.org) (last visited Feb. 3, 2013).
84. Organization of American States, Petition and Case System: Informational Brochure (2010)
85. U.S. Department of State, 2010 Human Rights Report: Trinidad (Apr. 2011).
86. U.S. Department of State, 2010 Human Rights Report: Antigua and Barbuda (May 2012).

Websites

87. Website of the Caribbean Court of Justice. Available at http://www.caribbeancourtofjustice.org/court-instruments. Last visited 22 Jan 2013.
88. Website of the Commonwealth of Nations. Available at www.commonwealthofnations.org. Last visited 4 Feb 2013.
89. Website of the Judicial Committee of the Privy Council. Available at http://www.jcpc.gov.uk/. Last visited 3 Feb 2013.

Chapter 8
Legal Status of Same-Sex Couples Within the Framework of Turkish Civil Law

Başak Başoğlu

Abstract Same-sex couples are not formally recognized in Turkey. In the last years, however, visibility of LGBTI individuals has increased. This Chapter is an overview of family law regulations in Turkey, and how they affect same-sex couples. It provides an account of legal spaces that could eventually allow for same-sex couples to start slowly enjoying spaces of legal protection. To a great extent these possibilities stem from the influence of the European Union and its strong stance against discrimination on the basis of sexual orientation and gender identity. This Chapter presents an overview of Family Law in Turkey and it specifically analyzes the marriage contract with the aim of showing spaces for recognition of same-sex couples in general and, eventually, same-sex marriage in particular.

8.1 Introduction

In the last decade, the social visibility of Lesbian, Gay Bisexual, Transgender and Transsexual and Intersex (LGBTI) people in Turkey increased. LGBTI people are still, however, marginalized.[1] A large number of Turkish people views

[1] For instance, Halil İbrahim Dinçdağ, who is a gay referee, has been suspended from duty by the Turkish Soccer Federation and he was barred from performing military service for being "gay". For a news account, see http://www.bianet.org/bianet/toplumsal-cinsiyet/141409-onun-dudugu-onun-karari. Moreover, in 2013 "*twelve LGBTI hate murders were reported in Turkey, and several lynching attempts and incidents of torture, rape, ill-treatment, domestic violence, harassment, and cyber-attacks against LGBTIs.*" For more information, see Communication From the Commission to the European Parliament and the Council: Enlargement Strategy And Main Challenges 2013–2014 Final Commission Staff Working Document Turkey 2013 Progress Report Accompanying the Document Com (2013) 700, Brussels, 16.10.2013 [Hereinafter, *Progress Report 2013*] at 59 available at http://www.abgs.gov.tr. For news account on the LGBT community in Turkey see the websites: http://www.bianet.org/bianet/lgbtt and http://www.lambdaistanbul.org

B. Başoğlu (✉)
Faculty of Law, Istanbul Kemerburgaz University, Mahmutbey Dilmenler Caddesi, No:26, 34217 Boğcılar, Istanbul, Turkey
e-mail: basakbasoglu@gmail.com

M. Sáez (ed.), *Same Sex Couples - Comparative Insights on Marriage and Cohabitation*, Ius Gentium: Comparative Perspectives on Law and Justice 42,
DOI 10.1007/978-94-017-9774-0_8

homosexuality as an "illness"[2] and LGBTI population faces discrimination in many different areas. The lack of provisions protecting people from discrimination on the basis of sexual orientation violates the basic rights and freedoms of LGBTI populations.[3]

In 2001 Turkey signed Protocol 12 to the European Convention on Human Rights for the Protection of Human Rights and Fundamental Freedoms. The Protocol, however, is not enforced or reflected in local legislation.[4] For example, during the Parliamentary discussions in preparation for a new Turkish Constitution, members of Parliament proposed to include a new definition of marriage that would read "all persons have a right to get married and establish a family." Other members of Parliament opposed to this definition because it could lead to same-sex marriages.[5] Another important example is the legal action presented to ban Lambdaİstanbul LGBT Solidarity Association. The trial court held that Turkish society did not approve Lambdaİstanbul LGBT Solidarity Association and that such organization went against the morality of Turkish society.[6] Furthermore, the court explained that the association's activities were a threat to the Turkish Constitution, which protects family and children, and it stipulates the rights and freedoms of the youth.[7] The Court of Cassation, however, overturned the trial court decision by stating that everyone had a right to establish an association in accordance with Article 20 of the Universal Declaration of Human Rights, Article 22 of the International Covenant on Civil and Political Rights, and Article 11 of the European Convention on Human Rights.[8] The Court of Cassation also stated in its decision that according to Article 10 of the Turkish Constitution everyone was equal before the law regardless of language, religion, ethnical background, gender and political view and all people

---

[2]Karadağ, Nevra; Cinsel Azınlıkların Bireysel Hakları, XII Levha Yayıncılık, Istanbul, 2008, 121 [Hereinafter, *Karadağ*]. For example, Court of Cassation has stated in a decision that "the reason for divorce is "homosexuality" which can never be accepted by Turkish society. Giving the custody of the girl to a woman who has such diseased habit which amount to illness could endanger the future of the child." [Decision of the Second Civil Chamber of the Court of Cassation dated 21, June, 1982, and numbered 5077/5531 (available at www.hukukturk.com)].

[3]Karadağ, *Ibid.*, pp. 121–122.

[4]Progress Report 2013 at 48. Moreover, it has been stated in this Progress Report that "*The Penal Code and the Law on Misdemeanours were used against transgender persons in a discriminatory and arbitrary manner. The Law on the Internet was used against some LGBTI and other websites which were considered politically and morally unsuitable. The Penal Code provision against resisting an officer in the course of his duty was frequently used to counter accusations of harassment.*" Progress Report 2013 at 59.

[5]For the news dated 11.11.2012 please see http://www.haberturk.com/polemik/haber/792977-ya-kopeklerle-evlenirlerse

[6]Beyoğlu 3rd Civil Court, 190/236, May 29, 2008. For detailed information and case analysis, please see Gülmez, Mesut, "Dernek Özgürlüğü ve Cinsel Yönelime Dayalı Ayrımcılık Sorunu: Lambdaİstanbul Davası Kararları (Karar İncelemesi)", Çalışma ve Toplum Dergisi, 2009/3(22): 195–230 at 200–209.

[7]*Ibid.*

[8]Court of Cassation, 7th Civil Chamber, 4109/5196, November 25, 2008.

had a right to establish an association or be part of an association. In addition to the Court of Cassation's decision in the Lambdaİstanbul case, other courts have recognized that European countries provide legal protection to same-sex couples and have referred to the importance of such protection within the framework of human rights and equality.[9]

8.2 Framework of Turkish Family Law

Turkish family law only recognizes specific family relations. This means that couples seeking legal protection can only access those relationships recognized by the Turkish Civil Code.[10] These are "engagement" and "marriage." Under Turkish family law, cohabitation does not carry any legal consequences regardless of whether the couple is of different or same-sex.[11] The only contract available to couples is marriage, interpreted by courts as the union between a man and a woman. The Turkish Civil Code does not clearly indicate that marriage is only established between a man and a woman,[12] Turkish courts, however, have interpreted that the wording of the Turkish Civil Code can only apply to the union between a man

---

[9]For an example see the decision of 4th Chamber of Court of Cassation dated 22.2.2000 and numbered 1598, available at http://www.hukukturk.com

[10]Akıntürk, Turgut/Ateş Karaman, Derya; Türk Medeni Hukuku Aile Hukuku İkinci Cilt, 15. Edition, Beta Yayıncılık, Istanbul 2013, 10–11 [Hereinafter, *Akıntürk/Ateş Karaman*]; Dural, Mustafa/Öğüz, Tufan/Gümüş, Alper, Türk Özel Hukuku, Cilt III, Aile Hukuku, 5. Edition, Filiz Kitabevi, Istanbul, 2012, 4 [Hereinafter, *Dural/Öğüz/Gümüş*]; Feyzioğlu, Feyzi Ncmeddin, Aile Hukuku, 3. Edition, Istanbul, Filiz Kitabevi, 1986, 14–15 [Hereinafter, *Feyzioğlu*]; Oğuzman, Kemal/Dural, Mustafa, Aile Hukuku, Filiz Kitabevi, Istanbul, 1998, 4 [Hereinafter, *Oğuzman/Dural*]; Öztan, Bilge, Aile Hukuku, 5. Edition, Turhan Kitabevi, Ankara, 2004, 17 [Hereinafter, *Öztan*]; Zevkliler, Aydın/Acabey, Beşir/Gökyayla, Emre, Medeni Hukuk (Giriş, Başlangıç Hükümleri, Kişiler Hukuku, Aile Hukuku), Ankara, 1999, 672–673 [Hereinafter, *Zevkliler/Acabey/Gökyayla*].

[11]Hatemi, Hüseyin, Hukuka ve Ahlaka Aykırılık Kavramı, Istanbul, 1976, 383–384 [Hereinafter, *Hatemi, Hukuka ve Ahlâka Aykırılık*].

[12]Akıntürk/Ateş Karaman, supra note 9, at 195; Dural/Öğüz/Gümüş, supra note 9, at 47, 69; Feyzioğlu, supra note 9, 95; Köprülü, Bülent/Kaneti, Selim, Aile Hukuku, Istanbul Üniversitesi Yayınları, Istanbul, 1986, 96 [Hereinafter, *Köprülü/Kaneti*]; Oğuzman/Dural, supra note 9, at 24, 26; Öztan, supra note 9 at 321; Sayman, Yücel, Türk Devletler Hususî Hukukunda Evlenmenin Kuruluşu, Fakülteler Matbaası, Istanbul, 1982, 99–100 [Hereinafter, *Sayman*]; Schwarz, Andreas, Aile Hukuku I, Istanbul, 1946, 123 [Hereinafter, *Schwarz*]; Tekinay, Selahâttin Sulhi, Türk Aile Hukuku, Filiz Kitabevi, Istanbul, 1990, 108 [Hereinafter, *Tekinay*]; Tutumlu, Mehmet Akif, Yeni Türk Medenî Kanunu Hükümlerine Göre Evliliğin Butlanı, Boşanma ve Ayrılık Sebepleri ve Boşanmanın Hukukî Sonuçları, Adalet Yayınevi, Ankara, 2002, 67 [Hereinafter, *Tutumlu*]; Velideoğlu, Hıfzı Veldet, Türk Medeni Hukuku, C. 2, Aile Hukuku, 5. Edition, Istanbul Üniversitesi Yayınları, Istanbul, 1965, 281 [Hereinafter, *Velidedeoğlu*]; Zevkliler/Acabey/Gökyayla, supra note 9 at 834–835.

and a woman.[13] Also, Article 2 of the Marriage Regulation[14] describes marriage as "a legal contract concluded between a man and a woman with the intention to establish a family before an authorized marriage officer in the required procedure." Additionally, Articles 6, 11, 14, and 16 of the Marriage Regulation support Article 2's narrative. Finally, Turkish jurisprudence strongly supports this definition.[15] Furthermore, the presence of one man and one woman is considered an essential element of marriage.[16] The lack of this essential element means that the union is nonexistent and carries no legal consequences.[17]

The Turkish legislator prefers a framework where marriage is the exclusive institution of family formation. Cohabitation does not carry any legal consequences[18] and it is not possible to apply the provisions of marriage by analogy.[19] Turkish family law, therefore, is not applicable to any living arrangements other than marriage.[20] Although cohabitation carries no legal protection, it carries no criminal sanctions either. Same-sex couples, therefore, are free to form *de facto* unions, just as heterosexual couples are.

[13]Articles 124, 134, and 136 of the Turkish Civil Code.

[14]It is published in the Official Gazette dated 7.11.1985 numbered 18921.

[15]Akıntürk/Ateş Karaman, *supra* note 9, p. 61; Dural/Öğüz/Gümüş, *supra* note 9, p.15; Feyzioğlu, *supra* note 9, p. 83; Gençcan, Ömer Uğur; Aile Hukuku, Yetkin Yayınları, Ankara, 2011, 166, 364 [Hereinafter, *Gençcan*], Gönensay, A. Samim, Medenî Hukuk, C. 2, Kısım 1, Istanbul Üniversitesi Yayınları, Istanbul, 1937; 17 [Hereinafter, *Gönensay*]; Köprülü/Kaneti, *supra* note 11, p. 65; Oğuzman/Dural, *supra* note 9, p. 19; Öztan, *supra* note 9, p. 94; Saymen, Ferit H./Elbir, K. Halid, Türk Medenî Hukuku, C. III, Aile Hukuku, İsmail Akgün Matbaası, Istanbul, 1957, 30 [Hereinafter, *Saymen/Elbir*]; Schwarz, *supra* note 10, p. 25; Tekinay, *supra* note 10, p. 63; Velidedeoğlu, *supra* note 10, p. 49; Zevkliler/Acabey/Gökyayla, *supra* note 1, p. 707.

[16]Akıntürk/Ateş Karaman, *supra* note 9, p. 195; Dural/Öğüz/Gümüş, *supra* note 1, p. 69; Feyzioğlu, *supra* note 9, p. 96; Hatemi, Hüseyin/Serozan, Rona; Aile Hukuku, Filiz Kitabevi, Istanbul, 1993, 87 [Hereinafter, *Hatemi/Serozan*], Köseoğlu, Bilal/Kocaağa, Köksal; Aile Hukuku ve Uygulaması – Bilimsel Görüşler, Yargı İçtihatları, Ekin Basım Yayın Dağıtım, Bursa, 2011, 8 [Hereinafter, *Köseoğlu/Kocaağa*] Oğuzman/Dural, *supra* note 9, p. 88; Öztan, *supra* note 9, p. 321; Tekinay, *supra* note 10, p. 108; Zevkliler/Acabey/Gökyayla, *supra* note 9, p. 835.

[17]Akıntürk/Ateş Karaman, *supra* note 9, p. 197; Dural/Öğüz/Gümüş, *supra* note 1, p. 75; Hatemi/Serozan, id, at 87; Köseoğlu/Kocaağa, id, at 8, Oğuzman/Dural, supra note 9, at 89; Öztan, supra note 9, p. 320; Zevkliler/Acabey/Gökyayla, supra note 9, at 835.

[18]Köteli, M. Argun; Evliliğin Hukuki Niteliği ve Evlilik Dışı Beraberlikler, Istanbul, 1991, 145 [Hereinafter, *Köteli*].

[19]Köteli, ibid. at 169.

[20]Dural/Öğüz/Gümüş; *supra* note 1, p. 46; Oğuzman/Dural, *supra* note 9, p. 19.

8.3 Application of Family Law Provisions

8.3.1 Application of Marriage Regulations to Same-Sex Couples

The legislature's political choice was to provide different legal status to married and unmarried couples. Accordingly, Turkish law provides married couples with the legal protection of family law while cohabitating couples have no protection at all. The rationale behind this decision is to promote marriage and, therefore, application of marriage regulations by analogy or interpretation to unmarried couples would contradict this purpose. Moreover, application of these provisions to same-sex couples would be even more problematic since the legislator purposely avoided providing legal protection to same-sex couples.

Although Turkish law does not include a concept of family,[21] the legal doctrine has defined a family as the community formed by a married couple and its children.[22] At the same time, Article 8 of the European Convention on Human Rights does not limit "family life" solely to marriage-based relationships, but it may also encompass other *de facto* family ties formed outside marriage.[23] According to this Convention, therefore, unmarried couples living together could have family ties depending on their personal commitment and seriousness of their relationship.[24] Weighing such factors, same-sex couples could have family ties according to European standards. Turkish courts, however, are not willing to apply those standards. In fact, the Court of Cassation decided that an opposite-sex couple living together without being married was against Turkish moral values.[25] Moreover, the General Assembly of the Court of Cassation decided that same-sex

[21] Gençcan, *supra* note 14, p. 171.

[22] Akıntürk/Ateş Karaman, *supra* note 9, p. 5; Dural/Öğüz/Gümüş; *supra* note 1, p. 1.

[23] ECHR: Case of Keegan v. Ireland, No: 411/490, 19 April 1994, available at: http://www.unhcr.org/refworld/docid/3ae6b6ff8.html, N. 42-43-44.

[24] When deciding whether a relationship would amount to "family life", a number of factors may be relevant, including whether the couple lives together, the length of their relationship and whether they have demonstrated their commitment to each other by having children together or by any other means (ECHR: Case of Al-Nashif v. Bulgaria, Application No. 50963/99, Judgment of 20 June 2002, N. 94, available at http://hudoc.echr.coe.int/sites/eng/pages/search.aspx?i=001-60522). The couples that have children are especially considered to be a family since children constitute strong ties between the couples (ECHR: Case of Elsholz v. Germany Application no. 25735/94, Judgment of 13 July 2000, N. 43, available at http://hudoc.echr.coe.int/sites/eng/pages/search.aspx?i=001-58763). However, same-sex couples could not have children by adoption or in vitro fertilization or such artificial methods. Even same-sex couples living together.

[25] The decision of the 4th Chamber of the Court of Cassation dated 04/06/2012 and numbered 2012/9724 (available at http://www.hukukturk.com).

couples did not have a family but could only be considered living a "mistress life."[26] Based on these decisions, it is not possible to consider same-sex couples as a family unit.

At the same time, there are circumstances in which the term "family member" should apply to opposite and same-sex cohabitating couples in order to provide protection to the parties. For instance, Turkish courts should apply the Law on the Protection of the Family and Prevention of Violence against Woman[27] to opposite and same-sex cohabitants.[28] Article 1 of the law seeks to protect women, children, family members and victims of stalking. Also, the law establishes procedures to prevent violence. Even though opposite and same-sex cohabitants do not constitute family under Turkish law, the courts should interpret this statute broadly, in order to protect people who live together and share mutual living arrangements. Some lower courts have decided to apply the Law on the Protection of the Family to unmarried opposite-sex couples living together.[29] The courts compared opposite-sex couples to a religious matrimony (hereinafter, "Muslim marriage") which is, in fact, not equal to the officially sanctioned marriage, and does not enjoy any of the rights and obligations under Turkish family law.[30] These decisions give ground to an application of the statute to both opposite and same-sex cohabitations.

[26]The decision of the General Assembly of the Court of Cassation dated 26/05/1999 and numbered 9-307/467; please see the opposing view of one of the Members of the General Assembly (available at http://www.hukukturk.com).

[27]Hereinafter referred as "Law on the Protection of the Family." It is published in the Official Gazette dated 20.03.2012 numbered 28239.

[28]Köseoğlu/Kocaağa, supra note 15, at 592.

[29]Referring to the date of the decision, this is not the recent Law on Protection of the Family but it is the previous law published in the Official Gazette dated 17/01/1998 and numbered 23233.

[30]According to Article 143 of Turkish Civil Code, religious matrimony can only be made upon an officially sanctioned marriage. Therefore, no religious wedding ceremony is permitted prior to the civil ceremony. If a couple gets married solely with a religious matrimony, their marriage is nonexistent, as religious ceremony does no amount to a marriage before the authorized officer in the required procedure. Also cohabilitation with a sole religious matrimony is regulated as a crime under Turkish Criminal Code. [For further information on the Muslim marriage and the status of women in Muslim marriage, please see: Başoğlu, Başak/Paksoy, Meliha Sermin "Dini Nikâhlı Kadının Hukuki Durumu", in "Prof. Dr. Şener Akyol'a Armağan", Filiz Kitabevi, Istanbul, 2011, pp. 239–269.]

8.3.2 Application of Engagement Regulations to Same-Sex Couples

An engagement is a mutual promise to marry. Some scholars argue that courts could apply the rules of engagement to opposite-sex couples living together.[31] Since the Turkish Civil Code does not define marriage, courts should broadly interpret the promise to marry and view opposite-sex cohabitation as an engagement.[32] This interpretation could eventually lead to an inclusion of the rules of engagement to same-sex couples as well. Other scholars, however, argue that a promise to marry is only valid within a systematic interpretation of the Turkish Civil Code, and only valid between a man and a woman.[33] As the law does not allow same-sex marriage, same-sex couples' promises to marry could not constitute engagement. Thus, engagement of same-sex couples would be invalid because it would lack the element of heterosexuality.

Under this interpretation cohabitation of opposite sex couples cannot constitute an engagement either since the intention of the partners is to live together and not to get married. The aim of the engagement provisions is to provide legal consequences for the promise to marry, so that parties take the proposals seriously and execute the preparations to marry with the confidence of a legally binding promise. Therefore, it is not possible to apply the engagement provisions to same-sex couples because the parties lack the intention of getting married.[34]

According to Article 121 of Turkish Civil Code, the engaged parties have the right to claim non-pecuniary damages from each other in case the engagement is terminated due to fault by one of the parties. Arguably, in cases where one of the cohabitants infringes the personality rights of the other through dissolution of the cohabitation, it is possible for the other party to claim damages based on Article 25 of the Turkish Civil Code, which provides general protection in case of infringement of the personality rights of an individual. In a 2002 case regarding the dissolution of a Muslim marriage after 45 years, the Court of Cassation ruled that in order for the court to award compensation, there had to be a specific offense. One of the spouses must commit a crime against the honor and reputation of the other person

[31] Belgesay, Mustafa Reşit, "Filli Evliliğin ve Evlilik Dışında Doğan Çocukların Himayesi", MHAD, Year 2, Istanbul, 1958, pp. 21–24 (21) [Hereinafter, *Belgesay*]. For the criticism of this view, please see Hatemi, *supra* note 10, p. 369–373; Köprülü/Kaneti, *supra* note 11, p. 65; Köteli, *supra* note 17, p. 145–146.

[32] Belgesay, ibid., p. 24.

[33] Akıntürk/Ateş Karaman, *supra* note 9, p. 195; Dural/Öğüz/Gümüş, *supra* note 9, p. 47, 69; Feyzioğlu, *supra* note 9, p. 95; Köprülü/Kaneti, *supra* note 11, p. 96; Köteli, *supra* note 17, p. 55; Oğuzman/Dural, *supra* note 9, p. 24, 26; Öztan, *supra* note 9, p. 321; Sayman, *supra* note 10, p. 99–100; Schwarz, *supra* note 2, p. 123; Tekinay, *supra* note 10, p. 108; Velidedeoğlu, *supra* note 10, p. 281; Zevkliler/Acabey/Gökyayla, *supra* note 9, p. 834–835.

[34] Serozan, Rona, "Evlilik Dışı Birlikte Yaşam İlişkisi", Istanbul Barosu Dergisi Volume 57, No. 1–3, Istanbul, 1983, 5–17 (8) [Hereinafter, *Serozan*].

or her family or an infringement against personality. Compensation is warranted when dissolution of an engagement or a marriage occurs, a spouse denies paternity, or personal injury or death occurs. Courts, however, have stated that a person intentionally living in cohabitation without marriage may not claim infringement of personality rights.[35] Considering this and the approach of the Court of Cassation to same-sex couples, it would be hard to successfully argue that a person could claim compensation based on the general provisions protecting personality rights in case her or his partner of the same sex decided to leave.

With regards to pecuniary damages, the provisions on engagement state that parties can claim damages from each other in case one of them ends the engagement without legal grounds.[36] For the same reasons stated above, these provisions would not apply to same-sex couples either.

8.4 Possibility of Application of Contractual Provisions

8.4.1 Validity of the Contract

As observed, Turkish family law does not provide legal protection and rights to same-sex cohabitation. The freedom of contract, however, is one of the basic principles established in the Turkish Code of Obligations. As a result, same-sex couples could arrange their legal relations upon a contractual relationship, such as distribution of property in cases of death or separation. Turkish contract and property laws, therefore, provide a possible alternative for the protection of same-sex cohabitants.[37]

In fact, same-sex couples that want to share a mutual life can enter into a contractual relationship and can also contract with third parties. A same-sex couple may buy a house or household goods together, open a bank account or celebrate contracts with regards to the distribution of their shared property. There may be, however, problems with the liquidation of assets in case of separation.[38] The main issue is whether contracts celebrated by same-sex couples are valid.

[35]The decision of the 4th Chamber of Court of Cassation dated 24.04.2003 and numbered 2003/5289 (available at http://www.hukukturk.com).

[36]For instance, if one of the parties quits his/her job due to the engagement, then he/she could claim for compensation from the opposite party who has ended the engagement without legal grounds. Likewise if one of the parties specified his/her effort to the housework in order to avoid hiring help for the housework, then this party may claim for compensation as normative damages within the tort provisions. Serozan, *supra* note 31, p. 11.

[37]Başoğlu, Başak/Yasan, Candan; National Report: Turkey, 19 AM. U. J. Gender Soc. Pol'y & L., 2011, 319–328 (322) [Hereinafter, *Başoğlu/Yasan*].

[38]Köteli, *supra* note 17, pp. 121–122.

Turkish Code of Obligations, in Article 27 states that the subject matter of a legal transaction shall not be impossible or contrary to mandatory rules, public order, moral values and personality rights. In those cases, transactions will be deemed void.[39] As mentioned before, in several cases the Court of Cassation has ruled that opposite-sex cohabitation goes against Turkish moral values.[40] Legal doctrine criticized these decisions.[41] Furthermore, these cohabitations related to Muslim marriages which do not comply with legal regulations of marriage but are nonetheless acceptable unions by Turkish society. Considering these decisions, it is likely that Turkish courts would consider same-sex cohabitations against morality as well. Some legal scholars also claim that same-sex relationships go against moral values and any contracts entered in order to regulate mutual obligations or property would be deemed void.[42]

---

[39]Eren, Fikret, Borçlar Hukuku, Genel Hükümler, 14. Edition, Yetkin Yayınevi, Ankara, 2012, 333–336 [Hereinafter, *Eren*]; Kocayusufpaşaoğlu, Necip in Borçlar Hukuku Genel Bölüm, Birinci Cilt, Borçlar Hukukuna Giriş-Hukukî İşlem-Sözleşme, Kocayusufpaşaoğlu, Necip/Hatemi, Hüseyin/Serozan, Rona/Arpacı, Abdülkadir, 4. Edition, Filiz Kitabevi, Istanbul, 2008, 580–581 [Hereinafter, *Kocayusufpaşaoğlu Borçlar*]; Oğuzman, Kemal/Barlas, Nami; Medenî Hukuk – Giriş, Kaynaklar, Temel Kavramlar, 18. Edition, Vedat Kitapçılık, Istanbul, 2012, 221 [Hereinafter, *Oğuzman/Barlas*]; Oğuzman, Kemal/Öz, Turgut; Borçlar Hukuku Genel Hükümler Cilt I, 9. Edition, Vedat Kitapçılık, Istanbul, 2011, 87 [Hereinafter, *Oğuzman/Öz, v.1*]. In case that these contracts are deemed to be void, then the unjust enrichment provisions of the Turkish Code of Obligations shall be applied to the restitution. In accordance with Article 81 of the Turkish Code of Obligations, no right to restitution exists for the things given to produce an illegal or immoral outcome. **Ateş, Derya**; Borçlar Hukuku Sözleşmelerinde Genel Ahlâka Aykırılık, Turhan Kitabevi, Ankara, 2007, 318 et seq. [Hereinafter, *Ateş*]; Eren, id, at 899–900; **Serozan, Rona,** "Geçersiz Satım Sözleşmesinin Karşılıklı İfa Sonrası Çözülmesi", MHAD, Volume 3, No: 4 (1969), pp. 187–213 (188) [Hereinafter, *Serozan Geçersiz Satım*]; **Serozan, Rona** in Borçlar Hukuku, Genel Bölüm, Üçüncü Cilt, İfa Engelleri-Haksız Zenginleşme, Kocayusufpaşaoğlu, Necip /Hatemi, Hüseyin/ Serozan, Rona /Arpacı, Abdülkadir, Filiz Kitabevi, İstanbul, 2006, 331 [Hereinafter, *Serozan, İfa Engelleri*]; Hatemi, supra note 10, at 543 et seq; **Hatemi, Hüseyin/ Gökyayla, Emre**; Borçlar Hukuku Genel Bölüm, 2. Edition, Vedat Kitapçılık, İstanbul, 2012, 198 [Hereinafter, *Hatemi/ Gökyayla*]. Furthermore, it is stated that the Court may decide to assign these goods to the State Treasury. The Court of Cassation has found opposite- sex cohabitations illegitimate and decided that the donations may not be restituted upon the application of Article 81 (Decision of the 13th Chamber of the Court of Cassation dated 24.4.2006 and numbered 6349 (http://www.hukukturk.com).

[40]The Court of Cassation has decisions regarding the restitution of goods since it is hard prove that they were given for the assurance of the opposite sex cohabitation. Please see the decisions of the General Assembly of the Court of Cassation dated 18.4.1962 and numbered 46 (available at http://www.hukukturk.com); 3rd Chamber of the Court of Cassation 31.5.1988 and numbered 5973 (http://www.hukukturk.com); 4th Chamber of the Court of Cassation dated 20.1.1970 and numbered 818 (available at http://www.hukukturk.com).

[41]For the view that the opposite sex cohabitations may not be deemed to be against the moral values please see Köprülü/Kaneti, *supra* note 11, p. 65; Tekinay, Selahâttin Sulhi, Ölüm Sebebiyle Destekten Yoksun Kalma Tazminatı, Istanbul, Fakülteler Matbaası, 1963, 38–43 [Hereinafter, *Tekinay, Destekten Yoksun Kalma*].

[42]Gökyayla, K. Emre, Destekten Yoksun Kalma Tazminatı, Ankara, Seçkin Yayınevi, 2004, 121, 128 [Hereinafter, *Gökyayla*]; Hatemi, *supra* note 10, p. 353.

Morality, however, is not a univocal concept. Scholars provide different definitions for the concept of morality that would be legally applicable in Turkish law.[43] Turkish courts have broadly interpreted the concept of morality in order to provide a common understanding. The notions "morality" and "public order," however, have vague meanings and courts interpret such notions with the concepts of "legality" and "personality rights" in mind. In other words, the mere fact that a same-sex relation is against an understanding of morality by a group of people is not sufficient to deem the contract between same-sex couples void. The notion "immoral" must come attached to a conduct that can be illegal or that triggers an infringement of personality rights. Courts do not protect same-sex relations but they do not forbid these relations either. Therefore, courts cannot deem the mere existence of same-sex cohabitation as immoral.

In order to be immoral, cohabitation itself should have an illegal purpose or such cohabitation should infringe the personality rights of at least one of the parties. Accordingly, courts should examine each case separately.[44] For example, a court may deem a contract "immoral" if its purpose is to impose a sexual conduct on the other party or if made to provide sexual relations in exchange of money. Courts may deem these contracts void. In these cases immorality complements illegality, infringement of personality and free will.[45]

If the goal of a same-sex couple is to build a life together, a court could not deem it immoral because the goal of the contract would concern the private life of the parties. Turkish law made a policy decision not to regulate same-sex cohabitation. This legal policy choice contradicts the notion that same-sex cohabitation goes against moral values. Furthermore, if courts held that same-sex cohabitation goes against morality, this would punish same-sex cohabitants due to choices that affect their private lives.[46] It would actually be an interference of privacy as a societal value. Some scholars argue that in order to end the debate regarding the immorality

---

[43]For these different definitions, please see Ateş, supra note 37, at 83–87. Constitutional Court has defined moral values in one of its decisions as "*the rules, which indicates the acts related to the moral values and are easily understood and accepted in a certain time, by the majority of the certain society.*" (The decision of Constitutional Court dated 28.1.1964 and numbered 1964/8 available at http://www.anayasa.gov.tr/index.php?l=manage_karar&ref=show&action=karar&id=86&content).

[44]The legal doctrine claims that contrary to Article 27 of the Code of Obligations, in the application of Article 81, the purpose of forcing the beneficiary must be sought in the donor; see Oğuzman, Kemal/Öz, Turgut; Borçlar Hukuku Genel Hükümler, Cilt II, 9. Edition, Vedat Kitapçılık, Istanbul, 2012, 354 [Hereinafter, *Oğuzman/Öz v.2*]. However, in a cohabitation where both parties have donations regarding the maintenance of the living, it may be hard to determine such Hatemi, *supra* note 10, pp. 362–363.

[45]Ateş, *supra* note 37, p. 211.

[46]It is claimed in the legal doctrine that the purpose of Article 81 of the Turkish Code of Obligation is to provide a civil law punishment for the acts against to the moral values. Ateş, *supra* note 37, p. 317; Hatemi, *supra* note 10, p. 615; Serozan, Rona; Medeni Hukuk, Genel Bölüm Kişiler Hukuku, Istanbul, Vedat Kitapçılık, 2011, 22–23 [Hereinafter, Serozan, *Medeni Hukuk*].

of same-sex cohabitations, the legislature should grant legal status to these relations under marriage or granting them a status other than marriage.[47]

8.4.2 Donations Between Same-Sex Cohabitants

A donation has to have a *causa donandi*, a reason for the donor to give something to another person. The donation cannot have immoral purposes such as providing or maintaining sexual relations with the beneficiary. Such donation would be void. It is not, however, sufficient for the donor to have an immoral motivation, but it is also required that the beneficiary know and accept the motivation of the donation.[48] It is not legally possible to deem all cohabitations immoral and to state that all donations made between cohabitants are motivated by immoral purposes. Courts must interpret social morality principles with an understanding that such principles are compatible with the Constitution, human rights, and the basic values of Turkish laws. This interpretation gives a broader scope of action than interpreting morality principles according to society's general approach to moral values.[49] Courts, therefore, could not deem donations between same-sex cohabitants immoral unless it is clear that the donation was made with the direct intention of maintaining sexual relations.[50] When the purpose of the donation goes against morality, the donor may not be able to claim the restitution of the donation.[51] According to Article 81 of Turkish Code of Obligations, no right to restitution exists for the things given to produce an illegal or immoral outcome. The same Article states that a court may decide to assign those goods to the State Treasury.

Inheritance laws do not provide legal protection to cohabitants. Donations, therefore, could be used by same-sex couples to seek protection in case of death on one of the parties. Donations established to be effective after the death of the donor are governed by inheritance laws. Courts, however, treat these donations as void when they violate statutory entitlements of legal heirs.[52] Thus, only individuals

[47] Üskül-Engin, Zeynep Özlem, Türkiye'de Evlenmenin Evrimi, Beşir Kitabevi, Istanbul 2008, 306 [Hereinafter, *Üskül-Engin*].

[48] Kocayusufpaşaoğlu Borçlar, *supra* note 36, p. 556.

[49] Kocayusufpaşaoğlu Borçlar, *supra* note 36, p. 553; Serozan, *supra* note 31, p. 8.

[50] Hatemi, *supra* note 10, p. 386.

[51] However, this issue is debated in the legal doctrine. In accordance with the opposing view, in cases of invalidity due to immorality, both the obligational and the dispositional transactions are affected from invalidity. Accordingly, the ownership does not pass to the other party. Oğuzman/Öz v.2, *supra* note 44, p. 739 et seq.

[52] Legal heirs are regulated under Articles 495–501 of Turkish Civil Code as descendants, parental line, grandparental line, surviving spouse and government. The statutory entitlement of the legal heirs is regulated under Article 506 of Turkish Civil Code as follows: "The statutory entitlement is: 1. for any descendants, one-half of statutory succession rights; 2. for each parent, quarter of statutory succession rights; 3. for any siblings; one eighth of statutory succession rights; 4. for the

without legally mandated heirs could make donations that would replace inheritance regulations. Turkey inheritance law establishes a mandated set of legal heirs who have the right to inherit even against the will of the deceased.[53]

8.4.3 Labor Relationships Between Same-Sex Couples

Another reason to consider the validity of contracts celebrated between couples of the same sex is the need to protect valid labor relationships. For instance, in a case where a person worked as the secretary and driver of his partner of the same sex, the Court of Cassation discussed whether the parties had created a labor relation between them.[54] In accordance with Article 394 of Turkish Code of Obligations, courts consider that parties create an employment contract when an employer accepts the performance of work done in a certain period in his service and under circumstances in which the employee could reasonably expect a salary.[55] Accordingly, courts consider the actual status but not the intention of the parties to celebrate an employment contract.[56] In case one of the parties worked for the benefit of the other, that party is entitled to claim wages. However, in accordance with Article 147 of the Turkish Code of Obligations, claims for wages are subject to a 5 years statute of limitations.[57] At the same time, the parties cannot claim wages for the efforts and work done for the benefit of the other party.[58] In the case where one of the parties contributes significantly to the other party's work, the services may be considered part of a simple partnership. Thus, the law must consider the

surviving spouse, in case she/he is a heir with any of the linear kins, it is the whole of statutory succession rights; and in other circumstances it is the 3:4 of the statutory succession rights."

[53]Hatemi, *supra* note 10, p. 286, 387; However the Court of Cassation has decisions in which it is stated that donations made in a Muslim marriage and subject to the death of the donor do not constitute a valid ground since the intent to infringe the legal entitlement of the heirs do not exist (1st Chamber of the Court of Cassation dated 27.05.2009 and numbered 2009/6090).

[54]The decision of the General Assembly of the Court of Cassation dated 26/05/1999 and numbered 9-307/467 (available at http://www.hukukturk.com).

[55]This is a strict presumption and thus, otherwise could not be proved. Schmid; Jörg/Stöckli, Hubert; Schweizerisches Obligationenrecht Besonderer Teil, Schulthess, Zürich, 2010, N. 1419 [Hereinafter, *Schmid/Stöckli*].

[56]As explained above, the employment contract may be void due to immorality or illegality in accordance with Article 27 of the Code of Obligations.

[57]Five years of prescription period is only foreseen for claims for the wages. The claims other than wages of the employee are subject to the years of the prescription period. Erdem, Mehmet, Özel Hukukta Zamanaşımı, XII Levha Yayıncılık, Istanbul, 2010, 68–69 [Hereinafter, *Erdem*].

[58]Emmel, Stephen in Handkommentar zum Schweizer Privatrecht, Vertragsverhältnisse Teil 2: Arbeitsvertrag, Werkvertrag, Auftrag, GoA, Bürgschaft (Art. 319–529), Schulthess, Zurich, 2010, OR 320, N. 2; Portmann, Wolfgang, in Basler Kommentar Obligationenrecht I, Art. 1–529, Herausgeber: Honsell, Heinrich; Vogt, Nedim Peter; Wiegand, Wolfgang, 5. Edition, Helbing Lichtenhahn, Basel, 2007, Art 320, No. 22.

contribution of one of the parties to the work of the other. If the contribution is small, then the provisions of Article 395 of the Turkish Code of Obligation applies, whereas if the contribution is significant, then the simple partnership provisions apply.[59]

8.4.4 Simple Partnership

Some scholars consider that Turkish law could accept cohabitation of opposite sex couples as a simple partnership and the economic values that the parties bring to the partnership could be evaluated as contribution.[60] The provisions of the simple partnership could also apply to same-sex couples living together.[61]

Simple partnership is a contractual relationship in which two or more people combine their efforts or resources in order to achieve a common goal. Swiss Federal Courts[62] stated that it is possible for people to incorporate a simple partnership even when there is no intention to form one.[63] Under this interpretation it would be possible to apply the provisions of simple partnerships to same-sex cohabitations. The most important element for simple partnership is "mutual effort to achieve a common goal."[64] In same-sex cohabitation, the parties actually combine their efforts or resources in order to achieve their common goal to share a mutual life. In a simple partnership parties must show a common effort in order to achieve their common goal and must have a common economic unity. The latter is achieved by contributing capital and having a common budget.[65] For example, two students who only share

---

[59] It is also claimed in the legal doctrine that the labor, which is not related to sexual relation shall at least be claimed in accordance with the unjust enrichment provisions. Hatemi, *supra* note 10, p. 89.

[60] For this view, please see Gümüş, Alper; "*Yargıtay 2. ve 4. Hukuk Daireleri'nin Aile Hukukuna İlişkin Bir Kısım Kararları Üzerine Düşünceler*", Maltepe Üniversitesi Hukuk Fakültesi Dergisi, 2007/1, 423–424 [Hereinafter, *Gümüş*]. Also the Swiss Federal Court also has decisions on the application of the simple partnership during the liquidation of the cohabitations; please see the decisions of the Swiss Federal Court; BGE 108 II 204.

[61] BGE 108 II 204; BGE 109 II 230; Gümüş, *supra* note 57, p. 423.

[62] Since 1926, it is the legislature's political choice to adopt both Swiss Civil Code and its inseparably linked Code of Obligations. As Turkish Code of Obligations is adopted from Swiss Code of Obligations, Swiss jurisprudence and their interpretations of same laws is an important reference for the Turkish legal doctrine. [For further information on reception and development of the Swiss legislation in Turkey, please see Atamer, Yeşim M., "Rezeption und Weiterentwicklung des Schweizerischen Zivilgesetzbuches in der Türkei", Rabels Zeitschrift für ausländisches und internationales Privatrecht, Mohr Siebeck Publishers, RabelsZ 72 (2008), pp. 723–754.]

[63] BGE 108 II 204, p. 208.

[64] Barlas, Nami, Adi Ortaklık Temeline Dayalı Sözleşme İlişkileri, 3. Edition, Istanbul, 2012, 14 [Hereinafter, *Barlas*]; Yavuz, Cevdet/Acar, Faruk/Özen, Burak; Borçlar Hukuku Dersleri (Özel Hükümler), 10. Edition, Istanbul, 2012, 736 [Hereinafter, *Yavuz/Acar/Özen*].

[65] BGE 108 II 204, p. 206.

the same house will not constitute a simple partnership. Same-sex cohabitants with a common budget and sharing a life plan would fit into the definition of a simple partnership. The question is, however, if the "common goal" of same-sex cohabitants may be illegal under Turkish Law. In several cases Turkish courts have decided that a same-sex relationship constitutes prostitution when an exchange occurs to further a sexual relationship. Under that interpretation the common goal of the simple partnership would be illegal. Such narrow interpretation, however, does not restrict the possibility of broader ones in which the common goal of supporting each other is analyzed outside the realm of sexual intimacy. Those interpretations would deem the common goal legal.

The second element for the simple partnership is the economic contributions of the parties. According to Article 621 of the Turkish Code of Obligations, each partner must contribute something to the simple partnership. The contribution may be money, claims, other goods or labor. Goods that exist before the incorporation such as a house, a car, household goods and wages are evaluated as contribution. Housework, however, is evaluated as effort. The goods brought to the relationship are contributions and the goods acquired during the course of the relationship are profit. If the relationship can not be registered as a simple partnership it may be difficult to determine the contributions and profits. In order to overcome this evidence issue, courts could use the presumption that all goods in dispute will be treated as profit.

Another issue is whether the provisions of the simple partnership regarding the management, representation and reasons for dissolution apply to same-sex cohabitations.[66] In general, these provisions are parallel with the family provisions of the Turkish Civil Code and provide equality among the partners. Analogy treats two different legal concepts in the same manner by using similarities between two situations regarding the protected interests.[67] As the protected interest and the concepts of simple partnership and same-sex cohabitation are similar, courts can make analogies between the provisions of these concepts.[68]

---

[66]For these regulations, Yavuz/Acar/Özen, *supra* note 60, pp. 738–745.

[67]Serozan, Medeni Hukuk, *supra* note 34, p. 142.

[68]Conversely, the Turkish legislator purposely avoided regulating same-sex cohabitation under Turkish family law. Therefore, there is a premeditated loophole regarding cohabitation. Technically, this is not a legal loophole but a legal policy choice. Consequently, application of all provisions of the simple partnership by analogy would be unfavorable. As a matter of fact, such analogy would exceed its purpose because application of the simple partnership provisions to same-sex cohabitation is to provide protection to same-sex couples during the dissolution of their cohabitation. However, applying the whole concept of simple partnership to same-sex cohabitations leads to the problem of creating an institution, which competes with the provisions of marriage. That would lead to dangerous consequences, as such an analogy would infringe on the principle of *numerus clausus* of family law. Such would disregard the apparent intent and the policy choice of the Turkish legislator. Consequently, courts should carefully apply the provisions of the simple partnership by analogy to same-sex cohabitation limited to liquidation. In fact, the Swiss Federal Court has applied only the provision related to liquidation of the simple corporation to the cohabitations; please see BGE 108 II 204, p. 211.

8.5 Other Claims and Ways to Protect Same-Sex Couples

8.5.1 Claim for Compensation for the Loss of Support

According to Article 53 of the Turkish Code of Obligation, in case of a wrongful death, the court may award recovery of financial contributions of the deceased to his or her dependents. Damages arise due to the wrongful death of a person who provides support to others.[69] The claims for loss of support are relational loss regulated under Turkish law and accordingly a relationship of dependency or support must exist between the deceased ad the claimant in order to claim damages.[70] The relationship of support comes from a person who constantly and regularly takes care of another, economically supports the other person either totally or partially, and/or there is a definite expectation of support.[71] The law does not require the existence of a family relationship in order to claim damages for loss of support.[72]

Although same-sex cohabitation is not treated as family under Turkish law, there is clearly a constant and regular solidarity between the cohabitants. This solidarity falls within the scope of support and therefore, couples should be able to claim damages for loss of support in case of wrongful death of his or her same-sex partner. Just as with other areas, however, courts may deny damages for the loss of support if they consider same-sex cohabitations illegal.[73] The counter argument to this interpretation is that even though Turkish law does not accept same-sex cohabitation, these associations are not, *per se,* against public order. Some scholars claim that opposite sex cohabitations are not considered to be against morality unless one of the parties expects consideration or an impediment for marriage exists between the parties.[74] Accordingly, with cohabitants that have mutual cooperation, the partner who maintains and supports the couple should be accepted by courts as the supporting party.[75] In the case of wrongful death of one of the same-sex

---

[69]Eren, *supra* note 36, p. 755 et seq.; Oğuzman/Öz, v.2, *supra* note 37, p. 98.

[70]Eren, *supra* note 36, p. 753; Oğuzman/Öz, v.2, *supra* note 37, at 102–103.

[71]Eren, *supra* note 36, p. 755; Oğuzman/Öz, v.2, *supra* note 37, at 101; Tekinay, Selahattin Sulhi/Akman, Sermet/Burcuoğlu, Haluk/Altop, Atilla; Tekinay Borçlar Hukuku, Istanbul, 1993, 627–628 [Hereinafter, *Tekinay/Akman/Burcuoğlu/Altop*]; Köteli, *supra* note 17, p. 192.

[72]The decision of the General Assembly of the Court of Cassation dated 13.04.2011 and numbered 142; dated 21.04.1982 and numbered 412; the decision of the 4th Chamber of the Court of Cassation dated 08/03/2012 and numbered 2012/3755.

[73]Gümüş, *supra* note 57, p. 423.

[74]Tekinay/Akman/Burcuoğlu/Altop, *supra* note 69, p. 627–628; Oğuzman/Öz, v.1, *supra* note 36, p. 98; Köprülü/Kaneti, *supra* note 11, p. 65; Eren, *supra* note 36, p. 757; Hatemi, *supra* note 10, p. 100; Gökyayla, *supra* note 40, pp. 118–119.

[75]Oğuzman/Öz, v.1, id, p. 98; Tekinay/Akman/Burcuoğlu/Altop, *supra* note 58, pp. 627–628; Eren, *supra* note 36, p. 755; Köteli, supra note 17, p. 192.

cohabitants, the surviving partner has no rights under inheritance law. However, the surviving partner may claim compensation for loss of support. The last element to claim damages for loss of support is that the standard of living of the surviving partner must decrease due to the death of the partner.[76] Scholars who oppose an interpretation that would allow same-sex partners to claim damages use the same argument advanced so far against same-sex couples as going against Turkish morality.[77] This interpretation leaves the surviving party in a very difficult situation.

8.5.2 Claims for Compensation Due to Mental Anguish and Emotional Distress

According to Article 56 of the Turkish Code of Obligations, in case of wrongful death or injury, close relatives and acquaintances of the deceased may claim damages for their mental anguish and emotional distress. The old Turkish Code of Obligations only mentioned family members. Even then, however, courts broadly interpreted the provision in its application and extended the right to claim for damages to the spouse, children, parents, siblings and to the fiancé of the deceased. The new Turkish Code of Obligations expands this right to close relatives and acquaintances.

The purpose of non-pecuniary damages is to ease the pain of close relatives and acquaintances who suffer mental anguish and emotional distress due to the wrongful death of the deceased. As explained above, same-sex cohabitants share a life and have common goals. Their relations have the material, spiritual and social characteristics of a family relation even when not recognized by Turkish law as such. Mental anguish and emotional distress suffered by same-sex partners in case of wrongful death or injury of the other partner is no different than the mental anguish and emotional distress suffered by married couples. Accordingly, the law should place same-sex cohabitants within the scope of this article and grant them the right to claim damages.

8.5.3 Parental Rights

Under Turkish law *in vitro* fertilization is provided only to married couples. The law also forbids sperm/egg donations and surrogacy. Same-sex couples are not able to have children in Turkey using these methods of reproduction. Likewise, adoption is not an alternative for same-sex couples. Turkish Civil Code allows joint adoption

---

[76]Eren, *supra* note 36, p. 755; Oğuzman/Öz, v.1, *supra* note 31, p. 565; Tekinay/Akman/Burcuoğlu/Altop, supra note 69, pp. 627–628.

[77]Gökyayla, *supra* note 40, p. 121; Hatemi, *supra* note 10, p. 100.

between married couples. Same-sex couples may not adopt children together.[78] Adopting children as a single parent, however, is possible and there is no restriction for the adoption of a child by one of the partners of a same-sex couple.

Turkey is a party to the United Nations Convention on the Rights of the Child and it has undertaken not to discriminate against children on the basis, among others, sex, sexual orientation or sexual identity. During the assessment of adoptive parents, therefore, none of these considerations should be taken into account. Courts, however, should make their assessment thinking primarily on the interest of the adoptive children. Considering the approach of Turkish courts to homosexuality, the adoption of a child by a single homosexual parent may not be an easy process. In 1982, the Court of Cassation examined this situation. In that case, the lower court granted a divorce based on the lesbianism of wife but granted her child custody. The father appealed the custody decision and, subsequently, the Court of Cassation reversed the decision on the grounds that child custody to the mother could affect the future of the child as "homosexuality is a habit which amounts to illness and could not be accepted by society."[79] The court did not examine any arguments regarding the child's interest of living with her mother.[80]

8.6 Conclusion

Although the law does not forbid same-sex cohabitation, same-sex couples do not have any legal protection or rights under Turkish family law and so far same-sex relations are contrary to the Turkish concept of marriage as a union between a man and a woman.

Under Turkish Contracts and Obligations Law, it is possible for cohabitating parties to celebrate contracts such as loans, donations or distribution of the assets. In such cases, courts distribute the assets accordingly. However, if a contract does not exist between the parties, then courts can distribute the assets in accordance with the application of the liquidation provisions of the simple partnership by analogy.

Lastly, the acknowledgement of a same-sex marriage or a registered same-sex partnership in Turkey is not possible. Turkish Courts would refrain from evaluating same-sex marriages under Article 13 of the Turkish Private International and

[78]Yasan, Candan, "Eşcinsellerin Evlat Edinmesi", Prof. Dr. Belgin Erdoğmuş' Armağan, Der Yayınları, Istanbul, 2011, pp. 895–908 (906) [Hereinafter, *Yasan*].

[79]Decision of the Second Civil Chamber of the Court of Cassation dated 21, June, 1982, and numbered 5077/5531 (available at www.hukukturk.com). For the critic of the decision, please see Yasan, id, at 907.

[80]Court of Cassation stated that "the reason for divorce is "homosexuality" which can never be accepted by Turkish society. Giving the custody of the girl to a woman who has such diseased habit which amount to illness, could endanger the future of the child".

Procedural Law, which regulates conflict of rules regarding the marriage.[81] Even if it were evaluated under the said Article, acknowledgement of same-sex marriages and registered partnerships would be deemed to be against the public order.[82] There is, however, space for new interpretations and contract and obligations law provide a space for same-sex couples to seek some legal protections and fill part of the voids created by a rigid regulatory framework.

Bibliography

1. Atamer, Yeşim M. 2008. Rezeption und Weiterentwicklung des Schweizerischen Zivilgesetzbuches in der Türkei. Rabels Zeitschrift für ausländisches und internationales Privatrecht, Mohr Siebeck Publishers, RabelsZ 72, 723–754.
2. Akıntürk, Turgut, and Derya Ateş Karaman. 2013. Türk Medeni Hukuku Aile Hukuku İkinci Cilt, 15. Edition, Beta Yayıncılık, Istanbul.
3. Ateş, Derya. 2007. *Borçlar Hukuku Sözleşmelerinde Genel Ahlâka Aykırılık*. Ankara: Turhan Kitabevi.
4. Barlas, Nami. 2012. Adi Ortaklık Temeline Dayalı Sözleşme İlişkileri, 3. Edition, Istanbul, .
5. Başoğlu, Başak, and Candan Yasan. 2011. National Report: Turkey. American University Journal of Gender, Social Policy & the Law 19: 319–328.
6. Başoğlu, Başak, and Meliha SerminPaksoy. 2011. Dini Nikâhlı Kadının Hukuki Durumu. In Prof. Dr. Şener Akyol'a Armağan. Filiz Kitabevi, Istanbul, 239–269.
7. Belgesay, Mustafa Reşit. 1958. Filli Evliliğin ve Evlilik Dışında Doğan Çocukların Himayesi. MHAD, Year 2, Istanbul, 21–24.
8. Dural, Mustafa, Tufan Öğüz, and Alper Gümüş. 2012. Türk Özel Hukuku, Cilt III, Aile Hukuku, 5. Edition, Filiz Kitabevi, Istanbul.
9. Emmel, Stephen. 2010. in Handkommentar zum Schweizer Privatrecht, Vertragsverhältnisse Teil 2: Arbeitsvertrag, Werkvertrag, Auftrag, GoA, Bürgschaft (Art. 319–529), Schulthess, Zurich.
10. Erdem, Mehmet. 2010. *Özel Hukukta Zamanaşımı*. Istanbul: XII Levha Yayıncılık.
11. Eren, Fikret. 2012. Borçlar Hukuku, Genel Hükümler, 14. Edition, Yetkin Yayınevi, Ankara.
12. Feyzioğlu, Feyzi Necmeddin. 1986. Aile Hukuku, 3. Edition, Istanbul, Filiz Kitabevi.
13. Gençcan, Ömer Uğur. 2011. *Aile Hukuku*. Ankara: Yetkin Yayınları.
14. Gökyayla, K. Emre. 2004. *Destekten Yoksun Kalma Tazminatı*. Ankara: Seçkin Yayınevi.
15. Gönensay, A. Samim. 1937. Medenî Hukuk, C. 2, Kısım 1, Istanbul Üniversitesi Yayınları, Istanbul.
16. Gülmez, Mesut. 2009. Dernek Özgürlüğü ve Cinsel Yönelime Dayalı Ayrımcılık Sorunu: Lambdaİstanbul Davası Kararları (Karar İncelemesi). *Çalışma ve Toplum Dergisi* 3(22): 195–230.
17. Gümüş, Alper. 2007/1. Yargıtay 2. ve 4. Hukuk Daireleri'nin Aile Hukukuna İlişkin Bir Kısım Kararları Üzerine Düşünceler. Maltepe Üniversitesi Hukuk Fakültesi Dergisi, Istanbul, 423–424.
18. Hatemi, Hüseyin. 1976. *Hukuka ve Ahlaka Aykırılık Kavramı*. Istanbul: Sulhi Garan Matbaası.

[81] For detailed information on the issue, please see Sirmen, Kâzım Sedat; "Eş Cinsel Birliktelikler ve Bunların Kanunlar İhtilâfı Hukukunda Düzenlenişi", AÜHFM Volume 58 No. 4, Ankara, 2009, pp. 825–879 (857 et seq.) [Hereinafter, *Sirmen*]; Yasan, Candan, Milletlerarası Özel Hukukta Aynı Cinsiyetten Kişilerin Birliktelikleri, XII Levha Yayıncılık, Istanbul, 2013.

[82] Sirmen, *ibid.*, p. 869 et seq.

19. Hatemi, Hüseyin, and Emre Gökyayla. 2012. Borçlar Hukuku Genel Bölüm, 2. Edition, Vedat Kitapçılık, Istanbul.
20. Hatemi, Hüseyin, and Rona Serozan. 1993. *Aile Hukuku*. Istanbul: Filiz Kitabevi.
21. Karadağ, Nevra. 2008. *Cinsel Azınlıkların Bireysel Hakları*. Istanbul: XII Levha Yayıncılık.
22. Kocayusufpaşaoğlu, Necip. 2008. in Borçlar Hukuku Genel Bölüm, Birinci Cilt, Borçlar Hukukuna Giriş-Hukukî İşlem-Sözleşme, Kocayusufpaşaoğlu, Necip, Hüseyin Hatemi, Rona Serozan, and Abdülkadir Arpacı, 4. Edition, Filiz Kitabevi, Istanbul.
23. Köprülü, Bülent, and Selim Kaneti. 1986. *Aile Hukuku*. Istanbul: Istanbul Üniversitesi Yayınları.
24. Köseoğlu, Bilal, and Köksal Kocaağa. 2011. *Aile Hukuku ve Uygulaması – Bilimsel Görüşler, Yargı İçtihatları*. Bursa: Ekin Basım Yayın Dağıtım.
25. Köteli, M. Argun. 1991. *Evliliğin Hukuki Niteliği ve Evlilik Dışı Beraberlikler*. Istanbul: Kazancı Yayıncılık.
26. Oğuzman, Kemal, and Nami Barlas. 2012. Medenî Hukuk – Giriş, Kaynaklar, Temel Kavramlar, 18. Edition, Vedat Kitapçılık, Istanbul.
27. Oğuzman, Kemal, and Mustafa Dural. 1998. *Aile Hukuku*. Istanbul: Filiz Kitabevi.
28. Oğuzman, Kemal, and Turgut Öz. 2011. Borçlar Hukuku Genel Hükümler Cilt I, 9. Edition, Vedat Kitapçılık, Istanbul.
29. Oğuzman, Kemal, and Turgut Öz. 2012. Borçlar Hukuku Genel Hükümler, Cilt II, 9. Edition, Vedat Kitapçılık, Istanbul.
30. Öztan, Bilge. 2004. Aile Hukuku, 5. Edition, Turhan Kitabevi, Ankara.
31. Portmann, Wolfgang. 2007. in Basler Kommentar Obligationenrecht I, Art. 1–529, Herausgeber: Honsell, Heinrich, Nedim Peter Vogt, and Wolfgang Wiegand, 5. Edition, Helbing Lichtenhahn, Basel.
32. Sayman, Yücel. 1982. *Türk Devletler Hususî Hukukunda Evlenmenin Kuruluşu*. Istanbul: Fakülteler Matbaası.
33. Saymen, Ferit H., and K. Halid Elbir. 1957. Türk Medenî Hukuku, C. III, Aile Hukuku, İsmail Akgün Matbaası, Istanbul.
34. Schmid, Jörg, and Hubert Stöckli. 2010. *Schweizerisches Obligationenrecht Besonderer Teil*. Zürich: Schulthess.
35. Schwarz, Andreas. 1946. *Aile Hukuku I*. Istanbul: Istanbul Üniversitesi Yayınları.
36. Serozan, Rona. 2006. in Borçlar Hukuku, Genel Bölüm, Üçüncü Cilt, İfa Engelleri-Haksız Zenginleşme, Kocayusufpaşaoğlu, Necip/Hatemi, Hüseyin/Serozan, Rona/Arpacı, Abdülkadir, Filiz Kitabevi, Istanbul.
37. Serozan, Rona. 1983. Evlilik Dışı Birlikte Yaşam İlişkisi. Istanbul Barosu Dergisi Volume 57, No. 1–3, 1983, Istanbul, 5–17.
38. Serozan, Rona. 1969. Geçersiz Satım Sözleşmesinin Karşılıklı İfa Sonrası Çözülmesi. MHAD, Volume 3, No: 4, 1969, Istanbul, 187–213.
39. Serozan, Rona. 2011. *Medeni Hukuk, Genel Bölüm Kişiler Hukuku*. Istanbul: Vedat Kitapçılık.
40. Sirmen, Kâzım Sedat. 2009. Eş Cinsel Birliktelikler ve Bunların Kanunlar İhtilâfı Hukukunda Düzenlenişi. AÜHFM Volume 58 No. 4, Ankara, 825–879.
41. Tekinay, Selahâttin Sulhi. 1990. *Türk Aile Hukuku*. Istanbul: Filiz Kitabevi.
42. Tekinay, Selahattin Sulhi, Sermet Akman, Haluk Burcuoğlu, and Atilla Altop. 1993. *Tekinay Borçlar Hukuku*. Istanbul: Filiz Kitabevi.
43. Tekinay, Selahâttin Sulhi. 1963. *Ölüm Sebebiyle Destekten Yoksun Kalma Tazminatı*. Istanbul: Fakülteler Matbaası.
44. Tutumlu, Mehmet Akif. 2002. *Yeni Türk Medenî Kanunu Hükümlerine Göre Evliliğin Butlanı, Boşanma ve Ayrılık Sebepleri ve Boşanmanın Hukukî Sonuçları*. Ankara: Adalet Yayınevi.
45. Üskül-Engin, Zeynep Özlem. 2008. *Türkiye'de Evlenmenin Evrimi*. Istanbul: Beşir Yayıncılık.
46. Velidedeoğlu, Hıfzı Veldet. 1965. Türk Medeni Hukuku, C. 2, Aile Hukuku, 5. Edition, Istanbul Üniversitesi Yayınları, Istanbul.
47. Yasan, Candan. 2011. Eşcinsellerin Evlat Edinmesi. Prof. Dr. Belgin Erdoğmuş' Armağan, Der Yayınları, Istanbul, 895–908.

48. Yasan, Candan. 2013. *Milletlerarası Özel Hukukta Aynı Cinsiyetten Kişilerin Birliktelikleri*. Istanbul: XII Levha Yayıncılık.
49. Yavuz, Cevdet, Faruk Acar, and Burak Özen. 2012. Borçlar Hukuku Dersleri (Özel Hükümler), 10. Edition, Beta Yayınları, Istanbul.
50. Zevkliler, Aydın, Acabey Beşir, and Gökyayla Emre. 1999. *Medeni Hukuk (Giriş, Başlangıç Hükümleri, Kişiler Hukuku, Aile Hukuku)*. Ankara: Seçkin Yayınevi.

Printed by Printforce, the Netherlands